BULGARIAN-ENGLISH
ENGLISH-BULGARIAN
DICTIONARY

IVAN TCHOMAKOV

HIPPOCRENE BOOKS
New York

Hippocrene Books Edition.

Copyright© 1992 by Ivan Tchomakov.

Fourth printing, 2000.

For information, address:
HIPPOCRENE BOOKS, INC.
171 Madison Avenue
New York, NY 10016

ISBN 0-87052-145-4

Printed in the United States of America.

FOREWORD

This Bulgarian-English English-Bulgarian Dictionary is addressed to business people, travelers and students. It contains over 8,000 entries in Bulgarian and English.

The use of this Dictionary is facilitated by the adoption of a simple transliteration scheme. Each word is supplied by a transliteration in the alphabet of the other language. This, naturally, entails a degree of imprecision, particularly in differentiating the pronunciation of sounds unique to the English language, such as open, short or long "o." Only one graphic symbol is employed. In the English-Bulgarian Dictionary, a hyphen following the letter "a" is used to denote the sound (a) in words such as "sad" and "cat." In the Bulgarian-English Dictionary, the hyphen is used to divide two letters indicating that they are to be pronounced separately, rather than as one sound. Such is the case with the combination of the letters "z" and "h," which, if divided by a hyphen, should be pronounced as in "zero" and "hotel." If used in combination without a dividing mark, they sould be pronounced as the sound "zh" in the English word "measure." Duplication of characters is used to denote long vowels in English or separate pronunciation of the two identical sounds in Bulgarian.

I.T.

THE KEY TO PRONUNCIATION

Bulgarian symbol	English pronunciation	Example
а	a	harbor
б	b	boy
в	v	victory
г	g	grammar
д	d	door
е	e	net
ж	zh	division
з	z	zebra
и	i	little
й	i	young
к	k	kettle
л	l	lonely
м	m	money
н	n	never
о	o	opera
п	p	open
р	r	rest
с	s	still
т	t	touch
у	ou	youth
ф	f	fig
х	h	hotel
ц	ts	shuts
ч	ch	choose
ш	sh	shoe
щ	sht	fishtail
ъ	u	gum
ь	denotes softening of vowel "o"	
ю	yu	you
я	ya	yard

ABBREVIATIONS USED IN THIS DICTIONARY

adj	adjective
adv	adverb
conj	conjunction
f	feminine
interj	interjection
m	masculine
n	neuter (Bulgarian-English Section)
n	noun (English-Bulgarian Section)
num	numeral
part	particle
pl	plural
prep	preposition
pron	pronoun
v	verb

BULGARIAN-ENGLISH DICTIONARY

А

а [a] *conj* and, while, yet, but
абажу́р [abazhour] *m* lampshade
абонаме́нт [abonament] *m* subscription
абони́рам [aboniram] *v* subscribe to
абсолю́тен [absolyuten] *adj* absolute
абсу́рден [absourden] *adj* absurd
авантю́ра [avantyura] *f* adventure
ава́рия [avariya] *f* damage, break down
а́вгуст [avgoust] *m* August
авиа́ция [aviatsiya] *f* aviation, aircraft
автобу́с [aftobous] *m* bus, coach
автомати́чен [aftomatichen] *adj* automatic
автомоби́л [aftomobil] *m* motorcar
а́втор [aftor] *m* author
авторите́т [aftoritet] *m* authority, prestige
авторемо́нтна работи́лница [aftoremontna rabotilnitsa] *f* auto-repair shop
аге́нт [agent] *m* agent
аге́нция [agentsiya] *f* agency, bureau
а́гне [agne] *n* lamb
агре́сия [agresiya] *f* aggression
агроно́м [agronom] *m* agronomist, agriculturalist
ад [ad] *m* inferno, hell
адвока́т [advokat] *m* lawyer, solicitor, barrister

администра́ция [administratsiya] *f* administration, management

адре́с [adres] *m* address

аерога́ра [aerogara] *f* airport

аз [as] *pron* I

а́збука [azbouka] *f* alphabet

азиа́тски [aziatski] *adj* Asiatic

азо́т [azot] *m* nitrogen

акаде́мия [akademiya] *f* academy

акваре́л [akvarel] *m* watercolor

аква́риум [akvarium] *m* aquarium

ако́ [ako] *conj* if

акроба́т [akrobat] *m* acrobat

акт [akt] *m* act, deed, certificate

акти́вен [aktiven] *adj* active

активизи́рам [aktiviziram] *v* activate, rouse, stir up

аку́ла [akoula] *f* shark

акумула́тор [akoumoulator] *m* battery

акура́тен [akouraten] *adj* accurate, precise

аку́стика [akoustika] *f* acoustics

акуше́рка [akousherka] *f* midwife

акце́нт [aktsent] *m* accent, stress

а́лен [alen] *adj* scarlet

але́я [aleya] *f* alley, lane, walk

алкохо́л [alkohol] *m* alcohol

а́ло [alo] *intej* hello

алпини́зъм [alpinizum] *m* mountaineering, mountain climbing

алуми́ний [aluminii] *m* aluminum

алчен [alchen] *adj* greedy, avid, covetous
аматьо́рски [amatyorski] *adj* amateur
амбала́ж [ambalazh] *m* packing
амбицио́зен [ambitsiozen] *adj* ambitious
амби́ция [ambitsiya] *f* ambition
америка́нски [amerikanski] *adj* American
ана́лиз [analis] *m* analysis
анато́мия [anatomiya] *f* anatomy
ангажиме́нт [angazhiment] *m* commitment, engagement
а́нгел [angel] *m* angel
англи́йски [angliiski] *adj* English
анекдо́т [anekdot] *m* anecdote
анке́та [anketa] *f* inquiry, investigation
анони́мен [anonimen] *adj* anonymous
анса́мбъл [ansambul] *m* ensemble, group, company
анте́на [antena] *f* aerial
антра́кт [antrakt] *m* interval, intermission
антре́ [antre] *n* entrance hall
апара́т [aparat] *m* apparatus, appliance
апартаме́нт [apartament] *m* flat, rooms, apartment
апели́рам [apeliram] *v* appeal to
аперити́в [aperitif] *m* appetizer
апети́т [apetit] *m* appetite
аплоди́рам [aplodiram] *v* applaud, acclaim
апри́л [april] *m* April
апте́ка [apteka] *f* pharmacy, drugstore
апте́кар [aptekar] *m* chemist, druggist

аргуме́нт [argument] *m* argument
аресту́вам [arestouvam] *v* arrest, take into custody
аристокра́ция [aristokratsiya] *f* aristocracy
аритме́тика [aritmetika] *f* arithmetic
а́рка [arka] *f* arch
а́рмия [armiya] *f* army
арога́нтност [arogantnost] *f* arrogance
арома́т [aromat] *m* aroma, fragrance, perfume
арома́тен [aromaten] *adj* aromatic, fragrant
арте́рия [arteriya] *f* artery
артиле́рия [artileriya] *f* artillery
арти́ст [artist] *m* actor
археоло́гия [arheologiya] *f* archaeology
архи́ва [arhiva] *f* records
архите́кт [arhitekt] *m* architect
архитекту́ра [arhitektoura] *f* architecture
асансьо́р [asansyor] *m* lift, elevator
асисте́нт [asistent] *m* assistant
асоциа́ция [asotsiatsiya] *f* association
аспири́рам [aspiriram] *v* aspire
астроно́мия [astronomiya] *f* astronomy
ата́ка [ataka] *f* attack, assault, onset
атаку́вам [atakouvam] *v* attack, assault
ателие́ [atelie] *n* shop, work room, studio
атента́т [atentat] *m* attempt, on smb's life, outrage
атле́т [atlet] *m* athlete

атлети́чески състеза́ния [atleticheski sustezaniya] *noun pl* track-and-field events

аудие́нция [audientsiya] *f* audience

аудито́рия [auditoriya] *f* auditorium, lecture hall

афекти́рам се [afektiram se] *v* become overexcited, exasperated

афи́ш [afish] *m* poster, bill, placard

африка́нски [afrikanski] *adj* African

а́хвам [ahvam] *v* exclaim, gasp

Б

ба́ба [baba] *f* grandmother, old woman

ба́вен [baven] *adj* slow, tardy, sluggish

ба́вене [bavene] *n* delay, protraction

бага́ж [bagazh] *m* luggage, baggage

ба́гер [bager] *m* excavator

ба́гра [bagra] *f* color, tint, hue, shade

баде́м [badem] *m* almond

баджана́к [badzhanak] *m* brother-in-law

ба́за [baza] *f* base, basis

байр [bair] *m* hill, elevation

бака́лница [bakalnitsa] *f* grocery

бакши́ш [bakshish] *m* tip

бал [bal] *m* ball

бала́нс [balans] *m* balance

балдъ́за [balduza] *f* sister-in-law

балет [balet] *m* ballet

балкан [balkan] *m* mountain

балкон [balkon] *m* balcony

балон [balon] *m* balloon

балтон [balton] *m* overcoat, topcoat

банален [banalen] *adj* commonplace, ordinary, banal

банан [banan] *m* banana

банда [banda] *f* gang, band

банка [banka] *f* bank

банкнота [banknota] *f* banknote, bill

бански [banski] *adj* bathing

баня [banya] *f* bathroom, public baths

бар [bar] *m* bar, night club

барабан [baraban] *m* drum

барака [baraka] *f* shed

барета [bareta] *f* cap, beret

бариера [bariera] *f* barrier, bar

барут [barout] *m* gunpowder

басейн [basein] *m* swimming pool

баскетбол [basketbol] *m* basketball

баснословен [basnosloven] *adj* fabulous

басня [basnya] *f* fable

бастун [bastoun] *m* cane, walking stick

батерия [bateriya] *f* battery

баща [bashta] *m* father

бдителен [bditelen] *adj* vigilant, watchful, alert

бебе [bebe] *n* baby

бегач [begach] *m* runner

беда́ [beda] *f* misfortune, disaster, trouble
бе́ден [beden] *adj* poor, needy
бе́дност [bednost] *f* poverty, poorness
бедро́ [bedro] *n* thigh
бе́дствие [bedstvie] *n* calamity, disaster
бежане́ц [bezhanets] *m* refugee
бе́жов [bezhof] *adj* beige
без [bes] *prep* without, to
безбро́ен [bezbroen] *adj* countless,
innumerable
безво́ден [bezvoden] *adj* waterless, dry
безво́лев [bezvolev] *adj* weak–willed,
irresolute
безвре́ден [bezvreden] *adj* harmless,
innocuous
безвъзвра́тен [bezvuzvraten] *adj*
irretrievable, irrevocable
безвъзме́зден [bezvuzmezden] *adj* free
безграни́чен [bezgranichen] *adj* boundless,
infinite
безгри́жие [bezgrizhie] *n* unconcern, ease
безде́ен [bezdeen] *adj* inactive, passive, inert
бе́здна [bezdna] *f* chasm, abyss
бездо́мник [bezdomnik] *m* waif, homeless
person
безжи́знен [bezzhiznen] *adj* lifeless, dull
беззаве́тен [bezzaveten] *adj* devoted, selfless
безизхо́ден [bezis-hoden] *adj* hopeless
безизхо́дица [bezis-hoditsa] *f* impasse,
deadlock

безинтересен [bezinteresen] *adj*
uninterested, dull

безир [bezir] *m* linseed oil

безкористен [beskoristen] *adj* unselfish

безкрайност [beskrainost] *f* infinity,
boundlessness

безлихвен [bezlihven] *adj* free of interest

безлюден [bezlyuden] *adj* deserted, empty,
uninhabited

безмилостен [bezmilosten] *adj* merciless,
ruthless

безмитен [bezmiten] *adj* duty-free

безмълвен [bezmulven] *adj* silent, mute

безнравствен [beznravstven] *adj* immoral

безоблачен [bezoblachen] *adj* cloudless

безобразен [bezobrazen] *adj* repulsive,
hideous

безобразие [bezobrazie] *n* outrage, scandal,
disgrace

безопасен [bezopasen] *adj* secure, safe

безочлив [bezochlif] *adj* impudent

безплатен [besplaten] *adj* free

безплоден [besploden] *adj* fruitless, vain

безпокойствие [bespokoystvie] *n* uneasiness,
anxiety

безпокоя [bespokoya] *v* trouble, disturb,
worry

безполезен [bespolezen] *adj* useless, vain,
futile

безпомощен [bespomoshten] *adj* helpless

безпорядък [besporyaduk] *m* disorder, confusion

безпощаден [besposhtaden] *adj* ruthless, merciless

безпристрастен [bespristrasten] *adj* impartial, unbiased

безработен [bezraboten] *adj* unemployed, jobless

безразборно [bezrazborno] *adv* at random, indiscriminately

безразличие [bezrazlichie] *n* indifference

безредие [bezredie] *n* disorder, disturbance

безрезултатен [bezrezoultaten] *adj* ineffective, futile

безсилие [besilie] *n* impotence, weakness

безсмислен [besmislen] *adj* meaningless, senseless

безсмъртен [besmurten] *adj* immortal

безспирен [bespiren] *adj* incessant, continual

безспорно [besporno] *adv* indisputably, certainly

безсрамен [besramen] *adj* shameless, impudent

безсрочен [besrochen] *adj* termless, permanent

безстрашен [bestrashen] *adj* fearless

безсъзнание [besuznanie] *n* unconsciousness

безсъние [besunie] *n* sleeplessness, insomnia

безумен [bezoumen] *adj* mad, insane

безу́пречен [bezouprechen] *adj* flawless, impeccable

безуспе́шен [bezouspeshen] *adj* unsuccessful

безхаракте́рен [bes-harakteren] *adj* weak-willed

безцве́тен [bestsveten] *adj* colorless

безце́нен [bestsenen] *adj* priceless, precious

безчестя́ [beschestya] *v* disgrace, dishonor, defame

безчове́чен [beschovechen] *adj* inhuman, cruel

безчу́вствен [beschouvstven] *adj* unconscious, indifferent, insensitive

безшу́мен [beshoumen] *adj* noiseless

бе́лег [beleg] *m* scar, mark, sign

беле́жа [belezha] *v* mark, note, show, register

бележи́т [belezhit] *adj* notable, distinguished

бележни́к [belezhnik] *m* notebook

бельо́ [belyo] *n* underwear, linen

беля́ [belya] *f* nuisance, trouble

бензи́н [benzin] *m* petrol, gasoline

бензиноста́нция [benzinostantsiya] *f* gas station

бера́ [bera] *v* pick, gather

бесе́да [beseda] *f* talk, lecture, discourse

бето́н [beton] *m* concrete

би, бих [bi, bih] *v* would

библиоте́ка [biblioteka] *f* library, bookcase

би́блия [bibliya] *f* the Bible

бижу́ [bizhou] *n* jewel, gem
бик [bik] *m* bull
биле́т [bilet] *m* ticket
би́лка [bilka] *f* herb
бинт [bint] *m* bandage
биогра́фия [biografiya] *f* biography
биоло́гия [biologiya] *f* biology
би́ра [bira] *f* beer, ale
бис [bis] *m* encore
би́сер [biser] *m* pearl
би́стър [bistur] *adj* clear
бити́е [bitie] *n* being, existence
би́тка [bitka] *f* battle, fight
би́я [biya] *v* beat, lash, ring
благ [blag] *n* gentle, kind, sweet
благода́рен [blagodaren] *adj* thankful, grateful
благода́рност [blagodarnost] *f* gratitude
благодаря́ [blagodarya] *conj* thank
благода́тен [blagodaten] *adj* beneficial
благозву́чен [blagozvouchen] *adj* harmonious, melodious
благонаде́жен [blagonadezhen] *adj* reliable, dependable
благополу́чен [blagopolouchen] *adj* successful
благоприли́чие [blagoprilichie] *n* propriety, decency
благоприя́тен [blagopriyaten] *adj* favorable

благоразумие [blagorazoumie] *n* prudence, reasonableness, common sense

благороден [blagoroden] *adj* noble, generous

благородство [blagorodstvo] *n* nobility, generosity

благосклонен [blagosklonen] *adj* favorable, benevolent

благословия [blagosloviya] *f* blessing

благосъстояние [blagosustoyanie] *n* prosperity, well-being

благотворен [blagotvoren] *adj* beneficial

благотворителен [blagotvoritelen] *adj* charitable

благочестив [blagochestif] *adj* pious, devout

блажен [blazhen] *adj* blessed, happy

блато [blato] *n* marsh, swamp

бледен [bleden] *adj* pale

блестя [blestya] *v* sparkle, shine, glitter

блестящ [blestyasht] *adj* shining, brilliant

блещукам [bleshtoukam] *v* twinkle, glimmer

ближа [blizha] *v* lick

близнак [bliznak] *m* twin

близо [blizo] *adv* near

близък [blizuk] *adj* near, recent, future

блуждая [blouzhdaya] *v* roam, wander

блуза [blouza] *f* blouse

блъскам [bluskam] *v* push, shove

блюдо [blyudo] *n* dish

бог [bog] *m* God

богат [bogat] *adj* rich, wealthy

бога́тство [bogatstvo] *n* wealth, fortune

боготворя́ [bogotvorya] *v* worship, adore, deify

бо́дър [bodur] *adj* cheerful, lively

бо́ен [boen] *adj* military, fighting

боепри́паси [boepripasi] *noun pl* ammunition

божествен [bozhestven] *adj* divine

боза́йник [bozainik] *m* mammal

боза́я [bozaya] *v* suck

бой [boi] *m* beating, battle, fight

бо́йлер [boiler] *m* boiler, water-heater

боклу́к [boklouk] *m* rubbish, garbage

боледу́вам [boledouvam] *v* be ill, suffer

бо́лен [bolen] *adj* ill, sick

бо́лест [bolest] *f* sickness, disease

бо́лка [bolka] *f* pain, ache

бо́лница [bolnitsa] *f* hospital

болшинство́ [bolshinstvo] *n* majority

бо́мба [bomba] *f* bomb

бонбо́н [bonbon] *m* candy

бор [bor] *m* pine

борба́ [borba] *f* fight, struggle, wrestling

борд [bord] *m* deck

боре́ц [borets] *m* fighter, wrestler

бо́рса [borsa] *f* exchange

бо́ря се [borya se] *v* fight, wrestle

бос [bos] *adj* barefoot

бота́ника [botanika] *f* botany

боту́ш [botoush] *m* boot

боя́ [boya] *f* paint, dye

бояджи́я [boyadzhiya] *m* painter
боя́ се [boya se] *v* be afraid of, fear
бояди́свам [boyadisvam] *v* paint, dye
брава́ [brava] *f* lock
бра́два [bradva] *f* axe
брак [brak] *m* marriage, matrimony
бра́ня [branya] *v* defend, protect
брат [brat] *m* brother
братовче́д [bratovched] *m* cousin
брашно́ [brashno] *n* flour
бреза́ [breza] *f* birch
бре́ме [breme] *n* burden
бре́менна [bremenna] *adj* pregnant
бридж [bridzh] *m* bridge
брой [broy] *n* number, issue, copy
бро́ня [bronya] *f* armor
броя́ [broya] *v* count, reckon
брута́лен [broutalen] *adj* brutal, cruel
бръ́мбар [brumbar] *m* beetle
бръ́сна [brusna] *v* shave
бръсна́ч [brusnach] *m* razor
бряг [bryag] *m* coast, shore
бу́ден [bouden] *adj* awake, intelligent
буди́лник [boudilnik] *m* alarm clock
бу́дя [boudya] *v* wake, awaken
бу́ен [bouen] *adj* hot-tempered, violent
бу́за [bouza] *f* cheek
бу́ква [boukva] *f* letter
буква́лно [boukvalno] *adv* literally
булева́рд [boulevard] *m* avenue, boulevard

бу́лка [boulka] *f* bride, wife
бунт [bount] *m* revolt, riot, rebellion
бу́рен [bouren] *adj* stormy, violent, rapid
бурка́н [bourkan] *m* jar
бу́ря [bourya] *f* storm, tempest
бут [bout] *m* leg, round
бу́там [boutam] *v* push, shove
бути́лка [boutilka] *f* bottle
буто́н [bouton] *m* button
буча́ [boucha] *v* rumble, roar
бъ́брек [bubrek] *m* kidney
бъбри́в [bubriv] *adj* talkative
бъ́да [buda] *v* be
бъ́дещ [budesht] *adj* future, coming
бъ́деще [budeshte] *n* future
бъ́лгарски [bulgarski] *adj* Bulgarian
бърз [burs] *adj* fast, quick, rapid
бъ́рзам [burzam] *v* hurry, be in a hurry
бъ́ркам [burkam] *v* stir, mix, make a
mistake
бъркоти́я [burkotiya] *f* confusion, disorder
бъ́рша [bursha] *v* wipe
бю́ро [byuro] *n* desk, office
бя́гам [byagam] *v* run, fly
бя́гство [byagstvo] *n* flight, escape
бял [byal] *adj* white, fair

В

в [v] *prep* in, on, at, to
вагóн [vagon] *m* carriage, coach, car
вáдя [vadya] *v* pull out, take out
вáжен [vazhen] *adj* important, haughty
вáжност [vazhnost] *f* importance
вакáнция [vakantsiya] *f* holiday, vacation
ваксинúрам се [vaksiniram se] *v* be vaccinated
валú [vali] *v* it snows, it rains
валúден [validen] *adj* valid, good
валс [vals] *m* waltz
валýта [valouta] *f* currency
вáна [vana] *f* tub, bathtub
вар [var] *f* lime
варúрам [variram] *v* vary
варúола [variola] *f* smallpox
варя́ [varya] *v* boil, cook
вас [vas] *pron* you
ваш [vash] *pron* your
вбеся́вам се [vbesyavam se] *v* be furious, be enraged
вглéждам се [vglezhdam se] *v* stare, gaze
вдúгам [vdigam] *v* raise, lift
вдúшвам [vdishvam] *v* inhale, breathe in
вдлъ́бнат [vdlubnat] *adj* concave
вдовéц [vdovets] *m* widower
вдовúца [vdovitsa] *f* widow

вдъхновéние [vduhnovenie] *n* inspiration
вегетариáнец [vegetarianets] *m* vegetarian
веднáга [vednaga] *adv* immediately, at once, right away
веднъ́ж [vednuzh] *adv* once
вéжда [vezhda] *f* eyebrow
вéжлив [vezhlif] *adj* polite, civil, courteous
везни́ [vezni] *noun pl* scales, balance
век [vek] *m* century
вели́к [velik] *adj* great
великáн [velikan] *m* giant
Вели́кден [velikden] *m* Easter
великобритáнски [velikobritanski] *adj* British
великодýшен [velikodoushen] *adj* generous, noble
великолéпен [velikolepen] *adj* magnificient
вели́чествен [velichestven] *adj* majestic
велисипéд [velosiped] *m* bicycle
вéна [vena] *f* vein
вентилáтор [ventilator] *m* fan
венчáвка [venchafka] *f* wedding
вéрен [veren] *adj* correct, right, true, loyal
вери́га [veriga] *f* chain
вероизповедáние [veroizpovedanie] *n* faith, religion
веролóмен [verolomen] *adj* treacherous, perfidious
вероя́тен [veroyaten] *adj* probable, likely
вероя́тно [veroyatno] *adv* probably, likely

вертика́лен [vertikalen] *adj* vertical
ве́сел [vesel] *adj* cheerful, jolly
веселя́ се [veselya se] *v* enjoy oneself, have fun
весло́ [veslo] *n* oar
ве́стник [vesnik] *m* newspaper, journal
ве́хна [vehna] *v* fade, wither, languish
ве́че [veche] *adv* already
ве́чен [vechen] *adj* eternal, everlasting
ве́чер [vecher] *f* evening
вече́ря [vecherya] *f* supper, dinner
вече́рям [vecheryam] *v* have supper, dine
ве́чност [vechnost] *f* eternity
вещ [vesht] *f* thing
вещ [vesht] *adj* experienced, clever
вещество́ [veshtestvo] *n* matter, substance
вещина́ [veshtina] *f* experience, skill
ве́щица [veshtitsa] *f* witch
взаи́мен [vzaimen] *adj* mutual, reciprocal
взе́мам [vzemam] *v* take, get, pick up
взиска́телен [vziskatelen] *adj* exacting
взрив [vzrif] *m* explosion
вид [vid] *m* appearance, air
вид [vid] *m* kind, sort
ви́ден [viden] *adj* eminent, outstanding, notable
ви́дим [vidim] *adj* visible
ви́е [vie] *pron* you
вие́лица [vielitsa] *f* blizzard
ви́ждам [vizhdam] *v* see, realize

ви́за [viza] *f* visa
вик [vik] *m* cry, shout
ви́кам [vikam] *v* cry, call out, shout
ви́лица [vilitsa] *f* fork
вина́ [vina] *f* guilt, fault
ви́наги [vinagi] *adv* always, ever
ви́но [vino] *n* wine
вино́вен [vinoven] *adj* guilty
винт [vint] *m* screw
виня́ [vinya] *v* blame, find fault
виоле́тов [violetof] *adj* violet, purple
вире́я [vireya] *v* grow, flourish
висо́к [visok] *adj* high, tall, loud
висо́ко [visoko] *adv* high
високоговори́тел [visokogovoritel] *m* loudspeaker
височина́ [visochina] *f* height, altitude, hill
вися́ [visya] *v* hang
витри́на [vitrina] *f* shop window
виц [vits] *m* anecdote, funny story
включвам [fklyuchvam] *v* include, switch on
включи́телно [fklyuchitelno] *adv* including, inclusive
вкус [fkous] *m* taste
вку́сен [fkousen] *adj* tasty, delicious
вла́га [vlaga] *f* moisture, humidity
владе́тел [vladetel] *m* ruler, monarch
владе́я [vladeya] *v* rule, govern, possess, master, speak
влади́ка [vladika] *m* bishop

влак [vlak] *m* train
власт [vlast] *f* power, rule
влача [vlacha] *v* drag, pull, tow
влечение [vlechenie] *n* inclination, bent
влечуго [vlechougo] *n* reptile
влизам [vlizam] *v* enter, go in
влияние [vliyanie] *n* influence
влиятелен [vliyatelen] *adj* influential
влог [vlog] *m* deposit
влошавам [vloshavam] *v* make worse, aggravate
влюбвам се [vlyubvam se] *v* fall in love
вместо [vmesto] *adv* instead of
внасям [vnasyam] *v* bring in, import
внезапен [vnezapen] *adj* sudden, unexpected
внимавам [vnimavam] *v* pay attention, be careful
внимание [vnimanie] *n* attention, care
внук [vnouk] *m* grandson
внучка [vnouchka] *f* granddaughter
внушавам [vnoushavam] *v* suggest
внушение [vnoushenie] *n* suggestion
вода [voda] *f* water
водач [vodach] *m* leader, guide
водовъртеж [vodovurtezh] *m* whirlpool
водолаз [vodolas] *m* diver
водопад [vodopad] *m* waterfall
водоравен [vodoraven] *adj* horizontal
водорасли [vodorasli] *noun pl* seaweed
водород [vodorod] *m* hydrogen

во́дя [vodya] *v* lead, conduct
вое́нен [voenen] *adj* military
во́зя [vozya] *v* ride
война́ [voina] *f* war, warfare
войни́к [voinik] *m* soldier
войска́ [voiska] *f* army
во́лейбол [voleibol] *m* volleyball
во́лен [volen] *adj* free, unrestricted
во́лност [volnost] *f* liberty
во́ля [volya] *f* will
впечатле́ние [fpechatlenie] *n* impression
впро́чем [fprochem] *adv* anyhow, besides, by the way
врабче́ [vrabche] *n* sparrow
враг [vrag] *m* enemy, foe
враждебен [vrazhdeben] *adj* hostile
вра́на [vrana] *f* crow
врат [vrat] *m* neck
врата́ [vrata] *f* door
врата́р [vratar] *m* goalkeeper
вратовръ́зка [vratovruska] *f* necktie
вреда́ [vreda] *f* damage, injury, harm
вре́ден [vreden] *adj* harmful
вре́ме [vreme] *n* time, tense
вре́ме [vreme] *n* weather
вре́менен [vremenen] *adj* temporary
връ́зка [vruska] *f* string, lace, relation, connection, link
връх [vruh] *m* top, peak, height
връ́щам [vrushtam] *v* send back, return

всеки [fseki] *pron* everyone, anyone, each

всекидневен [fsekidneven] *adj* daily, everyday

вселена [fselena] *f* universe, cosmos

всемогъщ [fsemogusht] *adj* almighty, omnipotent

всенароден [fsenaroden] *adj* national, nationwide

всеобщ [fseobsht] *adj* universal, common, general

всички [fsichki] *pron* all, everybody

всичко [fsichko] *pron* all, everything

вследствие [fsledstvie] *conj* as a result of, owing to

всред [fsred] *adv* amid, among

всякакъв [fsyakakuv] *adj* various, of all kinds

всякога [fsyakoga] *adv* always, ever

всякъде [fsyakude] *adv* everywhere

втори [ftori] *adj* second

вторник [ftornik] *m* Tuesday

вход [fhod] *m* entrance

вчера [fchera] *adv* yesterday

въведение [vuvedenie] *n* introduction

въглерод [vuglerod] *m* carbon

въглища [vuglishta] *noun pl* coal

въже [vuzhe] *n* rope, cord, line

възбуждам [vuzbouzhdam] *v* excite

възвание [vuzvanie] *n* appeal

възглавница [vuzglavnitsa] *f* pillow, cushion

въздействие [vuzdeistvie] *n* effect, influence, impact

въздух [vuzdouh] *m* air

въздържам се [vuzdurzham se] *v* refrain, abstain

въздъхвам [vuzduhvam] *v* sigh

възел [vuzel] *m* knot

възклицавам [vusklitsavam] *v* exclaim

възклицание [vusklitsanie] *n* exclamation

възкресение [vuskresenie] *n* resurrection, Easter

възможен [vuzmozhen] *adj* possible, likely

възможност [vuzmozhnost] *f* possibility

възмущение [vuzmoushtenie] *n* indignation

възнаграждение [vuznagrazhdenie] *n* reward, remuneration

възпрепятствувам [vusprepyatstvouvam] *v* impede, prevent

възраждане [vuzrazhdane] *n* revival, renaissance

възраст [vuzrast] *f* age

възрастен [vuzrasten] *adj* elderly, old

възстановявам [vuzstanovyavam] *v* restore, recover, reconstruct

възхищавам се [vus-hishtavam se] *v* admire

възхищение [vus-hishtenie] *n* admiration

възход [vus-hod] *m* progress, advance

вълк [vulk] *m* wolf

вълна [vulna] *f* wool

вълна [vulna] *f* wave

вълне́ние [vulnenie] *n* riot, emotion, excitement

вълше́бен [vulsheben] *adj* magic, enchanting

вън [vun] *prep* out of

въ́ншност [vunshnost] *f* appearance

въображе́ние [vuobrazhenie] *n* imagination

въобразя́вам си [vuobrazyavam si] *v* imagine, fancy

въобще́ [vuobshte] *adv* in general, on the whole, at all

въоръжа́вам [vuoruzhavam] *v* arm

въоръже́ние [vuoruzhenie] *n* armament

въпреки [vupreki] *conj* in spite of, despite

въпро́с [vupros] *m* question

вървя́ [vurvya] *v* go, walk

въртя́ [vurtya] *v* turn, revolve

върху́ [vurhou] *prep* on, upon, over

въ́рша [vursha] *v* do

въста́ние [vustanie] *n* rebellion, uprising

въ́тре [vutre] *prep* in, inside, within

вя́рвам [vyarvam] *v* believe in, trust in

вя́рно [vyarno] *adv* truly, right

вя́тър [vyatur] *m* wind

Г

газ [gas] *m* gas

га́ля [galya] *v* caress, stroke

га́ра [gara] *f* railway station
гара́ж [garazh] *m* garage
гаранти́рам [garantiram] *v* guarantee, warrant
гара́нция [garantsiya] *m* warranty, guarantee
гардеро́б [garderob] *m* wardrobe
гари́рам [gariram] *v* park
га́ся [gasya] *v* put out, extinguish, turn off
га́танка [gatanka] *f* riddle
гащета [gashteta] *noun pl* trunks, pants
геогра́фия [geografiya] *f* geography
геоло́гия [geologiya] *f* geology
геоме́трия [geometriya] *f* geometry
герма́нски [germanski] *adj* German
герои́зъм [geroizum] *m* heroism, gallantry
герои́чен [geroichen] *adj* heroic
геро́й [geroi] *m* hero
ги [gi] *pron* them
гига́нт [gigant] *m* giant
гимна́зия [gimnaziya] *f* high-school
глава́ [glava] *f* head, chapter
гла́вен [glaven] *adj* chief, main, principal
главобо́лие [glavobolie] *n* headache
глаго́л [glagol] *m* verb
глад [glad] *m* hunger, famine
гла́ден [gladen] *adj* hungry
гладу́вам [gladouvam] *v* starve, be hungry
гла́дък [gladuk] *adj* smooth, even
гла́дя [gladya] *v* iron
глас [glas] *m* voice

гласу́вам [glasouvam] *v* vote, poll
гле́дам [gledam] *v* look at, watch, see, gaze
гле́зя [glezya] *v* spoil, behave badly
гло́ба [globa] *f* fine, penalty
глу́пав [gloupaf] *adj* foolish, silly, stupid
глух [glouh] *adj* deaf
гне́вен [gneven] *adj* angry, wrathful
гнездо́ [gnezdo] *n* nest
гни́я [gniya] *v* rot, decay
гняв [gnyav] *m* anger, wrath, rage
го [go] *pron* him
гове́ждо [govezhdo] *n* beef
го́вор [govor] *m* speech, dialect
говори́тел [govoritel] *m* speaker
гово́ря [govorya] *v* speak, talk
годени́к [godenik] *m* fiancé
годени́ца [godenitsa] *f* fiancée
годи́на [godina] *f* year
годи́шен [godishen] *adj* yearly, annual
годи́шно вре́ме [godishno vreme] *n* season
годи́шнина [godishnina] *f* anniversary
гол [gol] *adj* naked
голя́м [golyam] *adj* big, large, great
го́ня [gonya] *v* chase, pursue
гора́ [gora] *f* forest, wood
горд [gord] *adj* proud
го́рдост [gordost] *f* pride
го́ре [gore] *adv* above, up
го́рен [goren] *adj* upper, top
горе́щ [goresht] *adj* hot, fervent

горещина [goreshtina] *f* heat
гориво [gorivo] *n* fuel
горчив [gorchif] *adj* bitter
горчица [gorchitsa] *f* mustard
горя [gorya] *v* burn
господар [gospodar] *m* master
господин [gospodin] *m* Mr., Sir
госпожа [gospozha] *f* Mrs., Madam
госпожица [gospozhitsa] *f* Miss
гост [gost] *m* guest, visitor
гостоприемство [gostopriemstvo] *n*
hospitality
гостуване [gostouvane] *n* visit
готвач [gotvach] *m* cook
готвя [gotvya] *v* cook, prepare
готов [gotof] *adj* ready, prepared
грабеж [grabezh] *m* robbery, plunder
град [grad] *m* town, city
град [grad] *m* hail
градина [gradina] *f* garden
градус [gradous] *m* degree
гражданин [grazhdanin] *m* citizen
граждански [grazhdanski] *adj* civil, civilian
грамаден [gramaden] *adj* huge, enormous,
tremendous
грамотен [gramoten] *adj* literate
грамофонна плоча [gramofonna plocha] *f*
record, disc
граница [granitsa] *f* frontier, border
грах [grah] *m* peas

грацио́зен [gratsiozen] *adj* graceful
гра́ция [gratsiya] *f* grace
гре́шка [greshka] *f* mistake, error
гри́вна [grivna] *f* bracelet
гри́жа [grizha] *f* care
гри́жа се [grizha se] *v* take care of, worry, look after
грим [grim] *m* make-up
грип [grip] *m* influenza, flu
гроб [grob] *m* grave
гро́бище [grobishte] *n* cemetery
гро́зде [grozde] *n* grapes
гро́зен [grozen] *adj* ugly, plain
груб [groub] *adj* coarse, rude
гру́па [groupa] *f* group, party
гръб [grub] *m* back
гръбна́к [grubnak] *m* spine, backbone
гръд [grud] *f* breast, bosom
гръм [grum] *m* thunder
грях [gryah] *m* sin
губерна́тор [goubernator] *m* governor
гу́бя [goubya] *v* lose
гу́ма [gouma] *f* rubber, tire
гу́менки [goumenki] *noun pl* tennis shoes
гу́ша [gousha] *f* throat
гу́щер [goushter] *m* lizard
гъ́ба [guba] *f* mushroom
гъ́вкав [gufkav] *adj* flexible, pliable
гъ́лтам [gultam] *v* swallow
гъ́лъб [gulub] *m* pigeon, dove

гълъб [gulub] *m* pigeon, dove
гърло [gurlo] *n* throat
гъска [guska] *f* goose
гъст [gust] *adj* thick, dense

Д

да [da] *prep* to
да [da] *part* yes
давам [davam] *v* give, pass, grant
давя [davya] *v* drown
далеч [dalech] *adv* far, far away
дали [dali] *conj* if, whether
дама [dama] *f* lady
данни [danni] *noun pl* data
данък [danuk] *m* tax, rate
дарба [darba] *f* talent, gift
дата [data] *f* date
два [dva] *num* two
двадесет [dvadeset] *num* twenty
дванадесет [dvanadeset] *num* twelve
двигател [dvigatel] *m* motor, engine
движа се [dvizha se] *v* move, stir, work
двоен [dvoen] *adj* double
двоеточие [dvoetochie] *n* colon
дворец [dvorets] *m* palace
двоумя се [dvooumya se] *v* hesitate
дебел [debel] *adj* thick, fat

дебелоглав [debeloglaf] *adj* stubborn, obstinate

девер [dever] *m* brother–in–law

девет [devet] *num* nine

деветнадесет [devetnadeset] *num* nineteen

дейсност [deisnost] *f* activity, work

действие [deistvie] *n* action, operation, act

действителен [deistvitelen] *adj* real, actual, valid

декември [dekemvri] *m* December

декларирам [deklariram] *v* declare

деление [delenie] *n* division, partition

дело [delo] *n* case, suit

делфин [delfin] *m* dolphin

деля [delya] *v* divide

демокрация [demokratsiya] *f* democracy

ден [den] *m* day

депозирам [depoziram] *v* deposit

десен [desen] *adj* right

десетилетие [desetiletie] *n* decade

дете [dete] *n* child

дефект [defect] *m* defect, fault, flaw

джоб [dzhob] *m* pocket

джунгла [dzhoungla] *f* jungle

диагноза [diagnoza] *f* diagnosis

диамант [diamant] *m* diamond

див [dif] *adj* wild

диван [divan] *m* couch, sofa

дивен [diven] *adj* marvellous, wonderful

дивеч [divech] *m* game

диета [dieta] *f* diet
диктатура [diktatoura] *f* dictatorship
дим [dim] *m* smoke
диня [dinya] *f* watermelon
директор [direktor] *m* director, manager, principal
диригент [dirigent] *m* conductor
дискриминация [diskriminatsiya] *f* discrimination
дискусия [diskousiya] *f* discussion, debate
дисциплина [distsiplina] *f* discipline, subject
дишам [disham] *v* breathe
длан [dlan] *f* palm
длъжност [dluzhnost] *f* office, position
дневник [dnevnik] *m* diary
днес [dnes] *adv* today, at present
до [do] *prep* at, by, beside, to, till
добив [dobif] *m* production, crop
добитък [dobituk] *m* cattle, livestock
добре [dobre] *adv* good, well, right
добрина [dobrina] *f* goodness, kindness
доброволец [dobrovolets] *m* volunteer
добродетел [dobrodetel] *f* virtue
добър [dobur] *adj* good
доверие [doverie] *n* confidence, faith, trust
довечера [dovechera] *adv* tonight, this evening
довод [dovod] *m* argument
договор [dogovor] *m* contract, agreement, treaty

догоди́на [dogodina] *adv* next year
дого́нвам [dogonvam] *v* catch up
доказа́телство [dokazatelstvo] *n* proof, evidence
дока́звам [dokazvam] *v* prove
докла́д [doklad] *m* report, lecture, talk
докога́ [dokoga] *adv* how long, till when
доко́лкото [dokolkoto] *adv* as far as
доко́свам [dokosvam] *v* touch lightly
до́ктор [doktor] *m* doctor
докуме́нт [dokoument] *m* document
долина́ [dolina] *f* valley
до́лу [dolou] *adv* down, below
дом [dom] *m* home
домаки́н [domakin] *m* host
домаки́ня [domakinya] *f* housewife
дома́т [domat] *m* tomato
дона́сям [donasyam] *v* bring, fetch
допу́скам [dopouskam] *v* admit
допълне́ние [dopulnenie] *n* addition, supplement
дори́ [dori] *adv* even
доса́да [dosada] *f* boredom, tediousness
доса́ждам [dosazhdam] *v* bore, tire, bother
досе́щам се [doseshtam se] *v* guess, remember
доспи́ва ми се [dospiva mi se] *v* be sleepy
досрамя́ва ме [dosramyava me] *v* feel ashamed

до́ста [dosta] *adv* fairly, somewhat, very, quite

доста́вка [dostafka] *f* shipment, delivery

доста́вям [dostavyam] *v* supply, furnish, provide

доста́тъчен [dostatuchen] *adj* sufficient, enough

достове́рен [dostoveren] *adj* reliable, authentic

досто́йнство [dostoinstvo] *n* dignity

до́ход [dohod] *m* income, revenue

до́ходен [dohoden] *adj* profitable

дра́зня [draznya] *v* irritate, tease

дра́ма [drama] *f* drama

драмату́рг [dramatourg] *m* dramatist, playwright

дре́бен [dreben] *adj* small, fine

дре́вен [dreven] *adj* ancient, antique

дре́ха [dreha] *f* garment, clothes

дроб [drob] *m* lung, liver

друг [droug] *adj* other, different

дру́жество [drouzhestvo] *n* association, society

дръ́жка [druzhka] *f* handle

дузи́на [douzina] *f* dozen

ду́ма [douma] *f* word

ду́пка [doupka] *f* hole, cavity

ду́хам [douham] *v* blow

духо́вен [douhoven] *adj* spiritual, of the mind

духо́венство [douhovenstvo] *n* clergy, priesthood

душ [doush] *m* shower

душа́ [dousha] *f* soul, heart

душе́вен [dousheven] *adj* spiritual, mental

дъб [dub] *m* oak tree

дъ́вка [dufka] *f* chewing gum

дъ́вча [dufcha] *v* chew

дъга́ [duga] *f* rainbow

дъжд [duzhd] *m* rain

дълбо́к [dulbok] *adj* deep

дълбочина́ [dulbochina] *f* depth

дъ́лго [dulgo] *adv* for a long time

дължа́ [dulzha] *v* owe, be indebted

дължина́ [dulzhina] *m* length, longitude

дъ́лъг [dulug] *adj* long

дъ́нки [dunki] *noun pl* blue jeans

дъ́но [duno] *n* bottom

дървеси́на [durvesina] *f* wood

дърво́ [durvo] *n* tree

държа́ [durzha] *v* hold, support, keep

държа́ва [durzhava] *f* state, country

държа́ние [durzhanie] *n* behavior, manners

дъска́ [duska] *f* board, plank

дъщеря́ [dushterya] *f* daughter

дюше́к [dyushek] *m* mattress

дя́вол [dyavol] *m* devil

дя́до [dyado] *m* grandfather

дял [dyal] *m* share, part, branch

дя́сно [dyasno] *adv* right

Е

Ева́нгелие [evangelie] *n* gospel
евре́ин [evrein] *m* Jew
европе́йски [evropeiski] *adj* European
е́втин [eftin] *adj* cheap, inexpensive
егои́зъм [egoizum] *m* selfishness, egoism
еди́н [edin] *num* one
едина́десет [edinadeset] *num* eleven
едини́ца [edinitsa] *f* unit
едини́чен [edinichen] *adj* single
еди́нство [edinstvo] *n* unity
еднообра́зие [ednoobrazie] *n* uniformity
еднопосо́чна у́лица [ednoposochna oulitsa] *f*
one-way street
езда́ [ezda] *f* riding
е́зеро [ezero] *n* lake, pond
ези́к [ezik] *m* tongue, language, speech
екра́н [ekran] *m* screen
екску́рзия [ekskourziya] *f* excursion, hike,
trip
екскурзово́д [ekskourzovod] *m* guide
експериме́нт [eksperiment] *m* experiment,
test
експе́рт [ekspert] *m* expert, specialist
експло́зия [eksploziya] *f* explosion
експона́т [eksponat] *m* exhibit
ела́ [ela] *v* come
елега́нтен [eleganten] *adj* elegant, smart

електри́чески [elektricheski] *adj* electric
елемента́рен [elementaren] *adj* elementary
елха́ [elha] *f* Christmas tree
емигра́нт [emigrant] *m* emigrant
емигри́рам [emigriram] *v* emigrate
емо́ция [emotsiya] *f* emotion
енерги́чен [energichen] *adj* energetic
ене́ргия [energiya] *f* energy
енциклопе́дия [entsiklopediya] *f* encyclopedia
епиде́мия [epidemiya] *f* epidemic
епи́скоп [episkop] *m* bishop
ерге́н [ergen] *m* bachelor
е́сен [esen] *f* autumn, fall
есте́ствен [estestven] *adj* natural
есте́ствено [estestveno] *adv* certainly, of course
ета́ж [etazh] *m* floor, storey
ета́п [etap] *m* stage
е́тика [etika] *f* ethics
ефе́кт [efect] *m* effect, result
ефекти́вен [efektiven] *adj* effective, efficient
е́хо [eho] *n* echo

Ж

жа́ба [zhaba] *f* frog, toad
жа́ден [zhaden] *adj* thirsty

жа́жда [zhazhda] *f* thirst, lust
жела́ние [zhelanie] *n* wish, desire
жела́я [zhelaya] *v* wish, desire
железари́я [zhelezariya] *f* hardware
желе́зен [zhelezen] *adj* iron
желе́зница [zheleznitsa] *f* railway
желя́зо [zhelyazo] *n* iron
жена́ [zhena] *f* woman, wife
жесто́к [zhestok] *adj* cruel, fierce
живе́я [zhiveya] *v* live
живопи́с [zhivopis] *f* painting
живо́т [zhivot] *m* life
живо́тно [zhivotno] *n* animal
жиле́тка [zhiletka] *f* vest
жи́лище [zhilishte] *n* home, house
жи́то [zhito] *n* wheat
жи́ца [zhitsa] *f* wire
журна́л [zhournal] *m* magazine
журнали́ст [zhournalist] *m* journalist, pressman
жълт [zhult] *adj* yellow
жълтъ́к [zhultuk] *m* yolk
жъ́тва [zhutva] *f* harvest

З

за [za] *prep* to, for, till
забавле́ние [zabavlenie] *n* entertainment
заба́вям [zabavyam] *v* delay, retard

забележителен [zabelezhitelen] *adj* remarkable, notable

заблуждавам [zablouzhdavam] *v* mislead

забогатявам [zabogatyavam] *v* grow rich

забравям [zabravyam] *v* forget

забрана [zabrana] *f* prohibition, ban

забранявам [zabranyavam] *v* forbid, prohibit

заварвам [zavarvam] *v* find

завеса [zavesa] *f* curtain

завещание [zaveshtanie] *n* will, testament

завземам [zavzemam] *v* seize, capture, occupy

зависим [zavisim] *adj* dependent

зависимост [zavisimost] *f* dependence

завист [zavist] *f* envy

завися [zavisya] *v* depend on

завод [zavod] *m* plant, mill

завой [zavoi] *m* turn, curve

завоювам [zavoyuvam] *v* conquer, win

завръщане [zavrushtane] *v* return

заглавие [zaglavie] *n* title, heading

заговор [zagovor] *m* plot, conspiracy

загрижен [zagrizhen] *adj* worried, anxious

загриженост [zagrizhenost] *f* anxiety, concern, care

загуба [zagouba] *f* loss, damage

задавам [zadavam] *v* assign, ask

задача [zadacha] *f* task, problem

задоволителен [zadovolitelen] *adj* satisfactory, satisfying

задълбочен [zadulbochen] *adj* profound, thorough

задължение [zadulzhenie] *n* duty, obligation, engagement

задължителен [zadulzhitelen] *adj* obligatory, compulsory

заедно [zaedno] *adv* together, along with

заек [zaek] *m* rabbit, hare

заем [zaem] *m* loan

зает [zaet] *adj* busy, taken, occupied

заинтересован [zainteresovan] *adj* interested, concerned, partial

заканвам се [zakanvam se] *v* threaten

закачалка [zakachalka] *f* hat rack, hanger

закачам [zakacham] *v* hang up

заключвам [zaklyuchvam] *v* lock

заключение [zaklyuchenie] *n* conclusion

закон [zakon] *m* law, act

законен [zakonen] *adj* lawful, legitimate, legal

законодателство [zakonodatelstvo] *n* legislation

законопроект [zakonoproekt] *m* bill

закопчавам [zakopchavam] *v* button

закусвам [zakousvam] *v* have breakfast

закуска [zakouska] *f* breakfast, snack

закъснение [zakusnenie] *n* delay

закъснявам [zakusnyavam] *v* be late

залавям [zalavyam] *v* catch

залез [zales] *n* sunset

залепвам [zalepvam] *v* stick
залив [zalif] *m* bay, gulf
замесвам [zamesvam] *v* involve
замествам [zamestvam] *v* replace, substitute
заможен [zamozhen] *adj* well-to-do, well off
замразен [zamrazen] *adj* frozen
замразявам [zamrazyavam] *v* freeze, ice
замяна [zamyana] *f* exchange
занятие [zanyatie] *n* occupation
запад [zapad] *m* west
запалвам [zapalvam] *v* light, kindle
запалка [zapalka] *f* lighter
запалянко [zapalyanko] *m* fan
заплата [zaplata] *f* salary, pay, wages
заплаха [zaplaha] *f* threat, menace
заплашвам [zaplashvam] *v* threaten, menace
заповед [zapoved] *f* command, order
запознавам [zapoznavam] *v* acquaint, introduce
започвам [zapochvam] *v* begin, start
запушвам [zapoushvam] *v* plug, cork
зар [zar] *m* die
заравям [zaravyam] *v* bury
зараза [zaraza] *f* infection, contagion
зародиш [zarodish] *m* embryo, foetus
засада [zasada] *f* ambush
засаждам [zasazhdam] *v* plant
заседание [zasedanie] *n* conference, session
заспивам [zaspivam] *v* go to sleep
заставям [zastavyam] *v* force, compel

застрахо́вка [zastrahofka] *f* insurance
затва́рям [zatvaryam] *v* shut, close
затво́р [zatvor] *m* prison, jail
затво́рен [zatvoren] *adj* closed, shut
затво́рник [zatvornik] *m* prisoner
затова́ [zatova] *adv* therefore, that is why
зато́плям [zatoplyam] *v* warm up
затъмне́ние [zatumnenie] *n* black out, eclipse
затя́гам [zatyagam] *v* tighten, make fast
зауча́вам [zaouchavam] *v* learn
за́ушки [zaoushki] *noun pl* mumps
за́хар [zahar] *m* sugar
за́харна бо́лест [zaharna bolest] *f* diabetes
захарни́ца [zaharnitsa] *f* sugar bowl
защи́та [zashtita] *f* defence, protection
защища́вам [zashtishtavam] *v* defend, protect
защо́ [zashto] *conj* why, what for
защо́то [zashtoto] *conj* because, for, as
звезда́ [zvezda] *f* star
звук [zvouk] *m* sound
звуча́ [zvoucha] *v* ring, sound
звъне́ц [zvunets] *m* bell
звъня́ [zvunya] *v* ring
звяр [zvyar] *m* beast, wild animal
зда́ние [zdanie] *n* building
здрав [zdraf] *adj* healthy, strong, solid
здра́ве [zdrave] *n* health
зе́ле [zele] *n* cabbage
зеле́н [zelen] *adj* green, unripe
зеленчу́к [zelenchouk] *m* vegetables

земевладе́лец [zemevladelets] *m* landowner
земеде́лец [zemedelets] *m* farmer
земеде́лие [zemedelie] *n* agriculture, farming
земетресе́ние [zemetresenie] *n* earthquake
земя́ [zemya] *f* soil, earth, ground
зет [zet] *m* son-in-law, brother-in-law
зехти́н [zehtin] *m* olive oil
зид [zid] *m* wall
зи́ма [zima] *f* winter
зла́то [zlato] *n* gold
зло́ба [zloba] *f* spite, malice
злове́щ [zlovesht] *adj* sinister, ominous
злополу́ка [zlopolouka] *f* accident
злоупотре́ба [zlooupotreba] *f* abuse, misuse
змия́ [zmiya] *f* snake
знак [znak] *m* sign, mark, symbol
зна́ме [zname] *n* flag, banner
знамени́т [znamenit] *adj* famous, eminent
зна́ча [znacha] *v* mean
значе́ние [znachenie] *n* meaning, importance, significance
значи́телен [znachitelen] *adj* considerable, important
значка́ [znachka] *f* badge
зна́я [znaya] *v* know, be aware of
зоологи́ческа гради́на [zoologicheska gradina] *f* zoo
зооло́гия [zoologiya] *f* zoology
зре́ние [zrenie] *n* eyesight, vision
зре́я [zreya] *v* ripen, mature

зрител [zritel] *m* spectator, viewer
зрял [zryal] *adj* ripe, mature
зъб [zub] *m* tooth
зъбобол [zubobol] *m* toothache
зъболекар [zubolekar] *m* dentist
зърно [zurno] *n* grain

И

и [i] *conj* and, even, also, too
игла [igla] *f* needle
игра [igra] *f* game, play
играчка [igrachka] *f* toy
играя [igraya] *v* play
игрище [igrishte] *n* playground
идвам [idvam] *v* come
идеален [idealen] *adj* ideal, perfect
идея [ideya] *f* idea, notion, concept
идиот [idiot] *m* idiot, fool
избирател [izbiratel] *m* voter
избори [izbori] *noun pl* elections
избягвам [izbyagvam] *v* run away, escape, avoid
изваждане [izvazhdane] *n* removal, subtraction
известен [izvesten] *adj* famous, certain
извинение [izvinenie] *n* excuse, apology, forgiveness
извод [izvod] *m* deduction, conclusion

извор [izvor] *m* spring

извоювам [izvoyuvam] *v* win, gain

извън [izvun] *adv* outside, out of

изглед [izgled] *m* view

изгнание [izgnanie] *n* exile

изговор [izgovor] *m* pronunciation, articulation

изгода [izgoda] *f* advantage, interest, profit

изгоден [izgoden] *adj* advantageous, profitable

изгонвам [izgonvam] *v* drive away, expel

изготвям [izgotvyam] *v* prepare, make

изгрев [izgrev] *m* sunrise

изгрявам [izgryavam] *v* rise

изгубен [izgouben] *adj* lost, hopeless

издавам [izdavam] *v* betray, give away

издавам [izdavam] *v* publish, issue

издание [izdanie] *n* publication, edition

издател [izdatel] *m* publisher

издателство [izdatelstvo] *n* publishing house

издишвам [izdishvam] *v* exhale, expire, breathe out

издръжливост [izdruzhlivost] *f* tenacity, resistance

изисканост [iziskanost] *f* refinement, fineness, good taste

изисквам [iziskvam] *v* demand, require

изискване [iziskvane] *n* requirement

изказване [iskazvane] *n* statement, speech, contribution

изклю́чвам [isklyuchvam] *v* exclude, rule out, bar

изключе́ние [isklyuchenie] *n* exception

изку́ствен [iskoustven] *adj* artificial

изку́ство [iskoustvo] *n* art, skill

изкуша́вам [iskoushavam] *v* tempt, allure

изкуше́ние [iskoushenie] *n* temptation, allurement

изли́вам [izlivam] *v* pour out, empty

изли́зам [izlizam] *v* come out

изли́там [izlitam] *v* fly out, take off

изли́шен [izlishen] *adj* superfluous, redundant

изли́шък [izlishuk] *m* surplus, excess

изло́жба [izlozhba] *f* exhibition, show, display

изма́ма [izmama] *f* deceit, fraud, delusion

изма́мвам [izmamvam] *v* deceive, cheat, fool

изме́рвам [izmervam] *v* measure, weigh

измере́ние [izmerenie] *n* dimension

изме́ствам [izmestvam] *v* displace

изми́вам [izmivam] *v* wash

изми́слям [izmislyam] *v* invent, contrive, fabricate

изморе́н [izmoren] *adj* tired, weary

измори́телен [izmoritelen] *adj* tiresome

измръ́знал [izmruznal] *adj* frozen, chilled

измъ́чвам [izmuchvam] *v* torture, torment

изнаси́лвам [iznasilvam] *v* rape

изневя́ра [iznevyara] *f* unfaithfulness

изненада [iznenada] *f* surprise

износ [iznos] *m* export, exportation

изобилие [izobilie] *n* abundance, profusion, plenty

изобразително искуство [izobrazitelno iskoustvo] *n* painting

изобретателен [izobretatelen] *adj* inventive, resourceful

изобретение [izobretenie] *n* invention, device

изолация [izolatsiya] *f* insulation, isolation

изолирам [izoliram] *v* insulate, isolate

изоставам [izostavam] *v* fall behind, lose

изоставям [izostavyam] *v* desert, abandon

изпарение [isparenie] *n* evaporation, fumes

изпарявам [isparyavam] *v* evaporate

изпит [ispit] *m* examination

изплащам [isplashtam] *v* pay off

изповед [ispoved] *f* confession

изпотявам се [ispotyavam se] *v* sweat, perspire

изправен [ispraven] *adj* upright

изпразвам [isprazvam] *v* empty, discharge

изпробвам [isprobvam] *v* test, try, fit

изпускам [ispouskam] *v* drop

изпълнение [ispulnenie] *n* execution, fulfilment, performance

изравям [izravyam] *v* dig out, excavate

изражение [izrazhenie] *n* expression, air

изразходвам [izraz-hodvam] *v* spend, use up

изразя́вам [izrazyavam] *v* express, voice
изрече́ние [izrechenie] *n* sentence
изря́звам [izryazvam] *v* cut, clip
изска́чам [iskacham] *v* jump out, pop up
изсле́дване [isledvane] *n* study, investigation, research
изследова́тел [isledovatel] *m* researcher, explorer
и́зстрел [istrel] *m* shot, report
изтеза́вам [istezavam] *v* torture, torment
изтеза́ние [istezanie] *n* torture, torment
изти́чам [isticham] *v* run out, expire
и́зток [istok] *m* east
и́зточен [istochen] *adj* eastern, oriental
и́зточник [istochnik] *m* source
изтоща́вам [istoshtavam] *v* exhaust, drain
изтоще́ние [istoshtenie] *n* exhaustion
изтреби́тел [istrebitel] *m* fighter
изтри́вам [istrivam] *v* wipe, rub, erase
изтъ́кнат [istuknat] *adj* outstanding, distinguished, eminent
изтърва́вам [isturvavam] *v* drop, let fall
изуча́вам [izouchavam] *v* study, learn
изхвъ́рлям [is-hvurlyam] *v* throw out, eject
и́зход [is-hod] *m* exit, way out, outcome, issue
изче́звам [ischezvam] *v* disappear, vanish
изче́рпан [ischerpan] *adj* exhausted, out of print

изчерпа́телен [ischerpatelen] *adj* thorough, comprehensive

изчисле́ние [ischislenie] *n* calculation

изчисля́вам [ischislyavam] *v* calculate, estimate

изчи́ствам [ischistvam] *v* clean out, clear

изя́щен [izyashten] *adj* graceful, refined, exquisite

изя́щество [izyashtestvo] *n* grace, refinement

ико́на [ikona] *f* icon

ико́но́мика [ikonomika] *f* economy

икономи́свам [ikonomisvam] *v* save, economize, put aside

икономи́чен [ikonomichen] *adj* economical, thrifty

илю́зия [ilyuziya] *f* illusion

илюстра́ция [ilyustratsiya] *f* illustration

и́ма [ima] *v* there is, there are

и́мам [imam] *v* have, own, possess

и́ме [ime] *n* name

имо́т [imot] *m* property, belongings

имуните́т [imounitet] *m* immunity

иму́щество [imoushtestvo] *n* property

инвали́д [invalid] *m* invalid, disabled person

индиви́д [individ] *m* individual, specimen

индивидуа́лен [individoualen] *adj* individual, personal

инди́йски [indiiski] *adj* Indian

индустриа́лен [indoustrialen] *adj* industrial

инду́стрия [indoustriya] *f* industry

инжекция [inzhektsiya] *f* injection
инженер [inzhener] *m* engineer
инстинкт [instinkt] *m* instinct
институт [institout] *m* institute
инструкция [instrouktsiya] *f* instructions
инструмент [instroument] *m* instrument, tool
интелект [intelekt] *m* intellect, brains
интелектуален [intelektoualen] *adj*
intellectual
интелигентен [inteligenten] *adj* intelligent,
clever, bright
интензивен [intenziven] *adj* intensive
интервал [interval] *m* interval, space, gap
интервю [intervyu] *n* interview
интерес [interes] *m* interest
интересен [interesen] *adj* interesting
интимен [intimen] *adj* intimate, close
интимност [intimnost] *f* intimacy
инфекция [infektsiya] *f* infection
инфлация [inflatsiya] *f* inflation
информация [informatsiya] *f* information,
news
информирам [informiram] *v* inform, notify,
advise
ироничен [ironichen] *adj* ironical, derisive
иск [isk] *m* claim
искам [iskam] *v* want, require, demand
искрен [iskren] *adj* sincere, frank
искреност [iskrenost] *f* sincerity, frankness
истина [istina] *f* truth

и́стински [istinski] *adj* true, real, genuine
истори́чески [istoricheski] *adj* historical
исто́рия [istoriya] *f* history, tale, affair

К

ка́бел [kabel] *m* cable
каби́на [kabina] *f* cabin, booth
кабине́т [kabinet] *m* study
кави́чки [kavichki] *noun pl* quotation marks
кадифе́н [kadifen] *adj* velvet
каза́рма [kazarma] *f* barracks
ка́звам [kazvam] *v* say, tell
как [kak] *adv* how
кака́о [kakao] *n* cocoa
какво́ [kakvo] *adv* what
ка́кто [kakto] *adv* as
какъ́в [kakuf] *adv* what, what kind of
кал [kal] *f* mud, dirt
календа́р [kalendar] *m* calendar
камба́на [kambana] *f* bell
ками́ла [kamila] *f* camel
камио́н [kamion] *m* truck
камши́к [kamshik] *m* whip, lash
кана́л [kanal] *m* canal, channel
канапе́ [kanape] *n* sofa, couch
кандида́т [kandidat] *m* candidate
канцела́рия [kantselariya] *f* office
ка́ня [kanya] *v* invite, ask

капа́к [kapak] *m* lid, cover
капа́н [kapan] *m* trap
капиталовложе́ние [kapitalovlozhenie] *n* investment
ка́пка [kapka] *f* drop
ка́рам [karam] *v* drive
ка́рам се[karam se] *v* scold, quarrel
карамфи́л [karamfil] *m* carnation
карие́ра [kariera] *f* career
карикату́ра [karikatoura] *f* caricature, cartoon
ка́рта [karta] *f* card
карте́чница [kartechnitsa] *f* machine-gun
карти́на [kartina] *f* picture, painting
ка́ртичка [kartichka] *f* postcard
карто́н [karton] *m* cardboard, pasteboard
карто́ф [kartof] *m* potato
ка́са [kasa] *f* safe, cash-drawer
катало́г [katalog] *m* catalog
катастро́фа [katastrofa] *f* accident, crash, disaster
катастрофи́рам [katastrofiram] *v* crash, have an accident
катедра́ла [katedrala] *f* cathedral
ка́терица [kateritsa] *f* squirrel
кате́ря се [katerya se] *v* climb
като́ [kato] *v* like
като́лик [katolik] *m* catholic
ка́уза [kauza] *f* cause, idea
кафе́ [kafe] *n* coffee

кафене́ [kafene] *n* cafe
кафя́в [kafyav] *adj* brown
ка́цане [katsane] *n* landing
ка́цам [katsam] *v* land
ка́чество [kachestvo] *n* quality
ка́шлям [kashlyam] *v* cough, have a cough
квадра́т [kvadrat] *m* square
квадра́тен [kvadraten] *adj* square
квалифика́ция [kvalifikatsiya] *f* qualification
кварти́ра [kvartira] *f* lodging(s)
квартира́нт [kvartirant] *m* lodger, tenant
кей [kei] *m* quay
кера́мика [keramika] *f* ceramics, pottery
керами́да [keramida] *f* tile
ке́стен [kesten] *m* chestnut
ке́цове [ketsove] *noun pl* sneakers
кибри́т [kibrit] *m* match, box of matches
или́м [kilim] *m* carpet, rug
ки́но [kino] *n* cinema, movie
кинорежисьо́р [kinorezhisyor] *m* film director
кипя́ [kipya] *v* boil, seethe
ки́сел [kisel] *adj* sour, acid
киселина́ [kiselina] *f* acid
кислоро́д [kislorod] *m* oxygen
кит [kit] *m* whale
кита́йски [kitaiski] *adj* Chinese
кита́ра [kitara] *f* guitar
ки́фла [kifla] *f* roll, bun
ки́хам [kiham] *v* sneeze

клави́ш [klavish] *m* key, note
кла́денец [kladenets] *m* well
кла́мер [klamer] *m* paper-clip
клас [klas] *m* class, grade
класи́чески [klasicheski] *adj* classic
кла́тя [klatya] *v* shake, rock, dangle
клепа́ч [klepach] *m* eyelid
кле́пка [klepka] *f* eyelash
кле́тва [kletva] *f* oath, curse
кле́тка [kletka] *f* cage, cell
клие́нт [klient] *m* customer, patron
кли́мат [klimat] *m* climate
климати́чна инстала́ция [klimatichna
instalatsiya] *f* air-conditioning
клон [klon] *m* branch, bough
кло́ун [kloun] *m* clown, joker
клуб [kloub] *m* club
клю́ка [klyuka] *f* gossip, scandal
ключ [klyuch] *m* key
ключа́лка [klyuchalka] *f* lock
кмет [kmet] *m* mayor
кни́га [kniga] *f* book
книжа́ [knizha] *noun pl* papers, documents
книжа́рница [knizharnitsa] *f* bookstore
коали́ция [koalitsiya] *f* coalition
кова́рство [kovarstvo] *n* treachery, perfidy
ковче́г [kofcheg] *m* coffin
кога́ [koga] *adv* when
ко́жа [kozha] *f* skin, fur, leather
ко́жен [kozhen] *adj* leather, fur

коза [koza] *f* goat
кой [koi] *pron* who, which
кокал [kokal] *m* bone
кокошка [kokoshka] *f* hen
колан [kolan] *m* bell
колебание [kolebanie] *n* hesitation, wavering
колебая се [kolebaya se] *v* hesitate, waver
колега [kolega] *m* colleague, mate
коледа [koleda] *f* Christmas
колекция [kolektsiya] *f* collection
колело [kolelo] *n* wheel, bicycle
количество [kolichestvo] *n* quantity, amount, number
колко [kolko] *adv* how much, how many
колкото [kolkoto] *adv* as, as much as, as many as
колона [kolona] *f* column, pillar, post
колония [koloniya] *f* colony
коля [kolya] *v* slaughter, kill, butcher
командир [komandir] *m* commander
комар [komar] *m* mosquito, gnat
комар [komar] *f* gambling
комедия [komediya] *f* comedy
коментар [komentar] *m* commentary, comment
коментирам [komentiram] *v* comment
комин [komin] *m* chimney
комисия [komisiya] *f* commission, committee, board
комитет [komitet] *m* committee

компа́с [kompas] *m* compass

компенса́ция [kompensatsiya] *f* compensation, recompense

компенси́рам [kompensiram] *v* compensate, make amends

компете́нтен [kompetenten] *adj* competent

компете́нтност [kompetentnost] *f* competence

компози́тор [kompozitor] *m* composer

комуни́зъм [komounizum] *m* communism

комфо́рт [komfort] *m* comfort, luxury

комюнике́ [komyunike] *n* communique, official statement

кон [kon] *m* horse, steed, knight

конгре́с [kongres] *m* congress

ко́нец [konets] *m* thread

конкуре́нт [konkourent] *m* competitor

конкуре́нция [konkourentsiya] *f* competition

конку́рс [konkours] *m* competition (in arts, sport)

ко́нница [konnitsa] *f* cavalry

консервати́вен [konservativen] *adj* conservative

консе́рвена кути́я [konservena koutiya] *f* tin, can

конспе́кт [konspekt] *m* syllabus

ко́нсулство [konsoulstvo] *n* consulate

консулти́рам [konsoultiram] *v* consult, see

контине́нт [kontinent] *m* continent

контраба́нда [kontrabanda] *f* smuggling, contraband

контраст [kontrast] *m* contrast
контрол [kontrol] *m* control, checking
конус [konous] *m* cone
конфитюр [konfityur] *m* jam, preserve
конфликт [konflict] *m* conflict
концерт [kontsert] *m* concert
коняк [konyak] *m* cognac, brandy
копая [kopaya] *v* dig
копие [kopie] *n* spear, pike
копие [kopie] *n* copy, duplicate
коприна [koprina] *f* silk
копче [kopche] *n* button
кора [kora] *f* bark, peal, crust
кораб [korab] *m* ship, boat
коректор [korektor] *m* proof-reader
корекция [korektsiya] *f* correction, amendment
корем [korem] *m* stomach, belly
корен [koren] *m* root
кореспондент [korespondent] *m* correspondent
коридор [koridor] *m* corridor
корица [koritsa] *f* cover
корона [korona] *f* crown
коса [kosa] *f* hair
космонавт [kosmonaft] *m* astronaut
кост [kost] *f* bone
костенурка [kostenourka] *f* turtle, tortoise
костюм [kostyum] *m* suit, costume
косъм [kosum] *m* hair

ко́тва [kotva] *f* anchor
ко́тка [kotka] *f* cat
ко́шница [koshnitsa] *f* basket
кра́ва [krava] *f* cow
крада́ [krada] *v* steal, lift
краде́ц [kradets] *m* thief
кра́жба [krazhba] *f* theft, burglary
кра́йник [krainik] *m* limb
кра́йност [krainost] *f* extreme, excess
крак [krak] *m* leg, foot
крал [kral] *m* king
крали́ца [kralitsa] *f* queen
кра́лство [kralstvo] *n* kingdom
краса́вица [krasavitsa] *f* beauty
краси́в [krasif] *adj* beautiful, lovely, handsome
красота́ [krasota] *f* beauty
кра́ставица [krastavitsa] *f* cucumber
кра́тък [kratuk] *adj* short, brief, concise
кра́чка [krachka] *f* step, pace
крева́т [krevat] *m* bed, bedstead
кре́дит [kredit] *m* credit
крем [krem] *m* cream
кре́нвирш [krenvirsh] *m* Frankfurter
кресло́ [kreslo] *n* armchair, easychair
креща́ [kreshtya] *v* scream, yell, shout
кривогле́д [krivogled] *adj* cross-eyed
кри́за [kriza] *f* crisis
крило́ [krilo] *n* wing
кримина́лен [kriminalen] *adj* criminal

криста́л [kristal] *m* crystal
крити́к [kritik] *m* critic
кри́я [kriya] *v* hide, conceal
крокоди́л [krokodil] *m* crocodile
кру́ша [krousha] *f* pear
кру́шка [kroushka] *f* light bulb
кръ́вно наля́гане [kruvno nalyagane] *n* blood pressure
кръг [krug] *m* circle
кръст [krust] *m* cross
кръст [krust] *m* waist
кръстосло́вица [krustoslovitsa] *f* crossword puzzle
кръ́чма [kruchma] *f* pub, tavern
кръще́лно свиде́телство [krushtelno svidetelstvo] *n* birth certificate
куб [koub] *m* cube
ку́ка [kouka] *f* hook, knitting needle
ку́кла [koukla] *f* doll
ку́ла [koula] *f* tower
култ [koult] *m* cult
култу́ра [koultoura] *f* culture, civilization
куп [koup] *m* heap, pile, stack
ку́па [koupa] *f* bowl, cup
купле́т [kouplet] *m* verse, couplet
купу́вам [koupouvam] *v* buy, get, purchase
купува́ч [koupouvach] *m* buyer, purchaser
курс [kours] *m* course
куршу́м [kourshoum] *m* bullet, lead
кути́я [koutiya] *f* box

ку́хня [kouhnya] *f* kitchen
ку́че [kouche] *n* dog
къде́ [kude] *adv* where
кълбо́ [kulbo] *n* ball, globe, sphere
към [kum] *adv* toward, to
къ́пя [kupya] *v* bathe
къ́рпа [kurpa] *f* cloth, handkerchief, towel
къс [kus] *adj* short, brief
къ́сен [kusen] *adj* late
късме́т [kusmet] *m* luck, fortune
късогле́д [kusogled] *adj* short-sighted
къ́ща [kushta] *f* home, house
кюфте́ [kyufte] *n* meatball

Л

лаборато́рия [laboratoriya] *f* laboratory
лави́на [lavina] *f* avalanche
ла́вка [lafka] *f* canteen
ла́гер [lager] *m* camp
ла́зя [lazya] *v* creep, crawl
лак [lak] *m* varnish, polish
ла́кът [lakut] *m* elbow
ла́мпа [lampa] *f* lamp
ла́па [lapa] *f* paw
ла́стик [lastik] *m* elastic, rubber band
лати́нски [latinski] *adj* Latin
ла́я [laya] *v* bark
ле́бед [lebed] *m* swan

леге́нда [legenda] *f* legend
легло́ [leglo] *n* bed
лед [led] *m* ice
лежа́ [lezha] *v* lie, recline, be situated
ле́кар [lekar] *m* physician, doctor
лека́рство [lekarstvo] *n* medicine, drug
леке́ [leke] *n* stain, spot
лекоми́слие [lekomislie] *n* frivolity
ле́ксика [leksika] *f* vocabulary
леку́вам [lekouvam] *v* cure, treat
ле́кция [lektsiya] *f* lecture
леля́ [lelya] *f* aunt
лепи́ло [lepilo] *n* gum, glue, paste
ле́пкав [lepkaf] *adj* sticky
ле́сен [lesen] *adj* easy, light
ле́сно [lesno] *adv* easily
лети́ще [letishte] *n* airport, airfield
летя́ [letya] *v* fly, soar
ли́жа [lizha] *v* lick
лила́в [lilav] *adj* purple, violet
лимо́н [limon] *m* lemon
лимона́да [limonada] *f* lemonade
лине́йка [lineika] *f* ambulance
ли́ния [liniya] *f* line, ruler, straightedge
ли́пса [lipsa] *f* lack, want, shortage
ли́псвам [lipsvam] *v* be wanting, be absent
ли́ра [lira] *f* pound
лиси́ца [lisitsa] *f* fox
лист [list] *m* leaf, petal, sheet
литерату́ра [literatoura] *f* literature

ли́хва [lihva] *f* interest
лицеме́рие [litsemerie] *n* hypocrisy
ли́чен [lichen] *adj* personal, private, eminent
ли́чност [lichnost] *f* personality
лов [lof] *m* hunting, shooting
лове́ц [lovets] *m* hunter
ловя́ [lovya] *v* catch, seize
ло́дка [lodka] *f* boat
ло́жа [lozha] *f* box
локомоти́в [lokomotif] *m* engine
лопа́та [lopata] *f* spade, shovel
лост [lost] *m* lever
лота́рия [lotariya] *f* lottery, raffle
лош [losh] *adj* bad, wicked, poor
луд [loud] *adj* mad, crazy, insane
лу́дост [loudost] *f* madness, insanity
лук [louk] *m* onion
лукс [louks] *m* luxury
лула́ [loula] *f* pipe
луна́ [louna] *f* moon
лу́па [loupa] *f* magnifying glass
лъв [luv] *m* lion
лъ́жа [luzha] *v* lie
лъжа́ [luzha] *f* lie, falsehood
лъжи́ца [luzhitsa] *f* spoon
лъч [luch] *m* ray, beam
любе́зен [lyubezen] *adj* polite, kind
любе́зност [lyubeznost] *f* kindness, courtesy
люби́мец [lyubimets] *m* favorite

любител [lyubitel] *m* lover, amateur
любов [lyubov] *f* love, affection, romance
любовник [lyubovnik] *m* lover, sweetheart
любовница [lyubovnitsa] *f* mistress, sweetheart
любопитен [lyubopiten] *adj* curious, inquisitive
любопитство [lyubopitstvo] *n* curiosity
любя [lyubya] *v* make love to, be in love with
люлка [lyulka] *f* swing, cradle
люляк [lyulyak] *m* lilac
лют [lyut] *adj* hot, pungent
ляв [lyaf] *adj* left
лягам [lyagam] *v* lie down
лято [lyato] *n* summer

М

магазин [magazin] *m* shop, store
магаре [magare] *n* donkey, ass
магнетофонен запис [magnetofonen zapis] *m* recording, tape
маза [maza] *f* cellar, basement
мазнина [maznina] *f* fat, grease
май [mai] *m* May
майка [maika] *f* mother
маймуна [maimouna] *f* monkey, ape
майор [mayor] *m* major

ма́йчинство [maichinstvo] *n* motherhood, maternity

мака́р [makar] *adv* though, if

макаро́ни [makaroni] *noun pl* macaroni

максима́лен [maksimalen] *adj* maximum, utmost

мали́на [malina] *f* raspberry

ма́лко [malko] *adv* little, some, few

малцинство́ [maltsinstvo] *n* minority

ма́лък [maluk] *adj* small, little, tiny

манасти́р [manastir] *m* monastery

маниа́к [maniak] *m* lunatic, maniac

манше́т [manshet] *m* cuff, turn-up

маргари́н [margarin] *m* margarine

маргари́та [margarita] *f* daisy

ма́рка [marka] *f* stamp

марку́ч [markouch] *m* hose

март [mart] *m* March

мару́ля [maroulya] *f* lettuce

ма́са [masa] *f* table

маса́ж [masazh] *m* massage

ма́ска [maska] *f* mask

масли́на [maslina] *f* olive

ма́сло [maslo] *n* butter, oil

масти́ло [mastilo] *n* ink

матема́тика [matematika] *f* mathematics

материа́л [material] *m* material, stuff

мате́рия [materiya] *f* matter, substance

матра́к [matrak] *m* mattress

ма́хам [maham] *v* wave, remove

мач [mach] *m* match
маши́на [mashina] *f* machine, engine
машинопи́сец [mashinopisets] *m* typist
маща́б [mashtab] *m* scale
ме [me] *pron* me
ме́бел [mebel] *f* piece of furniture
мебелиро́вка [mebelirofka] *f* furniture, furnishings
мед [med] *m* honey
мед [med] *f* copper
меда́л [medal] *m* medal
медици́на [meditsina] *f* medicine
медици́нски [meditsinski] *adj* medical
между́ [mezhdou] *prep* between, among
междувре́менно [mezhdouvremenno] *adv* meanwhile
междуме́тие [mezhdoumetie] *n* interjection
междунаро́ден [mezhdounaroden] *adj* international
междуча́сие [mezhdouchasie] *n* recess, break, interval
мек [mek] *adj* soft, mellow
ме́лница [melnitsa] *f* mill
ме́нта [menta] *f* peppermint
меню́ [menyu] *n* menu
ме́ря [merya] *v* measure, weigh
меса́р [mesar] *m* butcher
ме́сец [mesets] *m* month
ме́сечен [mesechen] *adj* monthly
месо́ [meso] *n* meat

ме́стен [mesten] *adj* local, native
ме́стност [mestnost] *f* locality, place, country
местожи́телство [mestozhitelstvo] *n* residence
местоиме́ние [mestoimenie] *n* pronoun
местонахожде́ние [mestonahozhdenie] *n* location, whereabouts
месторожде́ние [mestorozhdenie] *n* birthplace
ме́стя [mestya] *v* move, transfer
мета́ [meta] *v* sweep
мета́лен [metalen] *adj* metal
метеороло́гия [meteorologiya] *f* meteorology
метла́ [metla] *f* broom
ме́тод [metod] *m* method
метро́ [metro] *n* subway
меха́ник [mehanik] *m* mechanic
мехле́м [mehlem] *m* ointment, cream
меч [mech] *m* sword
ме́чка [mechka] *f* bear
мечта́ [mechta] *f* day-dream
мечта́я [mechtaya] *v* dream of, long for
ми́вка [mifka] *f* wash-basin, sink
ми́да [mida] *f* mussel, clam
мизе́рия [mizeriya] *f* misery, poverty
микро́б [mikrob] *m* microbe, germ
микроско́п [mikroskop] *m* microscope
микрофо́н [mikrofon] *m* microphone
мил [mil] *adj* dear, nice, kind
милиа́рд [miliard] *m* billion
милио́н [milion] *m* million
милионе́р [milioner] *m* millionaire

ми́лост [milost] *f* mercy, pity, compassion
ми́ля [milya] *f* mile
ми́на [mina] *f* mine
мина́вам [minavam] *v* pass, go by, be over
ми́нало [minalo] *n* past
минера́л [mineral] *m* mineral
минима́лен [minimalen] *adj* minimum
министе́рство [ministerstvo] *n* ministry, department
мини́стър [ministur] *m* minister, secretary of state
мину́та [minouta] *f* minute, moment, instant
миньо́р [minyor] *m* miner
мир [mir] *m* peace
мири́зма [mirizma] *f* smell, odor, scent
мири́ша [mirisha] *v* smell
ми́сия [misiya] *f* mission
ми́сля [mislya] *v* think, reason, intend
ми́съл [misul] *f* thought, reflection, idea
ми́тинг [miting] *m* rally
ми́тница [mitnitsa] *f* custom house
ми́то [mito] *n* duty
ми́шка [mishka] *f* mouse
ми́я [miya] *v* wash, clean
млад [mlad] *adj* young
мла́дост [mladost] *f* youth
мле́чен [mlechen] *adj* milky, of milk
мля́ко [mlyako] *n* milk
мне́ние [mnenie] *n* opinion
мно́го [mnogo] *adv* much, many, plenty

многолю́ден [mnogolyuden] *adj* crowded, populous

мно́жество [mnozhestvo] *n* multitude, great number

мо́га [moga] *v* can, be able to, may

могъ́щ [mogusht] *adj* powerful, mighty

мо́да [moda] *f* fashion, vogue

моде́л [model] *m* model, pattern, design

моде́рен [moderen] *adj* modern, contemporary, fashionable

мо́же [mozhe] *v* may

мо́зък [mozuk] *m* brain

мой [moi] *pron* my, mine

мо́кър [mokur] *adj* wet, damp

молба́ [molba] *f* request, application

мо́лив [molif] *m* pencil

моли́тва [molitva] *f* prayer

мо́ля [molya] *v* beg, ask, request

моме́нт [moment] *m* moment, instant

моми́че [momiche] *n* girl, lass

момче́ [momche] *n* boy, lad, youngster

моне́та [moneta] *f* coin

моноло́г [monolog] *m* monologue

мора́л [moral] *m* morality, morals

море́ [more] *n* sea

морепла́ване [moreplavane] *n* navigation

мо́рков [morkof] *m* carrot

моря́к [moryak] *m* sailor, seaman

мост [most] *m* bridge

мо́стра [mostra] *f* sample, specimen

мотéл [motel] *m* motel
мотоциклéт [mototsiklet] *m* motocycle, bike
мошéник [moshenik] *m* swindler, rascal
мощ [mosht] *f* might, power
мóщен [moshten] *adj* powerful
мрáвка [mrafka] *f* ant
мраз [mras] *m* frost, chill
мрáзя [mrazya] *v* hate, detest, dislike
мрáмор [mramor] *m* marble
мрéжа [mrezha] *f* net, network
мръсен [mrusen] *adj* dirty, soiled
мръсотия [mrusotiya] *f* dirt, squalor
му [mou] *pron* him
музéй [mouzei] *m* museum
музика [mouzika] *f* music
музикáлен [mouzikalen] *adj* musical
мускул [mouskoul] *m* muscle
мустáци [moustatsi] *noun pl* moustaches, whiskers
муха [mouha] *f* fly
мъглá [mugla] *f* mist, fog
мъдрост [mudrost] *f* wisdom, prudence
мъдър [mudur] *adj* wise, judicious
мъж [muzh] *m* man
мъжки [muzhki] *adj* male, masculine
мъка [muka] *f* pain, torment
мълчá [mulcha] *v* keep silence
мързел [murzel] *m* laziness, indolence
мързелив [murzelif] *adj* lazy, idle
мърмóря [murmorya] *v* mumble, grumble

мъртъв [murtuf] *adj* dead
мъх [muh] *m* moss, lichen
мъча [mucha] *v* torture, torment
мъченик [muchenik] *m* martyr
мярка [myarka] *f* measure, measurement
място [myasto] *n* place, room

Н

на [na] *prep* on, upon, to, at, of, by
наблюдавам [nablyudavam] *v* observe, watch
наблюдател [nablyudatel] *m* observer
наблюдение [nablyudenie] *n* observation, control
наблягам [nablyagam] *v* stress, emphasize
набожен [nabozhen] *adj* religious, devout
навеждам [navezhdam] *v* bend down
навик [navik] *m* habit, custom
наводнение [navodnenie] *n* flood
навън [navun] *adv* out, outside
навярно [navyarno] *adv* probably, most likely
навяхвам [navyahvam] *v* sprain
нагоре [nagore] *adv* upwards, uphill
награда [nagrada] *f* prize, award
награждавам [nagrazhdavam] *v* award, decorate
нагревател [nagrevatel] *m* heater
нагрубявам [nagroubyavam] *v* insult, be rude

нагря́вам [nagryavam] *v* heat, warm

над [nad] *prep* over, above

надале́ч [nadalech] *adv* far away, a long way off

надбя́гване [nadbyagvane] *n* race

наде́жда [nadezhda] *f* hope

на́дница [nadnitsa] *f* wage

надни́чам [nadnicham] *v* peep

на́дпис [nadpis] *m* inscription

надя́вам се [nadyavam se] *v* hope

надя́сно [nadyasno] *adv* on, to the right

на́ем [naem] *m* rent

нае́мам [naemam] *v* rent, hire

наема́тел [naematel] *m* tenant, lodger

напа́дам [napadam] *v* attack, assail

напада́тел [napadatel] *m* assailant, aggressor

нападе́ние [napadenie] *n* attack, assault

напеча́твам [napechatvam] *v* print

напи́вам се [napivam se] *v* get drunk

напосо́ки [naposoki] *adv* at random

напоя́вам [napoyavam] *v* irrigate, water, soak

напоя́ване [napoyavane] *n* irrigation

напра́во [napravo] *adv* straight, straight ahead

напра́зен [naprazen] *adj* vain, futile

напре́д [napred] *adv* forward, ahead

напре́дък [napreduk] *m* progress, advance

напреже́ние [naprezhenie] *n* tension, strain, effort

например [naprimer] *adv* for instance, for example

напу́квам [napoukvam] *v* crack

напъ́лно [napulno] *adv* completely, fully, quite

нараня́вам [naranyavam] *v* wound, injure, hurt

наре́дба [naredba] *f* regulation, instruction, order

нари́чам [naricham] *v* call, name

наро́д [narod] *m* people, nation

наро́чно [narochno] *adv* on purpose, deliberately

наруша́вам [naroushavam] *v* violate, break, transgress

наруше́ние [naroushenie] *n* breach, violation, offense

наруши́тел [naroushitel] *m* offender

наръ́чник [naruchnik] *m* handbook, manual, guide

нас [nas] *pron* us

наса́м [nasam] *adv* this way, here

насеко́мо [nasekomo] *n* insect

населе́ние [naselenie] *n* population, inhabitants

наси́лие [nasilie] *n* force, violation

наси́лствен [nasilstven] *adj* forcible

насле́дник [naslednik] *m* heir

насле́дствен [nasledstven] *adj* hereditary, inherited

насле́дственост [nasledstvenost] *f* heredity
насле́дство [nasledstvo] *n* inheritance, legacy
насле́дявам [nasledyavam] *v* inherit, succeed to

насме́шка [nasmeshka] *f* mockery, ridicule
насти́вам [nastivam] *v* catch cold
насти́гам [nastigam] *v* catch up with, overtake, reach
насто́йник [nastoinik] *m* guardian
насто́йчивост [nastoichivost] *f* insistence, perseverance
настоя́вам [nastoyavam] *v* insist, persist
настоя́ще [nastoyashte] *n* present
настрое́ние [nastroenie] *n* mood, temper, spirits
насърча́вам [nasurchavam] *v* encourage, reassure
на́тиск [natisk] *m* pressure
нати́скам [natiskam] *v* press
натова́рвам [natovarvam] *v* load, charge, entrust with
нау́ка [naouka] *f* science
науча́вам [naouchavam] *v* learn
нау́чен [naouchen] *adj* scientific, scholarly
наха́лен [nahalen] *adj* impertinent, saucy
наха́лство [nahalstvo] *n* impertinence, cheek
нахо́дка [nahodka] *f* find
нахо́дчив [nahodchif] *adj* resourceful, inventive, ingenious

нахо́дчивост [nahodchivost] *f*
resourcefulness, ingenuity
национа́лност [natsionalnost] *f* nationality
на́ция [natsiya] *f* nation
нача́лник [nachalnik] *m* head, chief, boss
нача́ло [nachalo] *n* beginning, start
наш [nash] *pron* our
наше́ственик [nashestvenik] *m* invader
наше́ствие [nashestvie] *n* invasion
не [ne] *part* no, not
небе́ [nebe] *n* sky, heaven
небре́жност [nebrezhnost] *f* carelessness,
negligence
неве́жество [nevezhestvo] *n* ignorance
невероя́тен [neveroyaten] *adj* improbable,
unbelievable
неви́дим [nevidim] *adj* invisible
неви́нен [nevinen] *adj* innocent
неви́нност [nevinnost] *f* innocence,
harmlessness
невнима́ние [nevnimanie] *n* carelessness
невнима́телен [nevnimatelen] *adj* careless,
thoughtless
невра́лгия [nevralgiya] *f* neuralgia
невро́за [nevroza] *f* neurosis
невро́лог [nevrolog] *m* neurologist
невъзмо́жен [nevuzmozhen] *adj* impossible
невъзпи́тан [nevuspitan] *adj* ill-bred,
bad-mannered

невъзпита́ние [nevuspitanie] *n* ill-breeding, bad manners

не́го [nego] *pron* him, it

не́гов [negof] *pron* his, its

негодува́ние [negodouvanie] *n* indignation, remonstrance

неграмо́тност [negramotnost] *f* illiteracy

не́гър [negur] *m* black person

неде́ля [nedelya] *f* Sunday

недове́рие [nedoverie] *n* mistrust, suspicion

недово́лен [nedovolen] *adj* dissatisfied, displeased

недово́лство [nedovolstvo] *n* discontent, dissatisfaction

недовъ́ршен [nedovurshen] *adj* unfinished, incomplete

недопусти́м [nedopoustim] *adj* inadmissible, unthinkable

недоразуме́ние [nedorazoumenie] *n* misunderstanding

недоста́тък [nedostatuk] *m* defect, fault, shortcoming

недоста́тъчен [nedostatuchen] *adj* insufficient, inadequate

недо́стиг [nedostik] *m* shortage, lack

недостъ́пен [nedostupen] *adj* inaccessible, out of reach

нежела́ние [nezhelanie] *n* reluctance, unwillingness

нежела́телен [nezhelatelen] *adj* undesirable, objectionable

не́жен [nezhen] *adj* tender, delicate, fine

неже́нен [nezhenen] *adj* unmarried, single

не́жност [nezhnost] *f* tenderness, delicacy

незаба́вно [nezabavno] *adv* immediately, at once

незави́сим [nezavisim] *adj* independent

незави́симост [nezavisimost] *f* independence

незако́нен [nezakonen] *adj* illegal, unlawful

незначи́телен [neznachitelen] *adj* insignificant, negligible

неизбе́жен [neizbezhen] *adj* inevitable

неизве́стен [neizvesten] *adj* unknown

неизлечи́м [neizlechim] *adj* incurable

неизме́нен [neizmenen] *adj* invariable, unchanging

неизпра́вен [neispraven] *adj* out of order

не́ин [nein] *pron* her

неквалифици́ран [nekvalifitsiran] *adj* unskilled

некомпете́нтен [nekompetenten] *adj* incompetent

нелоги́чен [nelogichen] *adj* illogical

не́мец [nemets] *m* German

немину́ем [neminouem] *adj* inevitable

немора́лен [nemoralen] *adj* immoral

не́мски [nemski] *adj* German

ненави́ждам [nenavizhdam] *v* hate, detest

ненáвист [nenavist] *f* hatred, abhorrence, dislike

необмѝслен [neobmislen] *adj* hasty, rash

необходѝм [neobhodim] *adj* necessary, indispensable

необходѝмост [neobhodimost] *f* necessity

необяснѝм [neobyasnim] *adj* inexplicable, unaccountable

неограничéн [neogranichen] *adj* unlimited, boundless

неодобрéние [neodobrenie] *n* disapproval

неомъ̀жена [neomuzhena] *adj* unmarried, single

неóпитен [neopiten] *adj* inexperienced, unpractised

неóпитност [neopitnost] *f* inexperience

неоснователен [neosnovatelen] *adj* groundless, unfounded

неоспорѝм [neosporim] *adj* indisputable, irrefutable

неосъществѝм [neosushtestvim] *adj* infeasible, impracticable

неотдáвна [neotdavna] *adv* recently, not long ago

неотдáвнашен [neotdavnashen] *adj* recent

неофициáлен [neofitsialen] *adj* informal, unofficial

неочáкван [neochakvan] *adj* unexpected, sudden

непобедѝм [nepobedim] *adj* invincible

неподвижен [nepodvizhen] *adj* immovable, motionless

неподходящ [nepodhodyasht] *adj* unsuitable, inappropriate

непознат [nepoznat] *adj* unknown, unfamiliar

непоносим [neponosim] *adj* intolerable, unbearable

непослушен [neposloushen] *adj* disobedient, naughty

непотребен [nepotreben] *adj* useless

неправда [nepravda] *f* injustice

неправилен [nepravilen] *adj* incorrect, wrong

непредвидлив [nepredvidlif] *adj* improvident

непредвидливост [nepredvidlivost] *f* improvidence

непредпазлив [nepredpazlif] *adj* imprudent, careless

непредпазливост [nepredpazlivost] *f* imprudence, carelessness

непредубеден [nepredoubeden] *adj* unprejudiced, unbiased

непрекъснато [neprekusnato] *adv* ceaselessly, incessantly

непривлекателен [neprivlekatelen] *adj* unattractive

неприемлив [nepriemlif] *adj* unacceptable, inadmissible

неприли́чен [neprilichen] *adj* indecent, improper

неприя́зън [nepriyazun] *f* hostility, ill-will

неприя́тел [nepriyatel] *m* enemy, foe

неприя́тен [nepriyaten] *adj* unpleasant, disagreeable

неприя́тност [nepriyatnost] *f* trouble, nuisance

непълноле́тен [nepulnoleten] *adj* under age, minor

нера́венство [neravenstvo] *n* inequality

неравноме́рен [neravnomeren] *adj* uneven, irregular

неразбира́ем [nerazbiraem] *adj* unintelligible

неразположе́ние [neraspolozhenie] *n* indisposition

неразу́мен [nerazoumen] *adj* unwise, unreasonable

нерв [nerf] *m* nerve

не́рвен [nerven] *adj* nervous

нерви́рам [nerviram] *v* get on someone's nerves

не́рвност [nervnost] *f* nervousness

нередо́вен [neredoven] *adj* irregular

нереши́телен [nereshitelen] *adj* irresolute, hesitating

нереши́телност [nereshitelnost] *f* indecision, irresolution

неръжда́ем [neruzhdaem] *adj* stainless

несигу́рен [nesigouren] *adj* uncertain, unreliable

несигу́рност [nesigournost] *f* uncertainty, insecurity

неспоко́ен [nespokoen] *adj* restless, uneasy

несполу́ка [nespolouka] *f* failure, bad luck

неспосо́бен [nesposoben] *adj* unable, incapable

неспосо́бност [nesposobnost] *f* inability, incapability

несправедли́в [nespravedlif] *adj* unjust, unfair

несправедли́вост [nespravedlivost] *f* injustice, unfairness

несръ́чен [nesruchen] *adj* clumsy, awkward

нестаби́лен [nestabilen] *adj* unstable, shaky

нестаби́лност [nestabilnost] *f* instability

несъвърше́н [nesuvurshen] *adj* imperfect

несъмне́но [nesumneno] *adv* doubtless, undoubtedly

не́то [neto] *n* net weight

нетърпели́в [neturpelif] *adj* impatient

нетърпе́ние [neturpenie] *n* impatience

неуваже́ние [neouvazhenie] *n* disrespect

неуве́рен [neouveren] *adj* uncertain

неуве́реност [neouverenost] *f* uncertainty

неудо́бен [neoudoben] *adj* uncomfortable, inconvenient

неудо́бство [neoudobstvo] *n* inconvenience, discomfort

неуме́л [neoumel] *adj* inept, incompetent
неуме́стен [neoumesten] *adj* irrelevant, inappropriate
неуми́шлен [neoumishlen] *adj* unintentional, unpremeditated
неуморе́н [neoumoren] *adj* untiring
неуспе́х [neouspeh] *m* failure, setback
неуспе́шен [neouspeshen] *adj* unsuccessful
неутра́лен [neoutralen] *adj* neutral
неутралите́т [neoutralitet] *m* neutrality
неучти́в [neouchtif] *adj* impolite
неучти́вост [neouchtivost] *f* impoliteness
нефт [neft] *m* petroleum, oil
нече́стен [nechesten] *adj* dishonest, unfair
нече́тен [necheten] *adj* odd
нечетли́в [nechetlif] *adj* illegible, unreadable
неща́стен [neshtasten] *adj* unhappy, miserable, unlucky
неща́стие [neshtastie] *n* misfortune, misery, unhappiness
не́що [neshto] *pron* something
не́я [neya] *pron* her
ни [ni] *pron* us, our
ни́ва [niva] *f* field
ниво́ [nivo] *n* level
ни́е [nie] *pron* we
ни́какъв [nikakuf] *adj* no, none
ни́кна [nikna] *v* grow, shoot
ни́кога [nikoga] *adv* never

ни́кой [nikoi] *pron* nobody, no one
ни́къде [nikude] *adv* nowhere
нима́ [nima] *adv* really, indeed
ни́ско [nisko] *adv* low
ни́сък [nisuk] *adj* low, short, undersized
нит [nit] *m* rivet
ни́шка [nishka] *f* thread
ни́що [nishto] *pron* nothing
но [no] *conj* but
нов [nof] *adj* new
нова́тор [novator] *m* innovator
новина́ [novina] *f* news
новодошъ́л [novodoshul] *m* newcomer
ное́мври [noemvri] *m* November
нож [nozh] *m* knife
но́жица [nozhitsa] *f* scissors
но́кът [nokut] *m* nail
но́мер [nomer] *m* number, size
норма́лен [normalen] *adj* normal
нос [nos] *m* nose
носи́лка [nosilka] *f* stretcher
но́ся [nosya] *v* carry, bring, wear
нощ [nosht] *f* night
но́щница [noshtnitsa] *f* nightgown
нрав [nraf] *m* temper, disposition
ну́жда [nouzhda] *f* need, necessity
нужда́я се [nouzhdaya se] *v* need, require
ну́жен [nouzhen] *adj* necessary, requisite
ну́ла [noula] *f* zero
ня́какъв [nyakakuf] *adj* some, some kind

нЯкога [nyakoga] *adv* once, formerly
нЯкой [nyakoi] *pron* somebody
нЯкъде [nyakude] *adv* somewhere
ням [nyam] *adj* dumb, mute
нЯма [nyama] *v* there is not, there are not

О

оáзис [oazis] *m* oasis
обáждам [obazhdam] *v* tell, inform, report
обáче [obache] *conj* but, however
обаЯние [obayanie] *n* fascination, charm
обвинéние [obvinenie] *n* accusation, charge
обвинЯвам [obvinyavam] *v* accuse, charge, blame
обвинЯем [obvinyaem] *m* defender
обгрáждам [obgrazhdam] *v* surround, encircle
обЯд [obyad] *m* lunch, dinner
обединéние [obedinenie] *n* union, society
обеднЯвам [obednyavam] *v* unite, combine
обезоръжáвам [obezoruzhavam] *v* disarm
обезпокоЯвам [obespokoyavam] *v* disturb, trouble
обезщетéние [obeshtetenie] *n* compensation, amends, damages
обезщетЯвам [obeshtetyavam] *v* compensate, indemnify
обéкт [obekt] *m* object

обекти́вен [obektiven] *adj* objective, unbiased

обекти́вност [obektivnost] *f* objectivity

обе́м [obem] *m* volume

обе́свам [obesvam] *v* hang

обеца́ [obetsa] *f* earring

обеща́вам [obeshtavam] *v* promise

обеща́ние [obeshtanie] *n* promise

обжа́лвам [obzhalvam] *v* appeal

обзаве́ждам [obzavezhdam] *v* furnish

обзала́гам се [obzalagam se] *v* bet, wager

обзо́р [obzor] *m* survey

оби́да [obida] *f* insult, affront

оби́ден [obiden] *adj* insulting, offensive

оби́ждам [obizhdam] *v* offend, insult

обика́лям [obikalyam] *v* go round, tour, travel over

обикнове́н [obiknoven] *adj* ordinary, usual

обикнове́но [obiknoveno] *adv* usually, as a rule

обико́лка [obikolka] *f* tour

оби́лен [obilen] *adj* abundant, plentiful

о́бир [obir] *m* robbery

обита́вам [obitavam] *v* inhabit, dwell in

обита́тел [obitatel] *m* inhabitant, dweller

обича́й [obichai] *m* habit, custom

оби́чам [obicham] *v* love, like

о́блак [oblak] *m* cloud

о́бласт [oblast] *f* district, region, sphere

о́блачен [oblachen] *adj* cloudy, overcast

облегáло [oblegalo] *n* back
облеклó [obleklo] *n* clothes, dress
облекчéние [oblekchenie] *n* relief
облигáция [obligatsiya] *f* share, bond, stock
облúчам [oblicham] *v* dress, clothe
облóг [oblok] *m* bet, wager
обля́гам [oblyagam] *v* lean, rest
обмéням [obmenyam] *v* exchange
обобщáвам [obobshtavam] *v* generalize, summarize
обобщéние [obobshtenie] *n* generalization, summary
обожáвам [obozhavam] *v* adore, worship
обожáтел [obozhatel] *m* admirer
обоня́ние [obonyanie] *n* smell
обрабóтвам [obrabotvam] *v* cultivate, process
обрабóтка [obrabotka] *f* treatment, processing
óбраз [obras] *m* shape, form, appearance, image
образóван [obrazovan] *adj* educated, well-read
образовáние [obrazovanie] *n* education
образовáтелен [obrazovatelen] *adj* educational
образу́вам [obrazouvam] *v* form, make
обрáт [obrat] *m* turn, change
обрáтно [obratno] *adv* back
обрéд [obred] *m* ritual, rite
óбрив [obrif] *m* rash

обръще́ние [obrushtenie] *n* address, appeal, circulation

обса́да [obsada] *f* siege

о́бсег [obseg] *m* sphere, range

обсервато́рия [observatoriya] *f* observatory

обстано́вка [obstanofka] *f* condition, situation

обстоя́телство [obstoyatelstvo] *n* circumstance

обсъ́ждам [obsuzhdam] *v* discuss, consider

обува́лка [obouvalka] *f* shoehorn

обу́вам се [obouvam se] *v* put on shoes

обу́вка [oboufka] *f* shoe

обуча́вам [obouchavam] *v* teach, instruct, train

общ [obsht] *adj* common, general

обще́ствен [obshtestven] *adj* social, public

обще́ственост [obshtestvenost] *f* public, society

общество́ [obshtestvo] *n* society

община́ [obshtina] *f* community

о́бщност [obshtnost] *f* community, commonwealth

о́бщо [obshto] *adv* generally, altogether

общоприе́т [obshtopriet] *adj* generally accepted

общопризна́т [obshtopriznat] *adj* universally acknowledged

объ́рквам [oburkvam] *v* mix, confuse

обя́ва [obyava] *f* announcement, notice

обявявам [obyavyavam] *v* announce, declare, proclaim

обядвам [obyadvam] *v* have lunch, dine

обяснение [obyasnenie] *n* explanation

обяснявам [obyasnyavam] *v* explain

овации [ovatsii] *noun pl* ovation, cheers, applause

овен [oven] *m* ram

овес [oves] *m* oats

овнешко [ovneshko] *n* mutton

овца [ovtsa] *f* sheep

овчар [ovchar] *m* shepherd

огладнявам [ogladnyavam] *v* grow hungry

огледало [ogledalo] *n* mirror, looking-glass

огнестрелно оръжие [ognestrelno oruzhie] *n* firearm

огнище [ognishte] *n* hearth, fireplace

ограбвам [ograbvam] *v* rob, plunder

ограда [ograda] *f* fence, enclosure

ограждам [ograzhdam] *v* fence in, enclose

ограничавам [ogranichavam] *v* limit, confine

огромен [ogromen] *adj* huge, enormous, immense

огън [ogun] *f* fire

огърлица [ogurlitsa] *f* necklace

одеколон [odekolon] *m* eau-de-cologne

одеало [odealo] *n* blanket

одобрение [odobrenie] *n* approval, sanction

одобрявам [odobryavam] *v* approve of, ratify

ожаднявам [ozhadnyavam] *v* become thirsty

озаглавя́вам [ozaglavyavam] *v* entitle
оздравя́вам [ozdravyavam] *v* recover, become well
океа́н [okean] *m* ocean
о́кис [okis] *m* oxide
окисля́вам [okislyavam] *v* oxidize
око́ [oko] *n* eye
око́лност [okolnost] *f* vicinity, surroundings
о́коло [okolo] *adv* around, about
оконча́ние [okonchanie] *n* ending
оконча́телен [okonchatelen] *adj* final, conclusive
о́кръг [okrug] *m* district, county, region
окръ́жност [okruzhnost] *f* circle
окто́мври [oktomvri] *m* October
окупа́ция [okoupatsiya] *f* occupation
окупи́рам [okoupiram] *v* occupy
олимпиа́да [olimpiada] *f* Olympiad
о́лио [olio] *n* oil
оло́во [olovo] *n* lead
олта́р [oltar] *m* altar
омагьо́свам [omagyosvam] *v* cast a spell on, bewitch
оме́квам [omekvam] *v* grow softer, get warmer
омле́т [omlet] *m* omelette
омра́за [omraza] *f* hate, hatred
омра́зен [omrazen] *adj* hateful, odious
омъ́жвам [omuzhvam] *v* marry
опа́звам [opazvam] *v* preserve

опа́зване [opazvane] *n* preservation
опако́вам [opakovam] *v* pack up, wrap up
опако́вка [opakofka] *f* packing
опа́сен [opasen] *adj* dangerous, perilous
опасе́ние [opasenie] *n* fear, apprehension
опа́сност [opasnost] *f* danger, peril
опа́шка [opashka] *f* tail, queue
о́пера [opera] *f* opera
опера́тор [operator] *m* cameraman
опера́ция [operatsiya] *f* operation
опере́та [opereta] *f* musical
опери́рам [operiram] *v* operate
о́пис [opis] *m* list, inventory
описа́ние [opisanie] *n* description
опи́свам [opisvam] *v* describe, portray
о́пит [opit] *m* attempt, test
опи́твам [opitvam] *v* try, make an attempt
о́питен [opiten] *adj* experienced, skilled, experimental
о́питност [opitnost] *f* experience, proficiency
опла́квам се [oplakvam se] *v* complain
опла́кване [oplakvane] *n* complaint
оповестя́вам [opovestyavam] *v* announce
опози́ция [opozitsiya] *f* opposition
опозна́вам [opoznavam] *v* get to know
опо́ра [opora] *f* support, bulwark
оправда́вам [opravdavam] *v* excuse, vindicate
оправда́ние [opravdanie] *n* justification, vindication

опрове́ргавам [oprovergavam] *v* refute, disprove

опроверже́ние [oproverzhenie] *n* refutation, denial

опроща́вам [oproshtavam] *v* pardon, remit

опъ́вам [opuvam] *v* stretch, pull, strain

ора́ [ora] *v* plough

ора́нжев [oranzhef] *adj* orange

о́рбита [orbita] *f* orbit

организа́ция [organizatsiya] *f* organization

организи́рам [organiziram] *v* organize

органи́зъм [organizum] *m* organism

органи́чен [organichen] *adj* organic

оре́л [orel] *m* eagle

о́рех [oreh] *m* walnut

оригина́лен [originalen] *adj* original

ори́з [oris] *m* rice

орке́стър [orkestur] *m* orchestra

оръ́дие [orudie] *n* instrument, tool

оръ́жие [oruzhie] *n* arms, weapons

ос [os] *f* axis

оса́ [osa] *f* wasp

осведомя́вам [osvedomyavam] *v* inform, notify, ask

освежа́вам [osvezhavam] *v* refresh

осве́н [osven] *prep* except for, but

осветле́ние [osvetlenie] *n* light

осветля́вам [osvetlyavam] *v* light up, illuminate

освободи́тел [osvoboditel] *m* liberator

освобожда́вам [osvobozhdavam] *v* liberate, free

освобожде́ние [osvobozhdenie] *n* liberation

осеза́ем [osezaem] *v* tangible

о́сем [osem] *num* eight

осемдесе́т [osemdeset] *num* eighty

осигуро́вка [osigourofka] *f* insurance, assurance

осиновя́вам [osinovyavam] *v* adopt

оскърбле́ние [oskurblenie] *n* insult

оскърбя́вам [oskurbyavam] *v* insult, offend, hurt

осно́ва [osnova] *f* foundation, base

основа́вам [osnovavam] *v* found

основа́ние [osnovanie] *n* grounds, reason

основа́тел [osnovatel] *m* founder

осно́вен [osnoven] *adj* basic, fundamental, thorough

осо́бен [osoben] *adj* special, peculiar, strange

осребря́вам [osrebryavam] *v* cash

оста́вам [ostavam] *v* remain

оста́вка [ostafka] *f* resignation

остаря́вам [ostaryavam] *v* grow old

остаря́л [ostaryal] *v* old

оста́тък [ostatuk] *m* remainder, rest

острие́ [ostrie] *n* edge, point

остри́лка [ostrilka] *f* pencil-sharpener

о́стров [ostrof] *m* island

о́стря [ostrya] *v* sharpen

о́стър [ostur] *adj* sharp, keen

осъждам [osuzhdam] *v* blame, sentence
осъществявам [osushtestvyavam] *v* realize, carry out
от [ot] *prep* out, of, from, off, than
отбор [otbor] *m* team
отбрана [otbrana] *f* defense
отбранителен [otbranitelen] *adj* defensive
отварям [otvaryam] *v* open, turn on
отверка [otverka] *f* screwdriver
отвесен [otvesen] *adj* vertical
отвор [otvor] *m* opening, hole
отворен [otvoren] *adj* open
отвратителен [otvratitelen] *adj* disgusting, repugnant
отвращение [otvrashtenie] *n* disgust, loathing
отвързвам [otvurzvam] *v* untie, undo
отговарям [otgovaryam] *v* answer, reply
отговор [otgovor] *m* answer, reply
отговорност [otgovornost] *f* responsibility
отгоре [otgore] *adv* upon, above
отдавна [otdavna] *adv* long ago
отдалечавам се [otdalechavam se] *v* move away
отдалечен [otdalechen] *adj* distant, remote
отдел [otdel] *m* department
отделен [otdelen] *adj* separate, individual
отделям [otdelyam] *v* separate, detach
отдясно [otdyasno] *adv* to the right
отегчавам [otegchavam] *v* bore
отегчение [otegchenie] *n* boredom

отзад [otzat] *adv* behind
отивам [otivam] *v* go
отказ [otkas] *m* refusal
отказвам [otkazvam] *v* refuse, decline
откак [otkak] *conj* since
отклонявам [otklonyavam] *v* divert, branch off
отключвам [otklyuchvam] *v* unlock
отколкото [otkolkoto] *pron* than
откривам [otkrivam] *v* open, discover, find out
откривател [otkrivatel] *m* discoverer, inventor
открит [otkrit] *adj* open
откритие [otkritie] *n* discovery, invention
откровен [otkroven] *adj* frank, sincere
откровеност [otkrovenost] *f* frankness, sincerity
откуп [otkoup] *m* ransom
отлагам [otlagam] *v* put off, postpone
отлитам [otlitam] *v* fly away
отличен [otlichen] *adj* excellent
отличие [otlichie] *n* distinction
отляво [otlyavo] *adv* to the left
отменям [otmenyam] *v* abolish, cancel, repeal
отмъщавам [otmushtavam] *v* revenge
отмъщение [otmushtenie] *n* revenge, vengeance
отначало [otnachalo] *adv* from the beginning
отново [otnovo] *adv* again

отноше́ние [otnoshenie] *n* relation, bearing
отопле́ние [otoplenie] *n* heating
отопля́вам [otoplyavam] *v* heat
отпо́р [otpor] *m* resistance
отпре́д [otpred] *adv* in front of
о́тпуск [otpousk] *m* holiday, leave
отпу́швам [otpoushvam] *v* open, unclog
отрица́телен [otritsatelen] *adj* negative,
unfavorable
отри́чам [otricham] *v* deny
отро́ва [otrova] *f* poison
отро́вен [otroven] *adj* poisonous
отря́звам [otryazvam] *v* cut
отсла́бвам [otslabvam] *v* grow weak, lose
weight
отстраня́вам [otstranyavam] *v* remove
отстъпле́ние [otstuplenie] *n* retreat
оттѐглям [otteglyam] *v* withdraw, retire
оттѐгляне [otteglyane] *n* withdrawal,
retirement
оттѐнък [ottenuk] *m* shade, tint, hue
оттога́ва [ottogava] *conj* since
отту́к [ottouk] *adv* from here, this way
отча́ян [otchayan] *adj* desperate, downcast
отча́яние [otchayanie] *n* despair,
despondency
отче́т [otchet] *m* account, report
офе́рта [oferta] *f* offer
офице́р [ofitser] *m* officer
охла́ждам [ohlazhdam] *v* cool, chill

о́хлюв [ohlyuf] *m* snail

охо́лен [oholen] *adj* rich, opulent

охра́на [ohrana] *f* guard, protection

оце́нка [otsenka] *f* valuation, estimation, mark

оценя́вам [otsenyavam] *v* evaluate, estimate, value

оце́т [otset] *m* vinegar

оча́квам [ochakvam] *v* expect, look forward to

оча́кване [ochakvane] *n* expectation

очаро́вам [ocharovam] *v* charm, enchant

очарова́телен [ocharovatelen] *adj* charming, fascinating

очеви́ден [ocheviden] *adj* obvious, evident, clear, conspicuous

оче́ртавам [ochertavam] *v* outline, describe

оче́ртание [ochertanie] *n* outline, delineation

очила́ [ochila] *noun pl* eye-glasses, spectacles

о́ще [oshte] *adv* more, still, yet

П

пава́ж [pavazh] *n* pavement

па́дам [padam] *v* fall

па́дане [padane] *m* fall

паза́р [pazar] *m* market

пазару́вам [pazarouvam] *v* buy, go shopping

пазаря́ се [pazarya se] *v* bargain
па́зя [pazya] *v* guard, protect, keep
пак [pak] *adv* again
паке́т [paket] *m* package, parcel
пала́тка [palatka] *f* tent
палачи́нка [palachinka] *f* pancake
па́лец [palets] *m* thumb
па́лма [palma] *f* palm
палто́ [palto] *n* coat, overcoat
па́луба [palouba] *f* deck
па́ля [palya] *v* light
паля́чо [palyacho] *m* clown, fool
па́мет [pamet] *f* memory
паме́тник [pametnik] *m* monument,
memorial
паму́к [pamouk] *m* cotton
пана́йр [panair] *m* fair
па́нделка [pandelka] *f* ribbon
па́ника [panika] *f* panic
пани́ца [panitsa] *f* bowl
панора́ма [panorama] *f* panorama, view
пансио́н [pansion] *m* boarding-house
панталóни [pantaloni] *noun pl* trousers,
pants
пантóфи [pantofi] *noun pl* slippers
па́па [papa] *m* pope
папага́л [papagal] *m* parrot
па́пка [papka] *f* portfolio
па́ра [para] *f* steam, vapor
пара́д [parad] *m* parade

парали́за [paraliza] *f* paralysis
парахо́д [parahod] *m* steamer
парашу́т [parashout] *m* parachute
пари́ [pari] *noun pl* money
парк [park] *m* park
парламе́нт [parlament] *m* parliament
па́ртер [parter] *m* ground floor
па́ртия [partiya] *f* party
парфю́м [parfyum] *m* perfume, scent
парца́л [partsal] *m* rag
парче́ [parche] *n* piece, fragment, slice
па́спорт [pasport] *m* passport
па́ста [pasta] *f* paste
пате́нт [patent] *m* patent
патрио́т [patriot] *m* patriot
патриоти́зъм [patriotizum] *m* patriotism
па́уза [paouza] *f* interval, pause
пацие́нт [patsient] *m* patient
па́як [payak] *m* spider
певе́ц [pevets] *m* singer
пе́ене [peene] *n* singing
пе́йка [peika] *f* bench
пека́ [peka] *v* bake, roast
пелена́ [pelena] *f* diaper
пенсионе́р [pensioner] *m* pensioner
пенсиони́рам се [pensioniram se] *v* retire
пе́пел [pepel] *m* ash
пе́пелник [pepelnik] *m* ash-tray
пеперу́да [peperouda] *f* butterfly
пера́ [pera] *v* wash

перáлня [peralnya] *f* washing machine, laundry

пердé [perde] *n* curtain

периóд [period] *m* period

пéрка [perka] *f* propeller, fin

пéрла [perla] *f* pearl

перó [pero] *n* feather

перóн [peron] *m* platform

перпендикуля́рен [perpendikoulyaren] *adj* perpendicular

перси́йски [persiiski] *adj* Persian

персонáл [personal] *m* personnel, staff

пéсен [pesen] *f* song

песимисти́чен [pesimistichen] *adj* pessimistic

пестели́в [pestelif] *adj* thrifty, sparing

пестя́ [pestya] *v* save

пет [pet] *num* five

петдесéт [petdeset] *num* fifty

петéл [petel] *m* rooster

петнáдесет [petnadeset] *num* fifteen

петнó [petno] *n* spot, stain

пéтък [petuk] *m* Friday

пехóта [pehota] *f* infantry

печáлба [pechalba] *f* gain, profit, prize

печáтам [pechatam] *v* print, publish

печатáр [pechatar] *m* printer

печáтница [pechatnitsa] *f* printing house

печéля [pechelya] *v* earn, gain, win

пéчка [pechka] *f* stove

пешехóдец [peshehodets] *m* pedestrian

пещ [pesht] *f* oven, furnace
пещера́ [peshtera] *f* cave
пе́я [peya] *v* sing
пиа́но [piano] *n* piano
пие́са [piesa] *f* play
пижа́ма [pizhama] *f* pyjamas
пила́ [pila] *f* file
пи́ле [pile] *n* chicken
пило́т [pilot] *m* pilot
пи́пам [pipam] *v* touch
пипе́р [piper] *m* pepper
пирами́да [piramida] *f* pyramid
писа́лка [pisalka] *f* pen
писмо́ [pismo] *n* letter
пи́ста [pista] *f* racetrack
пистоле́т [pistolet] *m* pistol
пи́там [pitam] *v* ask, question, inquire
пи́ша [pisha] *v* write
пи́я [piya] *v* drink, sip
пия́н [piyan] *v* drunk
плаж [plazh] *m* beach
плака́т [plakat] *m* poster
пла́мък [plamuk] *m* flame, blaze
план [plan] *m* plan, scheme, design
плане́та [planeta] *f* planet
планина́ [planina] *f* mountain
плани́рам [planiram] *v* plan, lay out
пла́стмаса [plastmasa] *f* plastics
пла́стмасов [plastmasof] *adj* plastic
плат [plat] *m* cloth, material

платѐж [platezh] *m* payment
плача [placha] *v* cry, weep
плѐме [pleme] *n* tribe
плѐменник [plemennik] *m* nephew
плѐменница [plemennitsa] *f* niece
плѐнник [plennik] *m* captive, prisoner
пленявам [plenyavam] *v* capture, take
prisoner
плета [pleta] *v* knit
плетиво [pletivo] *n* knitwear
плешив [pleshif] *adj* bald
плик [plik] *m* envelope
плитка [plitka] *f* plait, tress, braid
плитък [plituk] *adj* shallow
плод [plod] *m* fruit
плодороден [plodoroden] *adj* fertile
плодородие [plodorodie] *n* fertility
плодотворен [plodotvoren] *adj* fruitful
пломба [plomba] *f* filling
плосък [plosuk] *adj* flat
плоча [plocha] *f* slab, record
площ [plosht] *f* area
площад [ploshtad] *m* square
плувам [plouvam] *v* swim, sail
плътен [pluten] *adj* thick, dense
плътност [plutnost] *f* thickness, density
плъх [pluh] *m* rat
плюя [plyuya] *v* spit
пневмония [pnevmoniya] *f* pneumonia
по [po] *prep* along, on, over, by

побе́да [pobeda] *f* victory
победи́тел [pobeditel] *m* victor, winner
побежда́вам [pobezhdavam] *v* defeat, win
поби́рам [pobiram] *v* hold, contain
повди́гам [povdigam] *v* lift, raise
поведе́ние [povedenie] *n* conduct, behavior
повери́телен [poveritelen] *adj* confidential
по́вече [poveche] *adv* more
по́вечето [povecheto] *adv* most
пови́квам [povikvam] *v* call, summon, send for
по́вод [povod] *m* occasion, cause, ground
повръ́щам [povrushtam] *v* vomit, be sick
повъ́рхност [povurhnost] *f* surface
повъ́рхностен [povurhnosten] *adj* superficial
по́глед [pogled] *m* look, gaze, stare
погле́ждам [poglezhdam] *v* look at, glance
поглъ́щам [poglushtam] *v* swallow, absorb
погово́рка [pogovorka] *f* proverb, saying
погре́бвам [pogrebvam] *v* bury
погребе́ние [pogrebenie] *n* funeral, burial
под [pod] *m* floor
под [pod] *prep* under, below
по́даник [podanik] *m* subject
по́данство [podanstvo] *n* citizenship, nationality
пода́рък [podaruk] *m* present, gift
подаря́вам [podaryavam] *v* make a present
пода́тел [podatel] *m* sender
подво́дница [podvodnitsa] *f* submarine

подвъ́рзвам [podvurzvam] *v* bind
подго́твям [podgotvyam] *v* prepare, train
подгото́вка [podgotofka] *f* preparation
поддъ́ржам [poddurzham] *v* support, maintain
подзе́мен [podzemen] *adj* underground
подигра́вка [podigrafka] *f* mockery
по́диум [podioum] *m* platform
подкре́па [podkrepa] *f* support, backing
подкре́пям [podkrepyam] *v* support, back
подме́тка [podmetka] *f* sole
подна́сям [podnasyam] *v* serve, present, offer
подно́с [podnos] *m* tray
подобре́ние [podobrenie] *n* improvement
подобря́вам [podobryavam] *v* improve
подози́рам [podoziram] *v* suspect
подозре́ние [podozrenie] *n* suspicion
по́дпис [podpis] *m* signature
подпи́свам [podpisvam] *v* sign
подпра́вка [podprafka] *f* condiment, spice,
seasoning
подробе́н [podroben] *adj* detailed
подро́бност [podrobnost] *f* detail
подсла́ждам [podslazhdam] *v* sweeten
подсло́н [podslon] *m* shelter
поду́вам се [podouvam se] *v* swell
поду́т [podout] *adj* swollen
поду́швам [podoushvam] *v* scent, sniff
подхо́д [podhod] *m* approach
подходя́щ [podhodyasht] *adj* suitable,
appropriate

подхо́ждам [podhozhdam] *v* suit, fit

подценя́вам [podtsenyavam] *v* underestimate, underrate

подчерта́вам [podchertavam] *v* underline, emphasize, stress

по́дъл [podul] *adj* mean, base

пое́зия [poeziya] *f* poetry

пое́т [poet] *m* poet

пожа́р [pozhar] *m* fire

пожа́рен кран [pozharen kran] *m* fire hydrant

пожарника́р [pozharnikar] *m* fireman

пожела́вам [pozhelavam] *v* wish

пожела́ние [pozhelanie] *n* wish

по́за [poza] *f* pose, attitude

позволе́ние [pozvolenie] *n* permission, permit

позволя́вам [pozvolyavam] *v* allow, permit, let

по́здрав [pozdraf] *m* greeting, regards

поздравле́ние [pozdravlenie] *n* greeting, congratulation

поздравя́вам [pozdravyavam] *v* greet, congratulate

пози́ция [pozitsiya] *f* position, stand

позна́вам [poznavam] *v* guess, know

позна́ние [poznanie] *n* knowledge, learning

позна́т [poznat] *m* acquaintance

позна́т [poznat] *adj* well-known, familiar

позо́р [pozor] *m* disgrace, shame

показа́лец [pokazalets] *m* forefinger
показа́ние [pokazanie] *n* evidence, testimony
показа́тел [pokazatel] *m* index, indicator
пока́звам [pokazvam] *v* show, point, exhibit
пока́на [pokana] *f* invitation
пока́нвам [pokanvam] *v* invite, ask
покло́н [poklon] *m* bow
поколе́ние [pokolenie] *n* generation
по́крив [pokrif] *m* roof
покри́вам [pokrivam] *v* cover
поку́пка [pokoupka] *f* purchase
пол [pol] *m* sex
пола́ [pola] *f* skirt
поле́ [pole] *n* field
поле́зен [polezen] *adj* useful, beneficial
по́лет [polet] *m* flight
по́лза [polza] *f* advantage, benefit, use
полиле́й [polilei] *m* chandelier
полити́к [politik] *m* politician
полити́ка [politika] *f* politics
полица́й [politsai] *m* policeman
поли́ция [politsiya] *f* police
по́лов [polof] *adj* sexual
полови́на [polovina] *f* half
положе́ние [polozhenie] *n* position, situation
по́лски [polski] *adj* Polish
полукълбо́ [poloukulbo] *n* hemisphere
полуме́сец [poloumesets] *m* crescent
полуно́щ [polounosht] *m* midnight
полуо́стров [polouostrov] *m* peninsula

получавам [polouchavam] *v* get, receive, obtain

получател [polouchatel] *m* recipient, addressee

поляк [polyak] *m* Pole

помагам [pomagam] *v* help, assist, aid

помирение [pomirenie] *n* reconciliation

помощ [pomosht] *f* help, assistance, aid

помощник [pomoshtnik] *m* assistant, helper, deputy

помпа [pompa] *f* pump

поне [pone] *adv* at least

понеделник [ponedelnik] *m* Monday

понеже [ponezhe] *conj* because, since

понякога [ponyakoga] *adv* sometimes, occasionally

понятие [ponyatie] *n* concept, notion

поправка [poprafka] *f* correction, repairs

поправям [popravyam] *v* correct, repair, mend

популярен [popoulyaren] *adj* popular

порода [poroda] *f* breed, race

портативен [portativen] *adj* portable

портокал [portokal] *m* orange

портрет [portret] *m* portrait, picture

портфейл [portfeil] *m* wallet, pocketbook

порцелан [portselan] *m* china

поръчвам [poruchvam] *v* tell, ask, commission

посетител [posetitel] *m* visitor

посещáвам [poseshtavam] *v* visit, call on, attend

посещéние [poseshtenie] *n* visit, attendance

послáние [poslanie] *n* message

послáник [poslanik] *m* ambassador

послéден [posleden] *adj* last, final

послéдица [posleditsa] *f* consequence, result

послóвица [poslovitsa] *f* proverb, saying

посóка [posoka] *f* direction

посóлство [posolstvo] *n* embassy

посрéщам [posreshtam] *v* meet, welcome

пост [post] *m* post

постáвям [postavyam] *v* put, place, set, stage

постепéнен [postepenen] *adj* gradual

постепéнно [postepenno] *adv* gradually

постúгам [postigam] *v* achieve, attain

постижéние [postizhenie] *n* achievement, attainment

постоя́нен [postoyanen] *adj* constant, permanent, steady

постоя́нно [postoyanno] *adv* always, constantly

построя́вам [postroyavam] *v* build, construct

пот [pot] *f* sweat, perspiration

потвържда́вам [potvurzhdavam] *v* confirm

потвърждéние [potvurzhdenie] *n* confirmation

потóк [potok] *m* stream, brook

потъ́вам [potuvam] *v* sink, be lost in

потя́ се [potya se] *v* sweat, prespire

похвала [pohvala] *f* praise
почва [pochva] *f* soil, ground
почвам [pochvam] *v* begin, start
почерк [pocherk] *m* handwriting
почест [pochest] *f* honor
почетен [pocheten] *adj* honorary
почивам [pochivam] *v* rest, die
почивен ден [pochiven den] *m* day off
почти [pochti] *adv* almost, nearly,
practically
поща [poshta] *f* mail
появявам се [poyavyavam se] *v* appear,
come into view
правен [praven] *adj* legal
правилен [pravilen] *adj* regular, correct
правило [pravilo] *n* rule
правителство [pravitelstvo] *n* government
право [pravo] *n* right, law
правопис [pravopis] *m* spelling
православен [pravoslaven] *adj* orthodox
правоъгълен [pravougulen] *adj* rectangular
правя [pravya] *v* do, make
праг [prag] *m* threshold, doorstep
празник [praznik] *m* holiday
практика [praktika] *f* practice
практикувам [praktikouvam] *v* practise
практичен [praktichen] *adj* practical
прасе [prase] *n* pig
праскова [praskova] *f* peach
прах [prah] *m* dust, powder

прахосмука́чка [prahosmoukachka] *f* vacuum cleaner

пра́шен [prashen] *adj* dusty

пребива́вам [prebivavam] *v* stay, sojourn

пребива́ване [prebivavane] *n* stay

преброя́ване [prebroyavane] *n* census

преве́ждам [prevezhdam] *v* translate, interpret

превра́т [prevrat] *m* coup d'etat

пре́вод [prevod] *m* translation

превода́ч [prevodach] *m* translator, interpreter

пре́воз [prevos] *m* transport, shipping

прево́звам [prevozvam] *v* transport, carry, ship

прево́зно сре́дство [prevozno sredstvo] *n* vehicle

превръ́зка [prevruska] *f* bandage, dressing

превръ́щам [prevrushtam] *v* turn, change

превъзхо́дство [prevus-hodstvo] *n* superiority, excellence

превъзхо́ждам [prevus-hozhdam] *v* surpass, exceed

превъ́рзвам [prevurzvam] *v* dress, bandage

пре́глед [pregled] *m* survey, inspection, examination

прегле́ждам [preglezhdam] *v* examine

прегръ́дка [pregrudka] *f* embrace

прегръ́щам [pregrushtam] *v* embrace

пред [pred] *prep* before, in front of

предавам [predavam] *v* hand in, deliver, teach

предавам се [predavam se] *v* surrender

предавател [predavatel] *m* transmitter

преданост [predanost] *f* devotion, attachment

предател [predatel] *m* traitor, betrayer

предателство [predatelstvo] *n* treachery, betrayal

предварителен [predvaritelen] *adj* preliminary, beforehand

предговор [predgovor] *m* preface, foreword

предградие [predgradie] *n* suburb

преден [preden] *adj* front

преди [predi] *adv* before

предимство [predimstvo] *n* advantage, priority

предишен [predishen] *adj* previous, former

предлагам [predlagam] *v* offer, suggest, propose

предлог [predlog] *m* pretext, preposition

предложение [predlozhenie] *n* offer, proposal, suggestion

предмет [predmet] *m* object, topic

предпазвам [predpazvam] *v* protect, preserve

предпазен [predpazen] *adj* preventive

предпазлив [predpazlif] *adj* cautious, wary

предпазливост [predpazlivost] *f* caution, wariness

предписвам [predpisvam] *v* prescribe

предпола́гам [predpolagam] *v* suppose, guess
предположе́ние [predpolozhenie] *n*
supposition, conjecture
предпочи́там [predpochitam] *v* prefer
предпочита́ние [predpochitanie] *n* preference
предприя́тие [predpriyatie] *n* enterprise
предразсъ́дък [predrasuduk] *m* prejudice,
bias
председа́тел [predsedatel] *m* president,
chairman
предста́ва [predstava] *f* idea, notion
представи́тел [predstavitel] *m*
representative, agent
предста́вка [predstavka] *f* prefix
представле́ние [predstavlenie] *n* performance
предста́вям [predstavyam] *v* represent,
introduce
предубежде́ние [predoubezhdenie] *n*
prejudice, bias
предупрежда́вам [predouprezhdavam] *v*
warn, notify
предупрежде́ние [predouprezhdenie] *n*
warning, notice
предше́ственик [predshestvenik] *m*
predecessor, forerunner
пре́жда [prezhda] *f* yarn
през [prez] *conj* through, via
президе́нт [prezident] *m* president
прези́ме [prezime] *n* surname
прези́рам [preziram] *v* despise, scorn

презре́ние [prezrenie] *n* contempt, scorn
презри́телен [prezritelen] *adj*
contemptuous, scornful
прекале́н [prekalen] *adj* excessive, too great
прекра́сен [prekrasen] *adj* beautiful,
wonderful, splendid
прекъ́свам [prekusvam] *v* interrupt, break off
прекъ́сване [prekusvane] *n* interruption,
break
премие́ра [premiera] *f* first night
performance
пренебре́гвам [prenebregvam] *v* neglect,
disregard, ignore
пренощу́вам [prenoshtouvam] *v* spend the
night
преодоля́вам [preodolyavam] *v* overcome,
surmount
пре́пис [prepis] *m* copy
препи́свам [prepisvam] *v* copy
препода́вам [prepodavam] *v* teach
препода́ване [prepodavane] *n* teaching
преподава́тел [prepodavatel] *m* teacher
препоръ́ка [preporuka] *f* recommendation
препоръ́чвам [preporuchvam] *v* recommend
пре́сен [presen] *adj* fresh, new
пресе́чка [presechka] *f* crossing
пресле́дване [presledvane] *n* persecution,
pursuit
пресмя́там [presmyatam] *v* calculate
прести́лка [prestilka] *f* apron

престру́вам се [prestrouvam se] *v* pretend, make believe

престъ́пен [prestupen] *adj* criminal

престъ́пник [prestupnik] *m* criminal

престъпле́ние [prestuplenie] *n* crime

прете́нция [pretentsiya] *f* claim

преустановя́вам [preoustanovyavam] *v* stop, suspend

пре́ход [prehod] *m* transition

пре́ходен [prehoden] *adj* transitional

пре́чка [prechka] *f* obstacle, hindrance

при [pri] *prep* at, near, to

прибира́м [pribiram] *v* put away, gather

приближа́вам [priblizhavam] *v* bring near, approach

приблизи́телно [priblizitelno] *adv* approximately

привиле́гия [privilegiya] *f* privilege

привлека́телен [privlekatelen] *adj* attractive, appealing

привлека́телност [privlekatelnost] *f* attractiveness, charm

приго́твям [prigotvyam] *v* prepare, make ready

приготовле́ние [prigotovlenie] *n* preparation, arrangement

придружа́вам [pridrouzhavam] *v* accompany, escort

прие́м [priem] *m* reception

прие́млив [priemlif] *adj* acceptable, plausible

при́зив [prizif] *m* call, appeal

призна́вам [priznavam] *v* acknowledge, admit

призо́вка [prizofka] *f* summons

при́казка [prikaska] *f* tale, story

приключе́ние [priklyuchenie] *n* adventure

прила́гам [prilagam] *v* apply to, enclose

прилага́телно и́ме [prilagatelno ime] *n* adjective

при́мер [primer] *m* example

прими́рие [primirie] *n* armistice

примити́вен [primitiven] *adj* primitive

принадлежа́ [prinadlezha] *v* belong to

принадле́жност [prinadlezhnost] *f* belonging

при́нос [prinos] *m* contribution

принужда́вам [prinouzhdavam] *v* compel, force

принужде́ние [prinouzhdenie] *n* compulsion

принц [prints] *m* prince

принце́са [printsesa] *f* princess

при́нцип [printsip] *m* principle

припа́дам [pripadam] *v* faint

припо́мням [pripomnyam] *v* recall, bring to mind

приспособя́вам се [prisposobyavam se] *v* adapt, accommodate

приста́нище [pristanishte] *n* port, harbor

присти́гам [pristigam] *v* arrive

пристигане [pristigane] *n* arrival
пристъп [pristup] *m* fit, attack
присъда [prisuda] *f* sentence
присъединявам се [prisuedinyavam se] *v*
join, attach
присъствие [prisustvie] *n* presence,
attendance
притежание [pritezhanie] *n* possession
притежател [pritezhatel] *m* owner, possessor
притискам [pritiskam] *v* press
приход [prihod] *m* income, revenue
причина [prichina] *f* cause, reason
причинявам [prichinyavam] *v* cause, bring
about
приятел [priyatel] *m* friend
приятелски [priyatelski] *adj* friendly
приятелство [priyatelstvo] *n* friendship
приятен [priyaten] *adj* pleasant, agreeable,
nice
проба [proba] *f* trial, test, experiment
пробвам [probvam] *v* test
пробивам [probivam] *v* pierce, bore
проблем [problem] *m* problem
провалям [provalyam] *v* frustrate
проверка [proverka] *f* examination, check
up
проверявам [proveryavam] *v* verify, check,
examine
провинция [provintsiya] *f* province
проводник [provodnik] *m* conductor, wire

провокирам [provokiram] *v* provoke, instigate

прогноза [prognoza] *f* weather forecast

програма [programa] *f* program

прогрес [progres] *m* progress

продавам [prodavam] *v* sell

продавач [prodavach] *m* salesman

продажба [prodazhba] *f* sale, retail

продукт [prodoukt] *m* product

продукция [prodouktsiya] *f* production, output

продължавам [produlzhavam] *v* continue, go on

продължение [produlzhenie] *n* continuation, extension

проект [proekt] *m* project, design

проза [proza] *f* prose

прозорец [prozorets] *m* window

прозрачен [prozrachen] *adj* transparent

прозявам се [prozyavam se] *v* yawn

произвеждам [proizvezhdam] *v* produce, turn out

производител [proizvoditel] *m* producer

производителност [proizvoditelnost] *f* productivity

производство [proizvodstvo] *n* production, output

произношение [proiznoshenie] *n* pronunciation

произход [prois-hod] *m* origin, descent

произшествие [proizshestvie] *n* accident
прокурор [prokouror] *m* public prosecutor
пролет [prolet] *f* spring
променлив [promenliv] *adj* changeable, variable
променям [promenyam] *v* change, alter
промишлен [promishlen] *adj* industrial
промишленост [promishlenost] *f* industry
промяна [promyana] *f* change
прониквам [pronikvam] *v* penetrate, permeate
пропаст [propast] *f* precipice
проповед [propoved] *f* sermon
пропуск [propousk] *m* pass
прост [prost] *adj* simple, ordinary
просто [prosto] *adv* simply, merely, just
простота [prostota] *f* simplicity, plainness
пространство [prostranstvo] *n* space, area
простуда [prostouda] *f* cold, chill
прося [prosya] *v* beg
просяк [prosyak] *m* beggar
протест [protest] *m* protest, remonstrance
протестирам [protestiram] *v* protest
против [protif] *prep* against
противник [protivnik] *m* opponent, enemy
противореча [protivorecha] *v* contradict
противоречие [protivorechie] *n* contradiction
протокол [protokol] *m* protocol, report
професия [profesiya] *f* profession, trade
професор [profesor] *m* professor

процедура [protsedoura] *f* procedure
процент [protsent] *m* percentage
процес [protses] *m* process, course, trial
прошка [proshka] *f* forgiveness, pardon
прощавам [proshtavam] *v* forgive, pardon
пружина [prouzhina] *f* spring
пръст [prust] *f* earth, soil
пръст [prust] *m* finger, toe
пръстен [prusten] *m* ring
пръчка [pruchka] *f* stick
пряк [pryak] *m* nickname
психиатър [psihiatur] *m* psychiatrist
психология [psihologiya] *f* psychology
псувам [psouvam] *v* swear
птица [ptitsa] *f* bird
публика [poublika] *f* public, audience
публикувам [poublikouvam] *v* publish
пудра [poudra] *f* face powder
пуйка [pouika] *f* turkey
пуловер [poulover] *m* sweater
пулс [pouls] *m* pulse
пура [poura] *f* cigar
пустиня [poustinya] *f* desert
пуша [pousha] *v* smoke
пушач [poushach] *m* smoker
пушек [poushek] *m* smoke
пушка [poushka] *f* gun, rifle
пчела [pchela] *f* bee
пшеница [pshenitsa] *f* wheat
пълен [pulen] *adj* full, complete

пълномо́щно [pulnomoshtno] *n* power of attorney
пъ́лня [pulnya] *v* fill, stuff
пъ́пеш [pupesh] *m* melon
пъ́рви [purvi] *adj* first
пъ́ржа [purzha] *v* fry
пържо́ла [purzhola] *f* chop, cutlet
пъстъ́рва [pusturva] *f* trout
пъ́т [put] *m* road, path, track
пъ́тник [putnik] *m* traveller, passenger
пъ́тнически [putnicheski] *adj* passenger
пъту́вам [putouvam] *v* travel, voyage
пъту́ване [putouvane] *n* trip, journey, voyage
пя́на [pyana] *f* foam
пя́сък [pyasuk] *m* sand

Р

ра́бота [rabota] *f* work, job, labor
работи́лница [rabotilnitsa] *f* workshop
рабо́тник [rabotnik] *m* worker, workman
работода́тел [rabotodatel] *m* employer
рабо́тя [rabotya] *v* work
ра́вен [raven] *adj* even, level, equal
ра́венство [ravenstvo] *n* equality
равнина́ [ravnina] *f* plain
равни́ще [ravnishte] *n* level
равнове́сие [ravnovesie] *n* balance, equilibrium

ра́дио [radio] *n* radio

радиопреда́ване [radiopredavane] *n* broadcast

ра́дост [radost] *f* joy, gladness

ра́достен [radosten] *adj* joyful

ра́ждам [razhdam] *v* bear, give birth to, yield

разби́ра се [razbira se] *adv* of course

разби́рам [razbiram] *v* understand, realize, find out

разби́ране [razbirane] *n* understanding, comprehension, opinion

разва́лям [razvalyam] *v* spoil, damage, break

разве́ден [razveden] *adj* divorced

разве́ждам се [razvezhdam se] *v* divorce

разви́вам [razvivam] *v* develop

разви́тие [razvitie] *n* development, growth

развлече́ние [razvlechenie] *n* entertainment, amusement

разво́д [razvod] *m* divorce

развъ́рзвам [razvurzvam] *v* untie, undo

разгле́ждам [razglezhdam] *v* examine, look at, see

разгова́рям [razgovaryam] *v* talk, converse

ра́зговор [razgovor] *m* conversation, talk, chat

разгово́рен [razgovoren] *adj* colloquial

раздава́ч [razdavach] *m* postman

разде́лям [razdelyam] *v* divide, part

раздя́ла [razdyala] *f* parting

ра́зказ [raskas] *m* story, tale

разказвам [raskasvam] *v* tell, relate
разкривам [raskrivam] *v* reveal, disclose
разливам [razlivam] *v* spill
разлика [razlika] *f* difference
различавам [razlichavam] *v* distingiush, discern
различен [razlichen] *adj* different, various, diverse
размер [razmer] *m* size, degree, extent
размяна [razmyana] *f* exchange, barter
разнообразен [raznoobrazen] *adj* varied
разнообразие [raznoobrazie] *n* variety, diversity
разноски [raznoski] *noun pl* expenses
разобличавам [razoblichavam] *v* expose, unmask, lay bare
разоръжавам [razoruzhavam] *v* disarm
разоръжаване [razoruzhavane] *n* disarmament
разорявам [razoryavam] *v* ruin
разочаровам [razocharovam] *v* disappoint
разочарование [razocharovanie] *n* disappointment
разписка [raspiska] *f* receipt
разпит [raspit] *m* interrogation
разпитвам [raspitvam] *v* interrogate, question
разпределям [raspredelyam] *v* distribute
разпродажба [rasprodazhba] *f* sale
разрешавам [razreshavam] *v* allow, permit
разрешение [razreshenie] *n* permission, solution

разреши́телно [razreshitelno] *n* licence, permit

разруша́вам [razroushavam] *v* destroy, demolish

разруше́ние [razroushenie] *n* destruction, ruin

разсе́ян [raseyan] *adj* absent−minded

разстоя́ние [rastoyanie] *n* distance

разсъ́дък [rasuduk] *m* reason, sense

разсъжда́вам [rasuzhdavam] *v* reason

разсъ́мване [rasumvane] *n* dawn, daybreak

разтво́р [rastvor] *m* solution

разтопя́вам [rastopyavam] *v* melt

разтя́гам [rastyagam] *v* stretch

ра́зум [razoum] *m* sense, reason, mind

разу́мен [razoumen] *adj* sensible, reasonable

разхлади́телен [ras−hladitelen] *adj* cooling, refreshing

ра́зход [ras−hod] *m* expense, cost

разхо́дка [ras−hodka] *f* walk

разхо́ждам се [ras−hozhdam se] *v* take a walk

рай [rai] *m* paradise

райе́ [raie] *n* stripe

райо́н [raion] *m* district

рак [rak] *m* crab, cancer

раке́та [raketa] *f* rocket

ра́мка [ramka] *f* frame

ра́мо [ramo] *n* shoulder

ра́на [rana] *f* wound

ра́но [rano] *adv* early

ранявам [ranyavam] *v* wound
раса [rasa] *f* race
расизъм [rasizum] *m* racialism
растителност [rastitelnost] *f* vegetation
реактивен [reaktiven] *adj* jet
реализирам [realiziram] *v* make, realize
реалистичен [realistichen] *adj* realistic
ребро [rebro] *m* rib
ревер [rever] *m* lapel
ревматизъм [revmatizum] *m* rheumatism
ревнив [revnif] *adj* jealous
ревност [revnost] *f* jealousy
революция [revolyutsiya] *f* revolution
регистрирам [registriram] *v* register
ред [red] *m* order, line, row
редактор [redaktor] *m* editor
редица [reditsa] *f* row, series, number
редовен [redoven] *adj* regular
режа [rezha] *v* cut
режисирам [rezhisiram] *v* direct, produce
режисьор [rezhisyor] *m* director, producer
резервни части [reservni chasti] *noun pl*
spare parts
резултат [rezoultat] *m* result, outcome, score
рейс [reis] *m* bus
река [reka] *f* river, stream
реклама [reklama] *f* advertisement
рекламация [reklamatsiya] *f* claim
реколта [rekolta] *f* crop
рекорд [rekord] *m* record

релѝгия [religiya] *f* religion
рѐлса [relsa] *f* rail
ремо́нт [remont] *m* repairs
ремонтѝрам [remontiram] *v* repair
рентге́нов [rentgenof] *adj* X-ray
репетѝция [repetitsiya] *f* rehearsal
репорта́ж [reportazh] *m* report
репортьо́р [reportyor] *m* reporter
репу́блика [repoublika] *f* republic
рестора́нт [restorant] *m* restaurant
реце́пта [retsepta] *f* recipe, prescription
реч [rech] *f* speech, address
ре́чник [rechnik] *m* dictionary, vocabulary
ре́ша [resha] *v* comb
реша́вам [reshavam] *v* decide
реше́ние [reshenie] *n* decision, determination
рѝба [riba] *f* fish
риба́р [ribar] *m* fisherman
рибо́лов [ribolof] *m* fishing
рѝза [riza] *f* shirt
риску́вам [riskouvam] *v* risk
рису́вам [risouvam] *v* draw, paint
рису́нка [risounka] *f* drawing
рѝтам [ritam] *v* kick
роб [rob] *m* slave
рог [rog] *m* horn
ро́ден [roden] *adj* native, home
роде́н [roden] *adj* born
родѝтел [roditel] *m* parent
роднѝна [rodnina] *m* relation, relative

рожде́н ден [rozhden den] *m* birthday
ро́за [roza] *f* rose
ро́зов [rozof] *adj* pink, rosy
ро́кля [roklya] *f* dress, gown, frock
ро́ля [rolya] *f* part, role
рома́н [roman] *m* novel
роса́ [rosa] *f* dew
ру́да [rouda] *f* ore
рус [rous] *adj* blond
ру́син [rousin] *m* Russian
ру́ски [rouski] *adj* Russian
ръж [ruzh] *f* rye
ръка́ [ruka] *f* arm, hand
ръка́в [rukaf] *m* sleeve
ръкави́ца [rukavitsa] *f* glove
ръкопи́с [rukopis] *m* manuscript
ръку́вам се [rukouvam se] *v* shake hands with
ръст [rust] *m* stature, height, size
ря́дък [ryaduk] *adj* thin, rare

С

с [s] *prep* with, and, by, in, of
са́бя [sabya] *f* sword, sabre
садя́ [sadya] *v* plant
сако́ [sako] *n* coat, jacket
сакси́я [saksiya] *f* flower-pot
сала́м [salam] *f* sausage, salami

сала́та [salata] *f* salad
сам [sam] *adj* alone
са́мо [samo] *adv* only, solely, merely
самобръсна́чка [samobrusnachka] *f*
safety-razor
самоле́т [samolet] *m* airplane
самолетоноса́ч [samoletonosach] *m*
aircraftcarrier
самоли́чност [samolichnost] *f* identity
самооблада́ние [samoobladanie] *n*
self-control
самоотбра́на [samootbrana] *f* self-defense
самота́ [samota] *f* loneliness, solitude
само́тен [samoten] *adj* lonely, lonesome,
solitary
самоуби́йство [samooubiistvo] *n* suicide
самоуве́рен [samoouveren] *adj* self-confident
самоуве́реност [samoouverenost] *f*
self-confidence
самоуправле́ние [samooupravlenie] *n*
self-government
санда́л [sandal] *m* sandal
са́ндвич [sandvich] *m* sandwich
сантимента́лен [santimentalen] *adj*
sentimental
сапу́н [sapoun] *m* soap
сблъ́сквам се [sbluskvam se] *v* collide, clash
сблъ́скване [sbluskvane] *n* collision, conflict
сбо́гом [sbogom] *greet* good-bye, farewell
сбор [sbor] *m* sum

сборник [sbornik] *m* collection
свалям [svalyam] *v* take down, remove, take off
сватба [svatba] *f* wedding
сватбен [svatben] *adj* wedding, nuptial
свеж [svezh] *adj* fresh
свежест [svezhest] *f* freshness
свекър [svekur] *m* father-in-law
свекърва [svekurva] *f* mother-in-law
свет [svet] *adj* holy, sacred
светец [svetets] *m* saint
светкавица [svetkavitsa] *f* lightning
светлина [svetlina] *f* light
светло [svetlo] *adv* light, brightly
светя [svetya] *v* shine, beam
свещ [svesht] *f* candle
свещен [sveshten] *adj* holy, sacred
свещеник [sveshtenik] *m* priest, clergyman
свидетел [svidetel] *m* witness
свидетелство [svidetelstvo] *n* certificate
свинско месо [svinsko meso] *n* pork
свиня [svinya] *f* pig, swine
свирка [svirka] *f* whistle, pipe
свиря [svirya] *v* play, whistle
свобода [svoboda] *f* freedom, liberty
свободен [svoboden] *adj* free, vacant, unoccupied
свод [svod] *m* arch, vault
свой [svoi] *pron* one's own
свойство [svoistvo] *n* property, quality

свързвам [svurzvam] *v* connect, link, put in touch

свят [svyat] *m* world

сглобявам [sglobyavam] *v* assemble

сграда [sgrada] *f* building, house

сделка [sdelka] *f* transaction, bargain, deal

сдружение [sdrouzhenie] *n* corporation, society

се [se] *pron* oneself

север [sever] *m* north

северен [severen] *adj* northern

северозапад [severozapad] *m* northwest

североизток [severoistok] *m* northeast

сега [sega] *adv* now, at present

сегашен [segashen] *adj* present, current

седалка [sedalka] *f* seat, bench

седем [sedem] *num* seven

седемдесет [sedemdeset] *num* seventy

седемнадесет [sedemnadeset] *num* seventeen

седло [sedlo] *n* saddle

седмица [sedmitsa] *f* week

седмичен [sedmichen] *adj* weekly

седя [sedya] *v* sit, be seated

сезон [sezon] *m* season

сека [seka] *v* cut, chop, fell

секретар [sekretar] *m* secretary

секретен [sekreten] *adj* secret, confidential

сексуален [seksoualen] *adj* sexual, sex

секунда [sekounda] *f* second

селище [selishte] *n* settlement

село [selo] *n* village
селскостопански [selskostopanski] *adj* agricultural
селянин [selyanin] *m* peasant, countryman
семе [seme] *n* seed gram
семейство [semeistvo] *n* family
семинар [seminar] *m* seminar
сензация [senzatsiya] *f* sensation
сено [seno] *n* hay
септември [septemvri] *m* September
сервиз [servis] *m* set, service
сервирам [serviram] *v* serve, help
сервитьор [servityor] *m* waiter
сериозен [seriozen] *adj* serious, earnest, grave
серия [seriya] *f* series, set
сестра [sestra] *f* sister
сечиво [sechivo] *n* tool, instrument
сив [siv] *adj* gray
сигнал [signal] *m* signal
сигурност [sigournost] *f* certainty, security, safety
сила [sila] *f* strength, force, power
силен [silen] *adj* strong, powerful
символ [simvol] *m* symbol
симетрия [simetriya] *f* symmetry
симфония [simfoniya] *f* symphony
син [sin] *m* son
син [sin] *adj* blue
сипвам [sipvam] *v* pour

сирене [sirene] *n* cheese
система [sistema] *f* system
скала [skala] *f* rock, cliff
скандал [skandal] *m* scandal
скара [skara] *f* grill
скелет [skelet] *m* skeleton
скептичен [skeptichen] *adj* sceptical
ски [ski] *noun pl* ski
скиор [skior] *m* skier
склад [sklad] *m* storehouse, warehouse
склон [sklon] *m* slope
склонение [sklonenie] *n* declension
склонност [sklonnost] *f* inclination, propensity
сключвам [sklyuchvam] *v* conclude, contract
скоба [skoba] *f* clip, bracket
скок [skok] *m* jump, leap, spring
скоро [skoro] *adv* soon, presently, recently
скорост [skorost] *f* speed, rate, pace
скривалище [skrivalishte] *n* hiding place
скривам [skrivam] *v* hide, conceal
скрит [skrit] *adj* hidden, secret
скромен [skromen] *adj* modest, humble
скромност [skromnost] *f* modesty, humbleness
скръб [skrub] *f* sorrow, grief
скука [skouka] *f* boredom, tedium
скулптор [skoulptor] *m* sculptor
скулптура [skoulptoura] *f* sculpture
скъп [skup] *adj* dear, expensive

скъперник [skupernik] *m* miner, skinflint
скъпо [skupo] *adv* costly, dearly
скъпоценност [skupotsennost] *f* jewel, gem
скърбя [skurbya] *v* grieve, mourn
скъсвам [skusvam] *v* tear, wear out, break
слаб [slab] *adj* weak, slender, lean
слава [slava] *f* glory, fame
славянин [slavyanin] *m* Slav
славянски [slavyanski] *adj* Slavonic
сладкарница [sladkarnitsa] *f* pastry shop
сладки [sladki] *noun pl* pastry
сладолед [sladoled] *m* ice-cream
сладък [sladuk] *adj* sweet
слама [slama] *f* straw
следа [sleda] *f* track, trace, trail
следвам [sledvam] *v* follow, study, come after
следващ [sledvasht] *adj* next, following
следобед [sledobed] *m* afternoon
следствие [sledstvie] *n* investigation, inquiry
слива [sliva] *f* plum, prune
сливица [slivitsa] *f* tonsil
слово [slovo] *n* word, speech, address
словоред [slovored] *m* word order
сложен [slozhen] *adj* complex, complicated
сложност [slozhnost] *f* complexity
слой [sloi] *m* layer, stratum
слон [slon] *m* elephant
слонова кост [slonova kost] *f* ivory
слуга [slouga] *m* servant

служба [slouzhba] *f* work, employment
служебен [slouzheben] *adj* official, business
слух [slouh] *m* hearing, ear, rumor
случай [slouchai] *m* case, occasion, opportunity
случайно [slouchaino] *adv* accidentally
случайност [slouchainost] *f* chance, accident
слушалка [sloushalka] *f* receiver, stethoscope
слушател [sloushatel] *m* listener
слънчев [slunchev] *adj* sunny
сляп [slyap] *adj* blind
смел [smel] *adj* courageous, daring
смелост [smelost] *f* courage, boldness
смес [smes] *f* mixture, blend
смесвам [smesvam] *v* mix, blend
сметана [smetana] *f* cream
сметка [smetka] *f* account, profit
смешен [smeshen] *adj* funny, ridiculous, absurd
смея се [smeya se] *v* laugh
смисъл [smisul] *m* sense, meaning
смокиня [smokinya] *f* fig
смуча [smoucha] *v* suck
смърт [smurt] *f* death, decease
смъртен [smurten] *adj* mortal, deadly
смъртност [smurtnost] *f* mortality, death rate
смъртоносен [smurtonosen] *adj* deadly
смяна [smyana] *f* change, shift
смях [smyah] *m* laugh, laughter
снабдявам [snabdyavam] *v* provide, supply

снабдя́ване [snabdyavane] *n* supply, provisioning
снаря́д [snaryad] *m* shell, projectile
сна́сям [snasyam] *v* lay
снаха́ [snaha] *f* daughter-in-law, sister-in-law
сни́мка [snimka] *f* photograph, picture
сняг [snyag] *m* snow
со́бственик [sobstvenik] *m* owner, proprietor
со́бственост [sobstvenost] *f* property, possession
сода́ [soda] *f* soda
сок [sok] *m* juice
сол [sol] *f* salt
соле́н [solen] *adj* salty, saline
соля́ [solya] *v* salt
сос [sos] *m* sauce, gravy
социа́лен [sotsialen] *adj* social
социали́зъм [sotsializum] *m* socialism
спа́лня [spalnya] *f* bedroom
спана́к [spanak] *m* spinach
спасе́ние [spasenie] *n* rescue, salvation
спаси́тел [spasitel] *m* savior, rescuer
спестя́вам [spestyavam] *v* save, economize
спестя́вания [spestyavaniya] *noun pl* savings
специа́лен [spetsialen] *adj* special, particular
специали́ст [spetsialist] *m* specialist, expert
специалите́т [spetsialitet] *m* specialty
специа́лно [spetsialno] *adv* especially, in particular

специа́лност [spetsialnost] *f* specialty, subject

спе́шно [speshno] *adv* urgently, hastily

спе́шност [speshnost] *f* urgency

спира́чка [spirachka] *f* brake, curb

спи́рка [spirka] *f* stop, halt

спирт [spirt] *m* alcohol, spirit

списа́ние [spisanie] *n* magazine, journal

спи́сък [spisuk] *m* list

сплав [splaf] *f* alloy

спого́дба [spogodba] *f* agreement, accord

споко́ен [spokoen] *adj* calm, peaceful

споко́йствие [spokoistvie] *n* calmness, tranquility

спо́мен [spomen] *m* remembrance, recollection

спо́мням [spomnyam] *v* recall, call to mind

спор [spor] *m* dispute, argument

споразуме́ние [sporazoumenie] *n* agreement, understanding

спорт [sport] *m* sport

спорти́ст [sportist] *m* athlete

спо́ря [sporya] *v* dispute, argue

справедли́в [spravedlif] *adj* just, fair, equitable

справедли́вост [spravedlivost] *f* justice, equity

спра́вочник [spravochnik] *m* handbook, manual

спреже́ние [sprezhenie] *n* conjugation

спринцо́вка [sprintsofka] *f* syringe
спу́скам [spouskam] *v* lower, drop, descend
спя [spya] *v* sleep, slumber
сравня́вам [sravnyavam] *v* compare, check
сраже́ние [srazhenie] *n* fight, battle, action
срам [sram] *m* shame, disgrace
срамежли́в [sramezhlif] *adj* shy, bashful
срамувам се [sramouvam se] *v* be shy, be ashamed of
сребро́ [srebro] *n* silver
сред [sred] *prep* among, amidst
среда́ [sreda] *f* middle, environment
сре́дно [sredno] *adv* on the average
средновеко́вие [srednovekovie] *n* the Middle Ages
сре́дство [sredstvo] *n* means, device
сре́ща [sreshta] *f* meeting, appointment, date
сре́щам [sreshtam] *v* meet, see, encounter
срещу́ [sreshtou] *adv* against, opposite
сри́чка [srichka] *f* syllable
срок [srok] *m* term
сръ́чен [sruchen] *adj* dexterous, skilful
сръ́чност [sruchnost] *f* dexterity, skill
сря́да [sryada] *f* Wednesday
стаби́лен [stabilen] *adj* stable
стаби́лност [stabilnost] *f* stability
ста́ва [stava] *f* joint
ста́вам [stavam] *v* stand up, rise, happen, occur
ста́дий [stadii] *m* stage, phase

стадио́н [stadion] *m* stadium
ста́до [stado] *n* herd, flock
станда́ртен [standarten] *adj* standard
стар [star] *adj* old, ancient
ста́рец [starets] *m* old man
старе́я [stareya] *v* grow old
ста́рост [starost] *f* old age
ста́тия [statiya] *f* article
ста́туя [statouya] *f* statue
стафи́да [stafida] *f* raisin
ста́чка [stachka] *f* strike
ста́я [staya] *f* room
стена́ [stena] *f* wall
стеногра́фия [stenografiya] *f* shorthand
сти́гам [stigam] *v* reach, be sufficient, last out
стил [stil] *m* style
стипе́ндия [stipendiya] *f* scholarship
стих [stih] *m* verse, line
сто [sto] *num* one hundred
сто́йност [stoinost] *f* value, worth, cost
сто́ка [stoka] *f* commodity, wares
стол [stol] *m* chair
столе́тие [stoletie] *n* century
сто́лица [stolitsa] *f* capital, metropolis
столова́ [stolova] *f* diningroom
стома́на [stomana] *f* steel
стома́х [stomah] *m* stomach
стома́шен [stomashen] *adj* gastric
стопа́нски [stopanski] *adj* economic

стопанство [stopanstvo] *n* economy
страдам [stradam] *v* suffer
страдание [stradanie] *n* suffering
страна [strana] *f* side, aspect, country
странен [stranen] *adj* strange, odd, queer
страница [stranitsa] *f* page
страст [strast] *f* passion, ardor
стратегия [strategiya] *f* strategy
страх [strah] *m* fear, dread, apprehension
страхлив [strahlif] *adj* cowardly, timid
страшен [strashen] *adj* dreadful, terrible, awful
стрела [strela] *f* arrow, shaft
стрелка [strelka] *f* needle, hand
стрелям [strelyam] *v* shoot, fire
строг [strog] *adj* strict, severe
строго [strogo] *adv* strictly, severely
строител [stroitel] *m* builder
строителство [stroitelstvo] *n* building, construction
строя [stroya] *v* build, construct, put up
структура [strouktoura] *f* structure, texture
струна [strouna] *f* string, chord
струя [strouya] *f* stream, flush
стръмен [strumen] *adj* steep, precipitous
студ [stoud] *m* cold, chill
студен [stouden] *adj* cold, chilly
студент [stoudent] *m* undergraduate, student
студио [stoudio] *n* studio
стъкло [stuklo] *n* glass

стълб [stulb] *m* post, pole, column
стълба [stulba] *f* stairs, ladder
стълбище [stulbishte] *n* staircase
стъпало [stupalo] *n* step, stair, foot
стъпвам [stupvam] *v* tread, step
стъпка [stupka] *f* step, pace, footprint
сувенир [souvenir] *m* souvenir, keepsake
суверенитет [souverenitet] *m* sovereignty
суеверен [soueveren] *adj* superstitious
суеверие [soueverie] *n* superstition
суетност [souetnost] *f* vanity, foppery
сума [souma] *f* sum, amount
супа [soupa] *f* soup
суров [sourof] *adj* raw, severe
суровина [sourovina] *f* raw material
сутиен [soutien] *adj* brassiere, bra
сутрин [soutrin] *f* morning
сух [souh] *adj* dry, arid
суча [soucha] *v* suck
суша [sousha] *f* dry land, mainland
суша [sousha] *f* drought
сушен [soushen] *adj* dry, dried
схема [s-hema] *f* diagram
сходен [s-hoden] *adj* similar, analogous
сцена [stsena] *f* stage, scene
сценарий [stsenarii] *m* scenario, script
счетоводител [schetovoditel] *m* accountant
счетоводство [schetovodstvo] *n* book-keeping
счупвам [schoupvam] *v* break
събирам [subiram] *v* gather, collect, contain

съби́тие [subitie] *n* event

събли́чам [sublicham] *v* take off, undress, strip

съболезнова́ние [soboleznovanie] *n* condolence

съ́бота [subota] *f* Saturday

събра́ние [subranie] *n* meeting, assembly

събу́вам [subouvam] *v* take off

събу́ждам [subouzhdam] *v* wake, awake

съ́вест [suvest] *f* conscience

съ́вестен [suvesten] *adj* conscientious, scrupulous

съве́т [suvet] *m* advice, counsel

съве́твам [suvetvam] *v* advise, admonish

съве́тник [suvetnik] *m* adviser, counselor

съвме́стен [suvmesten] *adj* joint, combined

съвпа́дам [sufpadam] *v* coincide, concur

съвпаде́ние [sufpadenie] *n* coincidence, concurrence

съвре́менен [suvremenen] *adj* contemporary, modern, current

съвсе́м [sufsem] *adv* quite, entirely, altogether

съвърше́н [suvurshen] *adj* perfect, thorough

съгла́сие [suglasie] *n* consent, agreement

съгла́сно [suglasno] *adv* according to

съгра́жданин [sugrazhdanin] *m* fellow-citizen

съд [sud] *m* vessel, container, utensil

съд [sud] *m* court

съдба́ [sudba] *f* fate, fortune, destiny

съдбоно́сен [sudbonosen] *adj* fatal, fateful
съде́бен [sudeben] *adj* legal, judicial
съдия́ [sudiya] *m* judge, referee
съдру́жник [sudrouzhnik] *m* partner
съдъ́ржам [sudurzham] *v* contain, hold, comprise
съдържа́ние [sudurzhanie] *n* content
съ́дя [sudya] *v* judge, try, sue
съединя́вам [suedinyavam] *v* join, unite, connect
съжале́ние [suzhalenie] *n* regret, pity
съжаля́вам [suzhalyavam] *v* be sorry, regret, pity
създа́вам [suzdavam] *v* create, make, form
създа́ние [suzdanie] *n* creature, creation
създа́тел [suzdatel] *m* creator, founder
съзна́вам [suznavam] *v* realize, be aware of
съзна́ние [suznanie] *n* consciousness, awareness
съзна́телен [suznatelen] *adj* conscious, conscientious
съкраще́ние [sukrashtenie] *n* abbreviation
съкро́вище [sukrovishte] *n* treasury
сълза́ [sulza] *f* tear
съм [sum] *v* be, exist
съмне́ние [sumnenie] *n* doubt
съмни́телен [sumnitelen] *adj* doubtful, questionable
съмня́вам се [sumnyavam se] *v* doubt
сън [sun] *m* sleep, dream

сънаро́дник [sunarodnik] *m* compatriot, fellow-countryman

сънувам [sunouvam] *v* dream, have a dream

съобщавам [suobshtavam] *v* announce, tell

съобще́ние [suobshtenie] *n* announcement

съотве́тен [suotveten] *adj* corresponding, respective

съотве́тствувам [suotvetstvouvam] *v* correspond, fit

съотноше́ние [suotnoshenie] *n* correlation, ratio

съпе́рник [supernik] *m* rival

съпе́рничество [supernichestvo] *n* rivalry, competition

съпроти́ва [suprotiva] *f* resistance, opposition

съпротивле́ние [suprotivlenie] *n* resistance

съпру́г [suproug] *m* husband

съпру́га [suprouga] *f* wife

сърбе́ж [surbezh] *m* itch

сърбя́ [surbya] *v* itch

сърди́т [surdit] *adj* angry, cross

сърдя [surdya] *v* make angry

сърна́ [surna] *f* deer, doe

сърце́ [surtse] *n* heart

сърцевина́ [surtsevina] *f* core, heart

съсе́д [sused] *m* neighbor

съсе́ден [suseden] *adj* neighboring, next

съсе́дски [susedski] *adv* neighborly

съста́в [sustaf] *m* composition, cast

състезавам се [sustezavam se] *v* compete, contend

състезание [sustezanie] *n* contest, events, competition

състезател [sustezatel] *m* competitor

състоя се [sustoya se] *v* consist of, take place

състояние [sustoyanie] *n* condition, state

състояние [sustoyanie] *n* wealth, fortune

състрадание [sustradanie] *n* compassion, sympathy

състрадателен [sustradatelen] *adj* compassionate

съученик [suouchenik] *m* schoolmate

съхна [suhna] *v* dry, wither, fade

съчинение [suchinenie] *n* composition, work

съчинявам [suchinyavam] *v* compose, invent, make up

съчувствие [suchoufstvie] *n* sympathy

съчувствувам [suchoufstvouvam] *v* sympathize

съществително [sushtestvitelno] *n* noun

същество [sushtestvo] *n* being, creature, thing

съществуване [sushtestvouvane] *n* existence

съществувам [soushtestvouvam] *v* exist, be

също [sushto] *adv* also, too, as well

съюз [suyus] *m* union, alliance

сянка [syanka] *f* shadow, shade

сяра [syara] *f* sulphur

Т

табела [tabela] *f* sign-board
таблетка [tabletka] *f* tablet
таблица [tablitsa] *f* table
табло [tablo] *n* board
таван [tavan] *m* ceiling, attic
таен [taen] *adj* secret, covert
тази [tazi] *pron* this, that
тайна [taina] *f* secret, secrecy
такса [taksa] *f* fee
талант [talant] *m* talent, gift
талантлив [talantlif] *adj* talented, gifted
талия [taliya] *f* waist
там [tam] *adv* there
танк [tank] *m* tank
тантела [tantela] *f* lace
танц [tants] *m* dance
танцувам [tantsouvam] *v* dance
твой [tvoi] *pron* your
твърд [tvurd] *adj* hard, stiff, solid, firm
твърдение [tvurdenie] *n* assertion, allegation
твърдост [tvurdost] *f* firmness, hardness
те [te] *pron* they
театрален [teatralen] *adj* theatrical, theater
театър [teatur] *m* theater
теб [teb] *pron* to you
тебешир [tebeshir] *m* chalk
тегло [teglo] *n* weight

тѐгля [teglya] *v* weigh

тежа́ [tezha] *v* weigh, carry weight

тѐжък [tezhuk] *adj* heavy, weighty, hard, difficulty

тѐзи [tezi] *pron* these, those

тек [tek] *adj* odd

тека́ [teka] *v* flow, run, leak

текст [tekst] *m* text, words

тексти́л [tekstil] *m* textile

тел [tel] *m* wire

телѐ [tele] *n* calf

телеви́зия [televiziya] *f* television

телеви́зор [televizor] *m* television set

телегра́ма [telegrama] *f* telegram

телефо́н [telefon] *m* telephone

телефо́нен указа́тел [telefonen oukazatel] *m* telephone directory

телефо́нна слуша́лка [telefonna sloushalka] *f* receiver

тѐлешко [teleshko] *n* veal

тѐма [tema] *f* subject, theme, topic

темену́жка [temenouzhka] *f* violet

температу́ра [temperatoura] *f* temperature, fever

тѐнджера [tendzhera] *f* pot, saucepan

тѐнис [tenis] *m* tennis

теорѐма [teorema] *f* theorem

тео́рия [teoriya] *f* theory

террито́рия [teritoriya] *f* territory, area

тѐрмин [termin] *m* term

термоме́тър [termometur] *m* thermometer
те́рмос [termos] *m* vacuum flask, thermos
теро́р [teror] *m* terror, terrorism
те́сен [tesen] *adj* narrow, tight
тесто́ [testo] *n* dough, paste
тетра́дка [tetradka] *f* notebook
те́хен [tehen] *pron* their
техни́к [tehnik] *m* mechanic, technician
те́хника [tehnika] *f* technics, technique
техни́чески [tehnicheski] *adj* technical
те́чен [techen] *adj* liquid, fluid
те́чност [technost] *f* liquid, fluid
ти [ti] *pron* you, your
тига́н [tigan] *m* frying pan
ти́гър [tigur] *m* tiger
ти́ква [tikva] *f* pumpkin, squash
тип [tip] *m* type, pattern
тих [tih] *adj* quiet, still, calm
ти́чам [ticham] *v* run
тишина́ [tishina] *f* silence, stillness
тла́сък [tlasuk] *m* push, stimulus
то [to] *pron* it, that
тоале́тна [toaletna] *f* lavatory
това́ [tova] *pron* this, that
това́р [tovar] *m* load, burden, cargo
товари́телница [tovaritelnitsa] *f* bill of lading
това́ря [tovarya] *v* load, charge
тога́ва [togava] *adv* then, at that time
той [toi] *pron* he

ток [tok] *m* current, electricity
ток [tok] *m* heel
том [tom] *m* volume
тон [ton] *m* tone, shade
тон [ton] *m* ton
то́пка [topka] *f* ball
топло́та [toplota] *f* warmth, cordiality
топля́ [toplya] *v* warm, heat
топо́ла [topola] *f* poplar
то́пъл [topul] *adj* warm, mild, cordial
топя́ [topya] *v* melt, thaw
топя́ [topya] *v* dip, soak
тор [tor] *m* fertilizer
то́рта [torta] *f* cake
тост [tost] *m* toast
то́чен [tochen] *adj* exact, precise, punctual
то́чка [tochka] *f* point, period
то́чно [tochno] *adv* exactly, just, precisely
то́чност [tochnost] *f* precision, punctuality
траге́дия [tragediya] *f* tragedy
траги́чен [tragichen] *adj* tragic
тради́ция [traditsiya] *f* tradition
тракто́р [traktor] *m* tractor
транзи́стор [tranzistor] *m* transistor
трансп́орт [transport] *m* transport,
transportation
тра́ур [traour] *m* mourning
тра́я [traya] *v* last, endure
трева́ [treva] *f* grass
трево́жа [trevozha] *v* worry, be anxious

трезвен [trezven] *adj* sober
тренировка [trenirofka] *f* training, practice
треньор [trenyor] *m* trainer, coach
треперя [treperya] *v* tremble, shake, shudder
трети [treti] *adj* third
три [tri] *num* three
тридесет [trideset] *num* thirty
тримесечие [trimesechie] *n* quartet
тринадесет [trinadeset] *num* thirteen
трион [trion] *m* saw
триумф [trioumf] *m* triumph
триъгълник [triugulnik] *m* triangle
трия [triya] *v* rub, scrub
тровя [trovya] *v* poison
тропически [tropicheski] *adj* tropical
тротуар [trotouar] *m* pavement, sidewalk
труд [troud] *m* labor, work
труден [trouden] *adj* difficult, hard
трудност [troudnost] *f* difficulty, hardship
трудя се [troudya se] *v* labor, work
тръба [truba] *f* pipe, tube
тръгвам [trugvam] *v* start, set out, leave, depart
трън [trun] *m* thorn
трябва [tryabva] *v* must, have to, should
тук [touk] *adv* here
тунел [tounel] *m* tunnel
туризъм [tourizum] *m* tourism, hiking
турист [tourist] *m* tourist, hiker
турне [tourne] *n* tour

турни́р [tournir] *m* tournament
ту́хла [touhla] *f* brick
тъга́ [tuga] *f* sorrow, grief, sadness
тъгу́вам [tugouvam] *v* grieve, sorrow
тълку́вам [tulkouvam] *v* interpret
тълпа́ [tulpa] *f* crowd, throng
тъ́мен [tumen] *adj* dark
тъ́нък [tunuk] *adj* thin, slender, subtle
търг [turg] *m* auction, tender
търго́вец [turgovets] *m* merchant, dealer
търго́вия [turgoviya] *f* trade, commerce, business
търка́лям [turkalyam] *v* roll
тъ́ркам [turkam] *v* rub, polish
търпя́ [turpya] *v* bear, suffer, tolerate
тъ́рсене [tursene] *n* search, quest, demand
тъ́рся [tursya] *v* look for, search, seek
тъст [tust] *m* father-in-law
тъ́ща [tushta] *f* mother-in-law
тютю́н [tyutyun] *m* tobacco
тя [tya] *pron* she
тя́ло [tyalo] *n* body
тя́сно [tyasno] *adv* tight, closely
тях [tyah] *pron* them

У

у [ou] *prep* at, to, with, on, about
убежда́вам [oubezhdavam] *v* convince, persuade

убеждéние [oubezhdenie] *n* conviction, belief
убéжище [oubezhishte] *n* refuge, shelter, asylum
убúвам [oubivam] *v* kill, murder, assassinate
убúец [oubiets] *m* killer, murderer
убúйство [oubiiistvo] *n* murder, assassination
уважáвам [ouvazhavam] *v* respect, esteem, honor
уважéние [ouvazhenie] *n* respect, regard, esteem
уведомЯвам [ouvedomyavam] *v* inform, notify
увеличáвам [ouvelichavam] *v* increase, enlarge
увеличéние [ouvelichenie] *n* increase
увéрен [ouveren] *adj* sure, certain, assured
уверéние [ouverenie] *n* assurance, certificate
увéреност [ouverenost] *f* confidence, assurance, conviction
увú [ouvi] *interj* alas
увúвам [ouvivam] *v* wrap, wind
увод [ouvod] *m* introduction, preface
уводен [ouvoden] *adj* introductory
уволнéние [ouvolnenie] *n* dismissal, discharge
уволнЯвам [ouvolnyavam] *v* dismiss, fire
удар [oudar] *m* hit, blow, stroke, shock
ударéние [oudarenie] *n* accent, stress, emphasis
удóбен [oudoben] *adj* comfortable, convenient, handy

удо́бство [oudobstvo] *n* comfort, facilities
удовлетворя́вам [oudovletvoryavam] *v* satisfy, grant
удово́лствие [oudovolstvie] *n* pleasure
у́дрям [oudryam] *v* hit, strike, beat
удуша́вам [oudoushavam] *v* strangle, suffocate
удължа́вам [oudulzhavam] *v* prolong, extend
у́жас [ouzhas] *m* terror, horror, dread
ужа́сен [ouzhasen] *adj* awful, terrible, dreadful
узря́вам [ouzryavam] *v* ripen, mature
указа́тел [oukazatel] *m* index, directory
укра́са [oukrasa] *f* decoration
украше́ние [oukrashenie] *n* decoration, ornament
ула́вям [oulavyam] *v* catch, take hold of, seize
у́лица [oulitsa] *f* street
у́мен [oumen] *adj* clever, intelligent, bright
уме́ние [oumenie] *n* ability, skill
уме́рен [oumeren] *adj* moderate, temperate
уми́рам [oumiram] *v* die, pass away, depart
уми́съл [oumisul] *f* intention, design
уми́шлен [oumishlen] *adj* deliberate, intentional
умноже́ние [oumnozhenie] *n* multiplication
умо́ра [oumora] *f* weariness, fatigue
уморе́н [oumoren] *adj* tired, weary, worn out

умря́л [oumryal] *adj* dead, deceased
у́мствен [oumstven] *adj* mental, intellectual
универса́лен [ouniversalen] *adj* universal
университе́т [ouniversitet] *m* university
униже́ние [ounizhenie] *n* humiliation
унифо́рма [ouniforma] *f* uniform
унищожа́вам [ounishtozhavam] *v* destroy, annihilate
упла́ха [ouplaha] *f* fright, scare
упла́швам [ouplashvam] *v* frighten, scare
употре́ба [oupotreba] *f* use, usage
употребя́вам [oupotrebyavam] *v* use, make use of
упра́ва [ouprava] *f* management
управле́ние [oupravlenie] *n* management, administration, government
управля́вам [oupravlyavam] *v* govern, rule, run
упражне́ние [ouprazhnenie] *n* exercise, drill, practice
упражня́вам [ouprazhnyavam] *v* exercise, practise
упъ́тване [ouputvane] *n* direction
урага́н [ouragan] *m* hurricane, tornado
уро́к [ourok] *m* lesson
уси́лие [ousilie] *n* effort, exertion
ускоре́ние [ouskorenie] *n* acceleration
усло́вен [ousloven] *adj* conditional
усло́вие [ouslovie] *n* condition, stipulation
усложне́ние [ouslozhnenie] *n* complication

усложня́вам [ouslozhnyavam] *v* complicate
услу́га [ouslouga] *f* service, favor
услу́жвам [ouslouzhvam] *v* do a favor,
render a service
усми́вка [ousmifka] *f* smile
усми́хвам се [ousmihvam se] *v* smile
успе́х [ouspeh] *m* success, marks, grades
успе́шен [ouspeshen] *adj* successful
уста́ [ousta] *f* mouth
у́стен [ousten] *adj* oral, mouth
у́стна [oustna] *f* lip
усто́йчив [oustoichif] *adj* steady, firm, stable
усто́йчивост [oustoichivost] *f* stability,
firmness
утоля́вам [outolyavam] *v* satisfy, quench
уточня́вам [outochnyavam] *v* specify
у́тре [outre] *adv* tomorrow
ухо́ [ouho] *n* ear
у́ча [oucha] *v* learn, study, teach
уча́ствувам [ouchastvouvam] *v* participate,
take part in
уча́стие [ouchastie] *n* participation, share
уча́стник [ouchasnik] *m* participant
уче́бник [ouchebnik] *m* textbook
у́чен [ouchen] *m* scholar
учени́к [ouchenik] *m* student
учи́лище [ouchilishte] *n* school
учи́тел [ouchitel] *m* teacher, schoolmaster
учти́в [ouchtif] *adj* polite, civil

учти́вост [ouchtivost] *f* politeness, courtesy
учу́двам [ouchoudvam] *v* surprise, astonish
учу́дване [ouchoudvane] *n* surprise, astonishment
уязви́м [ouyazvim] *adj* vulnerable

Ф

фа́брика [fabrika] *f* factory, mill
фа́за [faza] *f* phase, period, stage
факт [fakt] *m* fact
фа́ктор [faktor] *m* factor, agent
факту́ра [faktoura] *f* invoice, bill
факу́лтет [fakoultet] *m* faculty, department
фали́рам [faliram] *v* bankrupt
фали́т [falit] *m* bankruptcy, crash, failure
фалши́в [falshif] *adj* false, coined, forged
фанати́зъм [fanatizum] *m* fanaticism, bigotry
фанта́зия [fantaziya] *f* imagination, fancy
фантасти́чен [fantastichen] *adj* fantastical, fabulous
фар [far] *m* lighthouse, beacon, headlights
фаса́да [fasada] *f* front, facade
фасу́л [fasoul] *m* beans
фата́лен [fatalen] *adj* fatal
фа́уна [faouna] *f* fauna
фаши́зъм [fashizum] *m* fascism
февруа́ри [fevrouari] *m* February
фене́р [fener] *m* lantern

фенерче [fenerche] *n* flashlight, electric torch

фиба [fiba] *f* hairpin

фигура [figoura] *f* figure

физик [fizik] *m* physicist

физика [fizika] *f* physics, physique

физически [fizicheski] *adj* physical, bodily

физкултура [fiskoultoura] *f* physical education

филателист [filatelist] *m* stamp-collector

филе [file] *n* loin, fillet

филия [filiya] *f* slice

филм [film] *m* film, motion picture

философ [filosof] *m* philosopher

философия [filosofiya] *f* philosophy

филтър [filtur] *m* filter, strainer

филхармония [filharmoniya] *f* philharmonic orchestra

фин [fin] *adj* fine, delicate

финансист [finansist] *m* financier

фирма [firma] *f* firm, sign-board

флора [flora] *f* flora

флота [flota] *f* fleet, navy

фоайе [foaie] *n* foyer, lobby

фокус [fokous] *m* trick, stut

фолклор [folklor] *m* folklore

фон [fon] *m* background

фонд [fond] *m* fund

форма [forma] *f* form, shape

формален [formalen] *adj* formal

формалност [formalnost] *f* formality
формат [format] *m* size, format
формула [formoula] *f* formula
формуляр [formoulyar] *m* form, blank
фотоапарат [fotoaparat] *m* camera
фотограф [fotograf] *m* photographer
фотографирам [fotografiram] *v* take a picture of
фотография [fotografiya] *f* photography, photo
фотьойл [fotyoil] *m* armchair, easy chair
фраза [fraza] *f* phrase
френски [frenski] *adj* French
фризьор [frizyor] *m* hairdresser
фронт [front] *m* front
фуния [founiya] *f* funnel
функционирам [founktsioniram] *v* function
функция [founktsiya] *f* function
фурма [fourma] *f* date
фурна [fourna] *f* bakery, oven
футбол [foutbol] *m* football, soccer
фъстък [fustuk] *m* peanut

X

хабя [habya] *v* waste, spoil
хавлия [havliya] *f* bathrobe, towel
хазарт [hazart] *m* gambling
хайвер [haiver] *m* roe, caviar

халка́ [halka] *f* ring
хамба́р [hambar] *m* barn, granary
хао́с [haos] *m* chaos, mess
ха́пя [hapya] *v* bite
хара́ктер [harakter] *m* character, temper, disposition
характе́рен [harakteren] *adj* characteristic, peculiar
харе́свам [haresvam] *v* like, enjoy
хармо́ния [harmoniya] *f* harmony
харти́я [hartiya] *f* paper
ха́рча [harcha] *v* spend
хва́ля [hvalya] *v* praise, commend
хе́рния [herniya] *f* hernia, rupture
хигие́на [higiena] *f* hygiene, sanitation
хиля́да [hilyada] *num* thousand
хими́к [himik] *m* chemist
химика́л [himikal] *m* chemical
химика́лка [himikalka] *f* ball-point pen
хими́ческо чи́стене [himichesko chistene] *n* dry cleaning
хи́мия [himiya] *f* chemistry
химн [himn] *m* hymn, anthem
хиру́рг [hirourg] *m* surgeon
хиру́ргия [hirourgiya] *f* surgery
хи́тър [hitur] *adj* sly, cunning, subtle
хлади́лник [hladilnik] *m* refrigerator, ice-box
хла́дък [hladuk] *adj* lukewarm, tepid
хлеба́рница [hlebarnitsa] *f* bakery

хлъ́згав [hluzgaf] *adj* slippery
хлъ́згам се [hluzgam se] *v* slip, slide
хляб [hlyab] *m* bread
хо́дя [hodya] *v* walk, go
холе́ра [holera] *m* cholera
хор [hor] *m* chorus, choir
хо́ра [hora] *noun pl* people
хоризо́нт [horizont] *m* horizon
хоте́л [hotel] *m* hotel
хра́брост [hrabrost] *f* bravery, courage
хра́бър [hrabur] *adj* brave, courageous
храм [hram] *m* temple
храна́ [hrana] *f* food, meal, board
хра́нене [hranene] *n* nutrition
хра́ня [hranya] *v* feed, nourish
храст [hrast] *m* bush, shrub
християни́н [hristiyanin] *m* Christian
Христо́с [hristos] *m* Christ
ху́бав [houbaf] *adj* nice, handsome,
good-looking
ху́бост [houbost] *f* good looks, beauty
худо́жник [houdozhnik] *m* artist, painter
хума́нен [houmanen] *adj* humane
хумани́зъм [houmanizum] *m* humanism
хуманита́рен [houmanitaren] *adj*
humanitarian
ху́мор [houmor] *m* humor
хълм [hulm] *m* hill
хъ́ркам [hurkam] *v* snore

Ц

цар [tsar] *m* king
царевица [tsarevitsa] *f* maize, corn
царица [tsaritsa] *f* queen
царство [tsarstvo] *n* kingdom
цвекло [tsveklo] *n* beet
цвете [tsvete] *n* flower
цвят [tsvyat] *m* color, blossom
цел [tsel] *f* aim, purpose, object, end
целзий [tselzii] *adj* centigrade
целина [tselina] *f* celery
целувам [tselouvam] *v* kiss
целувка [tseloufka] *f* kiss
целя [tselya] *v* aim at
цена [tsena] *f* price, cost
ценен [tsenen] *adj* valuable
ценност [tsenost] *f* value, worth
център [tsentur] *m* center
ценя [tsenya] *v* value, estimate, appreciate
цивилен [tsivilen] *adj* civil, civilian
цивилизация [tsivilizatsiya] *f* civilization
циганин [tsiganin] *m* gypsy
цигара [tsigara] *f* cigarette
цигулар [tsigoular] *m* violinist
цигулка [tsigoulka] *f* violin, fiddle
цимент [tsiment] *m* cement
цинизъм [tsinizum] *m* obscentity, cynicism
цинк [tsink] *m* zinc

цип [tsip] *m* zip-fastener
цирк [tsirk] *m* circus
цитат [tsitat] *m* quotation
цифра [tsifra] *f* figure
църква [tsurkva] *f* church
цъфтя [tsuftya] *v* bloom, blossom
цял [tsyal] *adj* entire, whole, all, full
цялост [tsyalost] *f* integrity, wholeness
цялостен [tsyalosten] *adj* entire, complete,
overall

Ч

чадър [chadur] *m* umbrella, parasol
чай [chai] *m* tea
чайка [chaika] *f* seagull
чайник [chainik] *m* teapot, tea-kettle
чакалня [chakalnya] *f* waitingroom
чакам [chakam] *v* wait, expect
чанта [chanta] *f* bag, briefcase
чар [char] *m* charm, fascination
чаршаф [charshaf] *m* sheet
час [chas] *m* hour, lesson, period
часовник [chasovnik] *m* clock, watch
част [chast] *f* part, portion, share
частен [chasten] *adj* private
чек [chek] *m* check
чело [chelo] *n* forehead
челюст [chelyust] *f* jaw

че́рвей [chervei] *m* worm
черве́н [cherven] *adj* red
черви́ло [chervilo] *n* lipstick
черво́ [chervo] *n* intestine, gut
че́рен [cheren] *adj* black
че́реп [cherep] *m* skull
черноко́ж [chernokozh] *adj* black, colored
черта́ [cherta] *f* line
черта́я [chertaya] *v* draw, trace
черте́ж [chertezh] *m* draft, sketch
черу́пка [cheroupka] *f* shell
чест [chest] *f* honor, credit
чест [chest] *adj* frequent, common
честву́вам [chestvouvam] *v* celebrate, commemorate
че́стен [chesten] *adj* honest, fair
че́стност [chestnost] *f* honesty
че́сто [chesto] *adv* often
че́сън [chesun] *m* garlic
чета́ [cheta] *v* read
че́твърт [chetvurt] *f* quarter
четвърти́т [chetvurtit] *adj* square
четвъ́ртък [chetvurtuk] *m* Thursday
че́тен [cheten] *adj* even
четиво́ [chetivo] *n* reading
че́тири [chetiri] *num* four
четири́десет [chetirideset] *num* forty
четирина́десет [chetirinadeset] *num* fourteen
четириъ́гълник [chetiriugulnik] *m* quadrangle

че́тка [chetka] *f* brush
чешма́ [cheshma] *f* tap
чин [chin] *m* desk, rank
чини́я [chiniya] *f* plate, dish
число́ [chislo] *n* number, figure
чист [chist] *adj* clean, neat
чиста́ч [chistach] *m* cleaner
чи́стене [chistene] *n* cleaning
чистота́ [chistota] *f* cleanliness
чи́стя [chistya] *v* clean
чита́тел [chitatel] *m* reader
чифт [chift] *m* pair, couple
член [chlen] *m* member
чове́к [chovek] *m* person, man
чове́шки [choveshki] *adj* human, humane
чора́п [chorap] *m* sock
чу́вам [chouvam] *v* hear, understand
чувстви́телен [choufstvitelen] *adj* sensitive
чу́вство [choufstvo] *n* feeling, emotion
чу́вствам [choufstvam] *v* feel
чу́до [choudo] *n* miracle, wonder
чу́дя се [choudya se] *v* wonder
чужби́на [chouzhbina] *f* abroad
чужд [chouzhd] *adj* alien, foreign
чужденéц [chouzhdenets] *m* foreigner
чук [chouk] *m* hammer
чу́кам [choukam] *v* knock, tap
чу́пя [choupya] *v* break
чу́шка [choushka] *f* pepper

Ш

шал [shal] *f* shawl
шама́р [shamar] *m* slap in the face
шампа́нско [shampansko] *n* champagne
шампио́н [shampion] *m* champion, title-holder
шампиона́т [shampionat] *m* championship
шампо́ан [shampoan] *m* shampoo
шанс [shans] *m* chance
ша́пка [shapka] *f* hat
шара́н [sharan] *m* carp
ша́рка [sharka] *f* measles
ша́хмат [shahmat] *m* chess
шев [shef] *m* seam, sewing, needlework
шега́ [shega] *f* joke, jest
шегу́вам се [shegouvam se] *v* joke
шедьо́вър [shedyovur] *m* masterpiece
шейна́ [sheina] *f* sledge, toboggan
ше́па [shepa] *f* handful
шепна́ [shepna] *v* whisper
шест [shest] *num* six
ше́ствие [shestvie] *n* procession, train
шестдесе́т [shestdeset] *num* sixty
шестна́десет [shestnadeset] *num* sixteen
шеф [shef] *m* chief, boss
шива́ч [shivach] *m* tailor
шип [ship] *m* thorn, spike
ширина́ [shirina] *f* width, breadth
широ́к [shirok] *adj* wide, broad, loose

шия [shiya] *v* sew
шия [shiya] *f* neck
шкаф [shkaf] *m* cupboard, locker
шлифер [shlifer] *m* raincoat
шоколад [shokolad] *m* chocolate
шосе [shose] *n* highway
шофьор [shofyor] *m* driver
шпионин [shpionin] *m* spy
шрифт [shrift] *m* type, font
шум [shoum] *m* noise, sound
шумен [shoumen] *adj* noisy, loud
шунка [shounka] *f* ham

Щ

щаб [shtab] *m* headquarters, staff
щанд [shtand] *m* counter, stall
щастие [shtastie] *n* happiness, luck
щастлив [shtastlif] *adj* happy, lucky,
fortunate
ще [shte] *v* will, shall
щедрост [shtedrost] *f* generosity, lavishness
щедър [shtedur] *adj* generous, lavish
щета [shteta] *f* damage
щипя [shtipya] *v* pinch
щит [shtit] *m* shield
щом [shtom] *adv* as soon as, if

Ъ

ъ́гъл [ugul] *m* angle

Ю

юбиле́й [yubilei] *m* anniversary
юг [yug] *m* south
ю́жен [yuzhen] *adj* southern
ю́ли [yuli] *m* July
юмру́к [yumrouk] *m* fist
ю́ни [yuni] *m* June
ю́ноша [yunosha] *m* teenager
ю́ношески [yunosheski] *adj* teenage, juvenile
юриди́чески [yuridicheski] *adj* legal,
juridical
юри́ст [yurist] *m* lawyer, jurist
ютия́ [yutiya] *v* iron

Я

я́бълка [yabulka] *f* apple
явле́ние [yavlenie] *n* phenomenon
я́года [yagoda] *f* strawberry
яд [yad] *m* anger
я́дрен [yadren] *adj* nuclear
ядро́ [yadro] *n* nucleus
я́зва [yazva] *f* ulcer

я́здя [yazdya] *v* ride
яйце́ [yaitse] *n* egg
яка́ [yaka] *f* collar
я́ке [yake] *n* jacket
ям [yam] *v* eat, have a meal
януа́ри [yanouari] *m* January
я́рък [yaruk] *adj* bright, brilliant
я́сен [yasen] *adj* clear, plain
я́стие [yastie] *n* dish
я́то [yato] *n* flock, flight

ENGLISH-BULGARIAN
DICTIONARY

A

abbreviation [ъбривиейшън] *n* съкращéние
ability [ъбѝлити] *n* спосóбност
able [éйбъл] *adj* спосóбен
abolish [ъбóлиш] *v* премáхвам,
унищожáвам
about [ъбáут] *adv* наóколо, почтѝ; *prep*
óколо, из, по, за, отнóсно
above [абъ̀в] *prep* над, пóвече от; *adv* гóре
absent [á-бсънт] *adj* отсъствуващ
absolute [á-бсълют] *adj* пълен,
неограничéн
absurd [á-бсърд] *adj* глýпав, смéшен
academical [áкадéмикал] *adj* академѝчен,
ýчен
academy [акá-деми] *n* акадéмия
accelerate [ъксéлерейт] *v* ускорáвам се
accent [á-ксент] *n* ударéние, ѝзговор
accept [ъксéпт] *v* приéмам, съгласáвам се
acceptable [ъксéптъбъл] *adj* приемлѝв
access [á-ксес] *n* дóстъп
accessories [ъксéсърис] *noun pl*
принадлéжности
accident [á-ксидент] *n* случáйност,
злополýка
accommodation [ъкóмодéйшън] *n* квартѝра
accompany [акъ̀мпани] *v* придружáвам,
съпровóждам

according to [акóрдинг ту] *prep* спорéд
account [акáунт] *n* смéтка, обяснéние; *v* дáвам смéтка, отчéт
accountant [акáунтънт] *n* счетоводи́тел
accuracy [áкюръси] *n* тóчност
accurate [áкюрът] *adj* тóчен
accusation [áкюзейшън] *n* обвинéние
accuse [акю́з] *v* обвиня́вам
ache [ейк] *n* бóлка; *v* боли́
achieve [ъчи́йв] *v* пости́гам, извъ́ршвам
achievement [ъчи́йвмънт] *n* постижéние
acid [á-сид] *n* киселинá
acquaint [ъкуéйнт] *v* запознáвам, осведомя́вам
acquaintance [ъкуéйнтънс] *n* запознáнство, познáт
acquit [ъкуи́т] *v* оправдáвам, освобождáвам
across [акрóс] *adv* напря́ко, отсрéща; *prep* през, отвъ́д, срещý
action [á-кшън] *n* дéйност, постъ́пка, сражéние
active [á-ктив] *adj* дéен, акти́вен
activity [ъкти́вити] *n* дéйност, акти́вност
actor [á-ктър] *n* арти́ст, актьóр
actress [á-ктрес] *n* актри́са, арти́стка
actually [á-кчуъли] *adv* наи́стина, в съ́щност
acute [ъкю́т] *adj* óстър, бъ́рз, проницáтелен
ad [а-д] *n* обявлéние

adapt [ъда́пт] *v* приспособя́вам,
пригодя́вам
add [ад] *v* приба́вям, съби́рам
addition [ъди́шън] *n* приба́вяне, съби́ране
address [а-дре́с] *v* обръщам се, адреси́рам
adjective [а́-джектив] *n* прилага́телно и́ме
adjust [аджъ́ст] *v* нагла́сям, приспособя́вам
adjustment [аджъ́стмент] *n* пригодя́ване
administration [адми́нистре́йшън] *n*
управле́ние, предписа́ние
admirable [а́-дмиръбъл] *adj* възхити́телен
admiration [а́дмире́йшън] *n* възхище́ние
admire [адма́йър] *v* възхища́вам се
admission [адми́шън] *n* вход, достъп,
призна́ние
admit [ъдми́т] *v* пу́скам да вле́зе,
призна́вам, допу́скам
adopt [адо́пт] *v* осиновя́вам, възприе́мам
adoption [адо́пшън] *n* осиновя́ване,
възприе́мане
adult [а́дълт] *n* възрастен
advance [ъдва́нс] *v* напре́двам; *n*
напре́дък, предпла́та
advanced [ъдва́нст] *adj* напре́днал,
напре́дничав
advantage [ъдва́нтъдж] *n* преди́мство, по́лза
adventure [ъдве́нчър] *n* приключе́ние
adverb [а́-двърб] *n* наре́чие
advice [ъдва́йс] *n* съве́т, изве́стие
advise [ъдва́йз] *v* съве́твам, известя́вам

adviser [ъдва́йзър] *n* съве́тник
aerial [е́риъл] *n* анте́на
affair [ъфе́р] *n* ра́бота, де́ло, въпро́с
affection [ъфе́кшън] *n* о́бич, привъ́рзаност
affectionate [ъфе́кшънът] *adj* любя́щ,
привъ́рзан
afford [афо́рд] *v* позволя́вам си
afraid [ъфре́йд] *adj* изпла́шен, боя́щ се
after [а́фтър] *prep* след, по, споре́д, за;
adv по́сле
afternoon [а́фтърну́н] *n* следобед
again [ъге́йн] *adv* отно́во, пак
against [ъге́йнст] *prep* срещу́, проти́в, о
age [ейдж] *n* въ́зраст, век, перио́д; *v* старе́я
agency [е́йджънси] *n* аге́нция
agenda [ъдже́ндъ] *n* дне́вен ред
agent [е́йджънт] *n* фа́ктор, предста́вител,
посре́дник
aggression [агре́шън] *n* агре́сия, нападе́ние
aggressive [агре́сив] *adj* агреси́вен
ago [аго́у] *adv* преди́
agony [а́-гъни] *n* аго́ния, си́лна мъка
agree [ъгри́] *v* съглася́вам се
agreement [ъгри́мънт] *n* съгла́сие, спого́дба
agricultural [а́-грикъ́лчъръл] *adj* земеде́лски
agriculture [а́-грикъ́лчър] *n* земеде́лие
aid [ейд] *v* пома́гам; *n* по́мощ, подкре́па
aim [ейм] *v* стремя́ се, преце́лвам се; *n*
намере́ние, цел

air [éър] *n* въздух; *v* проветрявам; *adj* въздушен

airplane [éърплейн] *n* самолет

airport [éърпорт] *n* летище, аерогара

alarm [аларм] *n* тревога; *v* тревожа, безпокоя

alcohol [á-лкохол] *n* алкохол, спирт

alive [ълáйв] *adj* жив, бодър, гъмжащ

all [ол] *adj* цял, всеки, всички

allow [алáу] *v* позволявам, допускам

allowance [алáуънс] *n* издръжка, отстъпка

alloy [áлой] *n* сплав

almost [óлмоуст] *adv* почти

alone [ълóун] *adj* сам, единствен

along [ълóнг] *adv* напред; *prep* по, край

alphabet [áлфабет] *n* азбука

already [олрéди] *adv* вече, преди това

also [óлсоу] *adv* също

although [олдóу] *conj* при все че, въпреки че

always [óлуейз] *adv* винаги

amaze [ъмейз] *v* слисвам, удивлявам

amazement [ъмéйзмънт] *n* удивление, силно учудване

ambassador [ъмбá-садър] *n* посланик

ambition [амбишън] *n* амбиция, честолюбие

ambitious [амбишъс] *adj* амбициозен

ambulance [áмбюлънс] *n* линейка

amount [ъмáунт] v възлизам, равнявам се; n количество, сума

amuse [ъмю́з] v забавлявам

amusement [ъмю́змънт] n забавление

amusing [ъмю́зинг] adj забáвен

analyse [áналайз] v анализирам

analysis [анáлисис] n анáлиз, разбóр

ancient [éйншънт] adj дрéвен

and [енд] conj и, а

angel [éйнджъл] n áнгел

anger [á-нгър] n гняв

angle [á-нгъл] n ъ́гъл

angry [á-нгри] adj гнéвен, сърди́т

animal [á-нимъл] n живóтно

anniversary [áнивъ̀рсари] n годи́шнина

announce [ънáунс] v съобщáвам, известявам

announcement [ънáунсмънт] n съобщéние

annual [á-нюъл] adj годи́шен, ежегóден

another [анáдър] adj друг

answer [áнсър] n óтговор; v отговáрям

ant [а-нт] n мрáвка

anxiety [ънкзáйъти] n безпокóйство, загри́женост, страх

anxious [á-нкшъс] adj разтревóжен, горя́щ от желáние

any [éни] pron всéки, някакъв

anybody [éнибъди] pron всéки, някой

anything [éнитинг] pron нéщо, всичко

apartment [апáртмънт] *n* апартамéнт, квартúра

apologize [апóлоджайз] *v* извинявам се

apology [апóлоджи] *n* извинéние, защúта

appear [апúър] *v* появявам се, изглéждам

appearance [апúърънс] *n* появяване, úзглед, въ́ншност

appetizer [áпетайзър] *n* мезé, аперитúв

applaud [ъплóд] *v* ръкоплáскам, аплодúрам

applause [ъплóуз] *n* ръкоплáскане, аплодисмéнти

apple [á-пъл] *n* ябълка

appliance [аплáйънс] *n* ýред, приспособлéние

appoint [апóйнт] *v* назначáвам, опредéлям

appointment [апóйнтмънт] *n* назначéние, опредéлена срéща

appreciation [апрúшиéйшън] *n* ценéне, благодáрност

approach [апрóуч] *v* приближáвам се; *n* подхóд, приближáване

appropriate [апрóприът] *adj* подходя́щ

approve [апрýв] *v* одобря́вам

approximately [ъпрóксимътли] *adv* приблизúтелно

April [éйпръл] *n* апрúл

arc [арк] *n* дъгá

architect [áркитект] *n* архитéкт

architecture [áркитекчър] *n* архитектýра

area [ериъ] *n* площ, област, район, обсег
arm [арм] *n* ръка, оръжие; *v* въоръжавам
armament [армамънт] *n* въоръжение
armchair [армчеър] *n* кресло
army [арми] *n* войска, армия
around [ъраунд] *adv* наоколо
arrest [арест] *v* арестувам, задържам
arrival [арайвъл] *n* пристигане
arrive [арайв] *v* пристигам
arrow [а-роу] *n* стрела
art [арт] *n* изкуство, сръчност, хитрина
artist [артист] *n* художник
artistic [артистик] *adj* художествен, изящен
as [а-з] *conj* като, както, докато
ash [а-ш] *n* пепел
ash-tray [а-штрей] *n* пепелник
ask [аск] *v* питам, моля, искам, каня
asleep [ъслийп] *adv* спящ, заспал
assemble [ъсембъл] *v* събирам, монтирам
assembly [ъсембли] *n* събрание
assist [асист] *v* подпомагам
assistance [асистънс] *n* помощ, съдействие
assistant [асистънт] *n* помощник
assure [ашуър] *v* уверявам
astonish [астониш] *v* учудвам
astonishing [астонишинг] *adj* удивителен
astonishment [астонишмънт] *n* учудване
at [а-т] *prep* при, на, в, у
attack [ата-к] *v* нападам; *n* нападение
attempt [ътемпт] *v* опитвам се *n* опит

attend [ътéнд] *v* внимáвам, посещáвам
attic [á-тик] *n* тавáн
attorney [атъ́рни] *n* пълномóщник, адвокáт
attract [атрá-кт] *v* привлѝчам
attraction [атрá-кшън] *n* привлѝчане, чар
attractive [атрá-ктив] *adj* привлекáтелен
auction [óкшън] *n* търг
audience [óдиънс] *n* пýблика
August [óгъст] *n* áвгуст
aunt [ант] *n* лéля, вýйна, стрѝнка
author [óтър] *n* áвтор
authority [отóрити] *n* авторитéт, власт
automobile [óтомобѝл] *n* автомобѝл
available [ъвéйлъбъл] *adj* налѝчен
avenue [áвеню] *n* алéя, булевáрд
avoid [ъвóйд] *v* избя́гвам, страня́
awake [ъуéйк] *v* бýдя, събýждам се
award [ъуóрд] *v* награждáвам *n* нагрáда
away [ъуéй] *adv* надалéче
awful [óфул] *adj* ужáсен
ax [а-кс] *n* брáдва

B

baby [бéйби] *n* бéбе
bachelor [бá-челър] *n* ергéн, бакалáвър
back [ба-к] *n* гръб, облегáло, óпако; *adv*
назáд, обрáтно; *v* подкрéпям
backbone [бá-кбоун] *n* гръбнáк

background [ба́-кграунд] *n* фон, произход, среда́

backward [ба́-куърд] *adj* обра́тен, изоста́нал

bacon [бе́йкън] *n* беко́н, слани́на

bad [ба-д] *adj* лош, развале́н

badge [ба-дж] *n* значка́,ембле́ма

baggage [ба́-гадж] *n* бага́ж

bake [бейк] *v* пека́

baker [бе́йкър] *n* пека́р, хлеба́р

balance [ба́-ланс] *n* равнове́сие, бала́нс

balcony [ба́-лкъни] *n* балко́н

ball [бол] *n* то́пка, кълбо́

bandage [ба́-ндъдж] *n* превръ́зка, бинт; *v* превръ́звам

bank [ба-нк] *n* ба́нка

bank [ба-нк] *n* бряг

bankrupt [ба́-нкръпт] *adj* фали́рал, разоре́н

bankruptcy [ба́-нкръпси] *n* фали́т, банкру́т

bar [бар] *n* прегра́да, адвокату́ра

barrel [ба́-ръл] *n* бъ́чва

barrier [ба́-риър] *n* препя́тствие, прегра́да, спънка

barter [ба́ртър] *n* разме́нна търгови́я

base [бейс] *n* осно́ва, ба́за; *v* основа́вам

basic [бе́йсик] *adj* осно́вен

basket [ба́скет] *n* ко́шница, кош

bath [бат] *n* ба́ня, къпане

bathroom [ба́трум] *n* ба́ня, тоале́тна

battle [ба-тл] *n* би́тка, сраже́ние

bay [бей] *n* за́лив
be [би] *v* съм, съществу́вам
beach [бийч] *n* мо́рски бряг, плаж
bean [бийн] *n* боб, фасу́л
beard [би́ърд] *n* брада́
beat [бийт] *v* би́я, у́дрям, побежда́вам
beautiful [бю́тифул] *adj* краси́в
beauty [бю́ти] *n* красота́, краса́вица
because [бико́уз] *conj* поне́же, защо́то
become [бикъ́м] *v* ста́вам, подхо́ждам
bed [бед] *n* легло́, кори́то, дъно, леха́
bedroom [бе́друм] *n* спа́лня
beef [бийф] *n* гове́ждо месо́
beer [би́ър] *n* би́ра
before [бифо́р] *adv* преди́
beg [бег] *v* про́ся, мо́ля
beggar [бе́гър] *n* про́сяк
begin [беги́н] *v* запо́чвам
beginner [беги́нър] *n* наче́ващ, нова́к
beginning [беги́нинг] *n* нача́ло
behave [бихе́йв] *v* държа́ се, постъ́пвам
behavior [бихе́йвиър] *n* поведе́ние, държа́не
belief [били́йф] *n* вя́ра, убежде́ние
believe [били́йв] *v* вя́рвам
bell [бел] *n* камба́на, звъне́ц
belong [било́нг] *v* принадлежа́
below [било́у] *prep* под; *adv* отдо́лу
belt [белт] *n* кола́н, по́яс
bench [бенч] *n* пе́йка, рабо́тна ма́са
bend [бенд] *v* наве́ждам, огъвам

beneath [бинийт] *prep* под; *adv* отдо́лу
beneficial [бенъфи́шъл] *adj* благотво́рен
benefit [бе́нъфит] *n* по́лза, изго́да; *v* по́лзувам
beside [биса́йд] *prep* край, до, извън
besides [биса́йдз] *prep* осве́н
bet [бет] *v* обзала́гам се; *n* бас, обло́г
betray [бетре́й] *v* преда́вам, изневеря́вам
between [биту́йн] *prep* между́
beyond [бийо́нд] *prep* отво́д, отта́тък, извън, след
Bible [ба́йбл] *n* Би́блия
bicycle [ба́йсикъл] *n* велосипе́д
big [биг] *adj* голя́м, ва́жен
bill [бил] *n* сме́тка, законопрое́кт, афи́ш
biography [байо́графи] *n* биогра́фия
biology [байо́лъджи] *n* биоло́гия
bird [бърд] *n* пти́ца
birth [бърт] *n* рожде́ние, ра́ждане
birthday [бъртдей] *n* рожде́н ден
biscuit [би́скит] *n* бискви́та
bishop [би́шъп] *n* епи́скоп
bite [байт] *v* ха́пя, заха́пвам
bitter [би́тър] *adj* горчи́в, озлобе́н
black [бла-к] *adj* че́рен
blade [блейд] *n* стрък, острие́
blame [блейм] *v* обвиня́вам; *n* вина́, у́прек
blanket [бла́нкет] *n* одея́ло
bleed [блийд] *v* кървя́, пу́скам кръв
bless [блес] *v* благосла́вям

blessing [блéсинг] *n* благодáт, благословиúя
blind [блайнд] *adj* сляп, безразсъден; *v*
ослепúявам, заслепéни
blindness [блáйнднис] *n* слепотá,
заслепúяване
blond [блонд] *adj* рус
blood [блъд] *n* кръв, проúзход,
темперамéнт
blossom [блóсъм] *n* цвят; *v* цъфтúя,
разцъфвам
blouse [блáуз] *n* блúуза
blue [блу] *adj* син, мрáчен, унúл
board [борд] *n* мáса, дъскá, хранá, съвéт
boarding—house [бóрдинг хáус] *n* пансиóн
boat [бóут] *n* лóдка, парахóд
body [бóди] *n* тúяло, грúупа, мáса
boil [бойл] *v* вря, кипúя, варúя
bomb [бом] *n* бóмба *v* бомбардúирам
bone [бóун] *n* кост, кóкал
bonus [бóунъс] *n* извънрéдно
възнаграждéние
book [бук] *n* книúга; *v* запúисвам, купúувам
boot [бúут] *n* висóка обúувка, ботúуш
booth [бúут] *n* бúудка, сергúия, кабúина
border [бóрдър] *n* грáница
bore [бóър] *v* пробúивам, досáждам
boredom [бóърдъм] *n* отегчéние, досáда
born [борн] *adj* родéн
boss [бос] *n* шеф
both [бот] *pron* и двáмата, и двéте

bother [бо́дър] *n* безпоко́йство; *v* безпокоя́, да́вам си труд
bottle [бо́тл] *n* бути́лка, шише́
bottom [бо́тъм] *n* дъно
boundary [ба́ундъри] *n* гра́ница, преде́л
bouquet [бу́кей] *n* буке́т
box [бокс] *n* кути́я, сандък, ло́жа
boy [бой] *n* момче́
bracelet [бре́йслит] *n* гри́вна
bracket [бра́кит] *n* ско́би, подпо́ра
brain [брейн] *n* мо́зък, ум, интеле́кт
branch [бранч] *n* клон, филиа́л
brandy [бра́-нди] *n* раки́я, коня́к
bra [бра] *n* сутие́н
brave [брейв] *adj* смел, хра́бър
bravery [бре́йвъри] *n* хра́брост
bread [бред] *n* хляб
break [брейк] *n* прекъсване, почи́вка
break [брейк] *v* чу́пя
breast [брест] *n* гърди́
breath [брет] *n* дъх, диха́ние, полъх
breathe [брийд] *v* ди́шам, лъхам, шептя́
brick [брик] *n* ту́хла
bride [брайд] *n* бу́лка
bridge [бридж] *n* мост
brief [брийф] *adj* кра́тък
bright [брайт] *adj* све́тъл, я́рък, у́мен
brightness [бра́йтнис] *n* бля́сък, я́ркост
bring [бринг] *v* но́ся, во́дя, дове́ждам
British [бри́тиш] *adj* брита́нски

broadcast [бро́удкаст] *v* разпространя́вам
broker [бро́укър] *n* комисионе́р
brother [бра́дър] *n* брат
brother-in-law [бра́дър ин ло] *n* зет, де́вер, шу́рей
brown [бра́ун] *adj* кафя́в
brush [бръш] *n* че́тка
buck [бак] *n* до́лар, еле́н
bucket [бъ́кет] *n* ко́фа, ведро́
budget [бъ́джит] *n* бюдже́т
build [билд] *v* строя́, изгра́ждам
builder [би́лдър] *n* строи́тел
building [би́лдинг] *n* зда́ние, изгра́ждане
bulb [бълб] *n* лу́ковица, електри́ческа кру́шка
bun [бън] *n* кръгла ки́фла, кок
burn [бърн] *v* горя́, изга́рям
bury [бе́ри] *v* зара́вям, погре́бвам
bus [бас] *n* автобу́с
bush [буш] *n* храст, гъстала́к
business [би́знис] *n* ра́бота, заня́тие, сде́лка
businessman [би́знисман] *n* търго́вец
butter [бъ́тър] *n* ма́сло
butterfly [бъ́търфлай] *n* пеперу́да
button [бъ́тън] *n* ко́пче, буто́н; *v* закопча́вам
buy [бай] *v* купу́вам
buyer [ба́йър] *n* купува́ч, заку́пчик
by [бай] *prep* до, при, с, чрез, покра́й

C

cab [ка-б] *n* файто́н, такси́
cabbage [ка́-бидж] *n* зе́ле
cable [ке́йбъл] *n* ка́бел, телегра́ма, ка́белна телеви́зия
café [кафе́] *n* кафене́, рестора́нт
cake [кейк] *n* кейк, то́рта
calculate [ка́-лкюлейт] *v* изчисля́вам, пресмя́там
calculation [ка́-лкюле́йшън] *n* изчисле́ние, пресмя́тане, обми́сляне
calendar [ка́-лендър] *n* календа́р
call [кол] *v* ви́кам, нари́чам, посеща́вам; *n* пови́кване, посеще́ние
calm [кам] *adj* тих, споко́ен
calmness [ка́мнис] *n* тишина́, споко́йствие
camera [ка́-мера] *n* фотоапара́т, ка́мера
can [ка-н] *v* мо́га; *n* тенеки́ена кути́я
canal [ка́нал] *n* изку́ствен кана́л
cancer [ка́-нсър] *n* рак
candid [ка́-ндид] *adj* и́скрен, открове́н
candidate [ка́-ндидейт] *n* кандида́т
candle [ка́-ндъл] *n* свещ
canned [ка-нд] *adj* консерви́ран
canvas [ка́-нвас] *n* платни́ще, брезе́нт
capability [ке́йпъби́лити] *n* спосо́бност
capable [ке́йпъбъл] *adj* спосо́бен

capacity [капá-сити] *n* вмести́мост, спосо́бност

capital [ка́-питал] *n* сто́лица, капита́л; *adj* гла́вен

car [кар] *n* кола́, автомоби́л, ваго́н

card [кард] *n* ка́рта за игра́, ка́ртичка

cardigan [ка́рдиган] *n* плéтена жилéтка

care [кéър] *n* грúжа, внимáние; *v* грúжа се, обúчам

career [карúър] *n* кариéра

careful [кéърфул] *adj* грижлúв, внимáтелен

careless [кéърлис] *adj* нехáен, лекомúслен

carelessness [кéърлиснис] *n* нехáйство

cargo [ка́рго] *n* товáр

carpet [ка́рпет] *n* килúм

carrier [ка́-риър] *m* самолетоно́сач

carrot [ка́-рът] *n* мо́рков

carry [ка́-ри] *v* но́ся, занáсям, държá се

cartoon [картýун] *n* карикатýра, мултипликацио́нен филм

case [кейс] *n* слýчай, процéс

cash [ка-ш] *n* парú

cashier [ка-шúър] *n* касиéр

cat [ка-т] *n* ко́тка

catalog [ка́-талог] *n* катало́г

catch [ка-ч] *v* хвáщам, ловя́, долáвям

cathedral [катúдрал] *n* катедра́ла

catholic [ка́-тълик] *adj* католúчески

cattle [ка-тл] *n* добúтък

cause [коз] *n* причи́на, ка́уза; *v* причиня́вам
cavity [ка́-вити] *n* кухина́, ду́пка
celebrate [се́лъбрейт] *v* че́ствувам, празну́вам, възхваля́вам
celebration [се́лъбре́йшън] *n* че́ствуване
celebrity [силе́брити] *n* изве́стност, знамени́тост
cell [сел] *n* кили́я, кле́тка
cellar [се́лър] *n* мазе́, и́зба
cemetery [се́митъри] *n* гро́бища
census [се́нсъс] *n* преброя́ване на населе́нието
central [се́нтрал] *adj* центра́лен, гла́вен
center [се́нтър] *n* це́нтър, среда́, сре́дище; *v* съсредоточа́вам
century [се́нчъри] *n* столе́тие, век
ceremony [се́ремъни] *n* о́бред, церемо́ния
certain [съ́ртън] *adj* си́гурен, уве́рен, несъмне́н
certainly [съ́ртънли] *adv* несъмне́но, разби́ра се
certificate [съртификът] *n* удостовере́ние, свиде́телство
certify [съ́ртифай] *v* уве́реност
chain [чейн] *n* вери́га *v* окова́вам
chair [че́ър] *n* стол
chairman [че́ърмън] *n* председа́тел
challenge [ча́лъндж] *n* предизви́кателство; *v* призова́вам на борба́

champagne [шáмпейн] *n* шампáнско

champion [чá-мпиън] *n* шампиóн, защи́тник

championship [чá-мпиъншип] *n* шампионáт, защи́та

chance [ча-нс] *n* слу́чай, случáйност; *v* слу́чвам се, риску́вам

change [чейндж] *n* промя́на, дрéбни пари́, рéсто; *v* промéням се

channel [чá-нъл] *n* канáл, потóк

chaos [кéъс] *n* хáос

character [кá-ръктър] *n* харáктер, бу́ква, дéйствуващо лицé

characteristic [кá-ръктери́стик] *adj* характéрен

charge [чардж] *v* обвиня́вам, напáдам; *n* обвинéние

charity [чá-рити] *n* благотвори́телност

charming [чáрминг] *adj* чарóвен, очаровáтелен

chase [чейс] *v* гóня, преслéдвам

cheap [чийп] *adj* éвтин, прост, долнокáчествен

cheat [чийт] *v* измáмвам; *n* измáма, измáмник

check [чек] *n* чек, провéрка

cheek [чийк] *n* бу́за, безóчливост

cheer [чи́ър] *v* аплоди́рам, насърчáвам

cheerful [чи́ърфул] *adj* бóдър, жизнерáдостен

cheese [чийз] *n* сѝрене, кашкавал
chemical [кѐмикъл] *adj* химѝчески
chemist [кѐмист] *n* химѝк, аптѐкар
chemistry [кѐмистри] *n* хѝмия
cherry [чѐри] *n* черѐша
chess [чес] *n* шахмат
chest [чест] *n* сандък, гръден кош
chestnut [чѐстнът] *n* кѐстен
chew [чу] *v* дъвча, предъвквам
chicken [чѝкън] *n* пѝле, пѝлешко месо
chief [чийф] *n* шеф, началник, вожд; *adj* главен
child [чайлд] *n* детѐ
childhood [чайлдхуд] *n* дѐтство, детѝнство
chimney [чѝмни] *n* комѝн, огнѝще
china [чайна] *n* порцелан
chips [чипс] *n* вид пържени картофи
chocolate [чоклът] *n* шоколад
choice [чойс] *n* ѝзбор
choose [чууз] *v* избѝрам, решавам
Christ [крайст] *n* Христос
Christianity [крѝсчианити] *n* християнство
Christmas [крѝсмъс] *n* Коледа
church [чърч] *n* църква
cigarette [сѝгърѐт] *n* цигара
cinema [сѝнема] *n* кѝно
circle [съркл] *n* кръг, окръжност; *v* кръжа, обикалям
circuit [съркит] *n* обиколка, електрѝческа верѝга

circumstance [съркъмстънс] *n* обстоя́телство

circus [съркъс] *n* кръ́гъл площа́д, цирк

citizen [си́тизън] *n* гра́жданин, по́даник

citizenship [си́тизъншип] *n* гра́жданство, по́данство

city [си́ти] *n* град

civic [си́вик] *adj* гра́ждански

civilian [сиви́лиън] *adj* циви́лен

civilization [си́вилизе́йшън] *n* цивилиза́ция

claim [клейм] *v* претенди́рам, твърдя́; *n* иск, прете́нция

clamp [кла-мп] *n* ско́ба *v* затя́гам

clarity [кла́-рити] *n* яснота́

class [кла-с] *n* кла́са, уче́бен час *v* класифици́рам

classic [кла́-сик] *adj* класи́чески, образцо́в

classical [кла́-сикъл] *adj* класи́чески, съвърше́н

classification [кла́-сификейшън] *n* класифика́ция

classroom [кла́-срум] *n* кла́сна ста́я

claw [кло] *n* но́кът, ла́па

clean [клийн] *adj* чист, изку́сен

cleaner [кли́йнър] *n* сре́дство за почи́стване

clear [кли́ър] *adj* я́сен, би́стър, прозра́чен, чист; *v* очи́ствам, избистрям

clearly [кли́ърли] *adv* я́сно, очеви́дно

clerk [кларк] *n* чино́вник

clever [кле́вър] *adj* у́мен, спосо́бен, изку́сен, хи́тър

climate [кла́ймът] *n* кли́мат
climb [клайм] *v* ка́чвам се, кате́ря се
clinic [кли́ник] *n* кли́ника
clip [клип] *n* ско́ба, кла́мер; *v* защи́пвам, пристя́гам
clock [клок] *n* часо́вник
close [кло́ус] *adj* бли́зък, те́сен, подро́бен
close [кло́уз] *v* затва́рям, свършвам
closely [кло́усли] *adv* отбли́зо, внима́телно
cloth [клот] *n* плат, покри́вка, парца́л
clothes [кло́удз] *n* дре́хи
clothing [кло́удинг] *n* облекло́
cloud [кла́уд] *n* о́блак; *v* заоблача́вам се, помрача́вам
cloudy [кла́уди] *adj* о́блачен, нея́сен, мътен
club [клаб] *n* клуб, тоя́га, па́лка
clutch [клъч] *v* сгра́бчвам; *n* ла́пи, амбреа́ж
coach [ко́уч] *n* кола́, ваго́н, треньо́р; *v* обуча́вам, трени́рам
coal [ко́ул] *n* въглища
coast [ко́уст] *n* мо́рски бряг, крайбре́жие
coat [ко́ут] *n* палто́, сако́, слой, мази́лка
cocktail [ко́ктейл] *n* кокте́йл
cocoa [ко́укоу] *n* кака́о
coconut [ко́укънът] *n* коко́сов о́рех
coffee [ко́фи] *n* кафе́
coffin [ко́фин] *n* ковче́г
coin [койн] *n* моне́та

coincide [кóуинсáйд] *v* съвпáдам

coincidence [кóуѝнсидънс] *n* съвпадéние

cold [кóулд] *adj* студéн; *n* студ, простýда

coldness [кóулднис] *n* студенинá

collar [кóлър] *n* якá

colleague [кóлиг] *n* колéга

collect [кълéкт] *v* събѝрам

collection [кълéкшън] *n* сбѝрка, колéкция

college [кóлидж] *n* колéж, колéгия

colonel [кърнъл] *n* полкóвник

color [кáлър] *n* цвят, руменинá; *v* оцветя́вам, изчервя́вам се

comb [кóум] *n* грéбен, чесáло; *v* рéша, срéсвам

combine [къмбáйн] *v* съчетáвам, комбинѝрам

come [към] *v* ѝдвам

comedy [кóмеди] *n* комéдия

comfort [кáмфърт] *n* утéха, удóбство; *v* утешáвам

comfortable [кáмфъртъбл] *adj* удóбен, спокóен

comic [кóмик] *adj* смéшен, комѝчен

comma [кóма] *n* запетáя

command [къмáнд] *v* заповя́двам, владéя, контролѝрам; *n* зáповед, комáнда

commander [къмáндър] *n* командѝр

comment [кóмент] *n* критѝческа белéжка, коментáр; *v* коментѝрам

commercial [къмъ́ршъл] *adj* търгóвски

commission [къми́шън] *n* коми́сия
commit [къми́т] *v* извършвам, преда́вам
commitment [къми́тмент] *n* задълже́ние, обвързване
committee [къми́ти] *n* коми́сия, комите́т
commodity [къмо́дити] *n* сто́ка
common [ко́мън] *adj* общ, обикнове́н
communicate [къмю́никейт] *v* съобща́вам, общу́вам
communication [къмю́никейшън] *n* съобще́ние, комуника́ция
community [къмю́нити] *n* обшина́, о́бщност, общество́
company [кѣмпъни] *n* компа́ния, тру́па, ро́та
comparatively [къмпа́ративли] *adv* сравни́телно
compare [къмпе́ър] *v* сравня́вам
comparison [къмпа́рисън] *n* сравне́ние
compassion [къмпа́-шън] *n* състрада́ние
compatible [къмпа́-тибл] *adj* съвмести́м
compensate [ко́мпенсейт] *v* обезщетя́вам, компенси́рам
compensation [ко́мпенсейшън] *n* обезщете́ние, компенса́ция
compete [къмпи́йт] *v* състеза́вам се, конкури́рам
competence [ко́мпитънс] *n* компете́нтност
competent [ко́мпитънт] *adj* компете́нтен
complain [къмпле́йн] *v* опла́квам се

complaint [къмплéйнт] *n* оплáкване, жáлба, бóлка

complete [къмплúйт] *v* завършвам; *adj* пълен, завършен

component [къмпóунънт] *n* състáвна част

composer [къмпóузър] *n* композúтор

composition [кóмпъзúшън] *n* съчинéние, композúция, състáв

comprehensive [кóмприхéнсив] *adj* простóрен, изчерпáтелен

comprise [къмпрáйз] *v* обхвáщам, включвам

compromise [кóмпръмайз] *v* прáвя компрóмис; *n* компрóмисно решéние

compulsory [къмпѐлсъри] *adj* задължúтелен, принудúтелен

concentrate [кóнсънтрейт] *v* съсредоточáвам, сгъстáвам

concentration [кóнсънтрéйшън] *n* съсредоточáване, стрýпване

concept [кóнсъпт] *n* понátие, схвáщане, предстáва

concern [кънсѐрн] *v* касáя се, засáгам, интересýвам се; *n* грúжа, загрúженост

concerning [кънсѐрнинг] *prep* отнóсно

concert [кóнсърт] *n* концéрт, съглáсие

condition [къндúшън] *n* услóвие, положéние, състоáние

conduct [къндáкт] *v* вóдя, провéждам, дирижúрам

conduct [кóндъкт] *n* поведéние, вóдене

confederation [конфѐдърѐйшън] *n* съюз,
конфедерáция

conference [кóнфърънс] *n* съвещáние,
конферéнция

confess [кънфéс] *v* признáвам, изповя́двам
се

confession [кънфéшън] *n* признáние,
ѝзповед

confidence [кóнфидънс] *n* довéрие,
увéреност, самонадéяност, тáйна

confident [кóнфидънт] *adj* увéрен,
самоувéрен, смел

confirm [кънфъ̀рм] *v* потвържда́вам

conflict [кóнфликт] *n* сблъскване,
конфлѝкт

conflict [кънфлѝкт] *v* сблъсквам се,
противореча́

confuse [кънфю́з] *v* смуща́вам, обърквам

confusion [кънфю́жън] *n* бъркотѝя, смут,
объркване

congratulate [кънгра́–чюлéйт] *v*
поздравя́вам, честитя́

congratulation [кънгра́–чюлéйшън] *n*
поздравлéние

congress [кóнгрес] *n* конгрéс

conjunction [кънджъ̀нкшън] *n* съединя́ване,
съюз

conscience [кóншънс] *n* съвест

conscientious [кóншиéншъс] *adj* съзна́телен,
добросъвестен

conscious [ко́ншъс] *adj* съзна́телен
consecutive [кънсе́кютив] *adj*
последова́телен, поре́ден
consequence [ко́нсикуенс] *n* сле́дствие,
резулта́т, значе́ние, ва́жност
consider [кънси́дър] *v* счи́там, обми́слям,
разгле́ждам
considerable [кънси́дъръбл] *adj* значи́телен
consideration [кънси́дъре́йшън] *n*
обми́сляне, съображе́ние, внима́ние
consist [кънси́ст] *v* състоя́ се, заключа́вам
се
consonant [ко́нсънънт] *n* съгла́сна бу́ква;
adj съзву́чен, хармони́чен
constant [ко́нстант] *adj* постоя́нен,
непоколеби́м
constantly [ко́нстантли] *adv* постоя́нно,
че́сто
constitution [ко́нститю́шън] *n* устро́йство,
органи́зъм, конститу́ция
construct [кънстрѣ́кт] *v* строя́, градя́
construction [кънстрѣ́кшън] *n* строе́ж,
постро́йка, констру́кция
constructive [кънстрѣ́ктив] *adj* гради́вен,
поле́зен
consult [кънсѣ́лт] *v* съве́твам се, допи́твам
се
consultation [ко́нсълте́йшън] *n* консулта́ция
consume [кънсю́м] *v* унищожа́вам,
консуми́рам

consumer [кънсю́мър] *n* потреби́тел, консума́тор

consumption [кънсъ́мпшън] *n* употре́ба, консума́ция, туберкуло́за

contact [ко́нта-кт] *n* до́пир, конта́кт

contain [кънте́йн] *v* съдържам, поби́рам, възпи́рам

container [кънте́йнър] *n* съд

contemporary [кънте́мпъръри] *adj* съвре́менен

contempt [кънте́мпт] *n* презре́ние, пренебреже́ние

content [ко́нтент] *n* съдържа́ние, вмести́мост

contest [кънте́ст] *v* състеза́вам се, спо́ря, бо́ря се

contest [ко́нтест] *n* състеза́ние, борба́, спор

continent [ко́нтинънт] *n* контине́нт

continental [ко́нтине́нтъл] *adj* контине́нтален, европейски

continuation [кънти́нюе́йшън] *n* продълже́ние

continue [кънти́ню] *v* продължа́вам, тра́я, прости́рам се

contract [ко́нтра-кт] *n* до́говор, контра́кт

contract [кънтра́-кт] *v* сключвам до́говор, сви́вам се

contractor [кънтра́-ктър] *n* предприема́ч

contradict [ко́нтръди́кт] *v* противореча́

contradiction [ко́нтръди́кшън] *n* противоре́чие, несъотве́тствие

contrary [ко́нтръри] *adj* противоположен; *adv* проти́вно на

contrast [ко́нтраст] *n* противополо́жност, контра́ст

contribute [кънтри́бют] *v* доприна́сям, съде́йствувам

contribution [ко́нтрибю́шън] *n* при́нос, уча́стие, сътру́дничество

control [кънтро́ул] *n* власт, надзо́р; *v* управля́вам, контроли́рам, обузда́вам

convenience [къпви́ниънс] *n* удо́бство

convenient [кънви́ниънт] *adj* удо́бен

convention [кънве́ншън] *n* събра́ние, конгре́с, споразуме́ние, усло́вност

conventional [кънве́ншънъл] *adj* общоприе́т, усло́вен, обикнове́н

conversation [ко́нвърсе́йшън] *n* ра́зговор, бесе́да

convict [кънви́кт] *v* осъждам

convict [ко́нвикт] *n* затво́рник

conviction [къпви́кшън] *n* осъждане, убежде́ние

convince [кънви́нс] *v* убежда́вам

cook [ку́ук] *v* го́твя, сваря́вам; *n* готва́ч

cool [ку́ул] *adj* хла́ден, спокое́н; *v* охла́ждам

cooperate [ко́упърейт] *v* сътру́днича, съде́йствувам

cooperation [коуо́пъре́йшън] *n* сътру́дничество, коопера́ция

coordinate [коуо́рдинейт] *v* съгласу́вам, координи́рам

cop [коп] *n* полица́й

copper [ко́пър] *adj* ме́ден

copy [ко́пи] *n* ко́пие, брой, екземпля́р; *v* копи́рам, препи́свам

cord [корд] *n* връв, шнур, стру́на

cordial [ко́рдиъл] *adj* сърде́чен

core [кор] *n* сърцевина́, същина́

cork [корк] *n* та́па, корк

corn [корн] *n* зърно, ца́ревица

corner [ко́рнър] *n* ъгъл, кът

correct [къре́кт] *adj* пра́вилен, то́чен; *v* попра́вям, кориги́рам

correction [къре́кшън] *n* попра́вка

correspondent [ко́ръспо́ндънт] *n* кореспонде́нт; *adj* съотве́тен

corridor [ко́ридор] *n* коридо́р

corrupt [к344ъпт] *adj* поква́рен, прода́жен; *v* покваря́вам, подку́пвам

corruption [къръ̀пшън] *n* покна́ра, кору́пция

cost [кост] *v* стру́вам; *n* цена́, сто́йност

costly [ко́стли] *adj* скъп

cotton [котн] *n* паму́к

couch [ка́уч] *n* дива́н, куше́тка

cough [коф] *v* ка́шлям; *n* ка́шлица

council [ка́унсъл] *n* съве́т, съвеща́ние

count [ка́унт] *v* броя́, счи́там

counter [ка́унтър] *n* тезгя́х, щанд

country [кънтри] *n* страна́, прови́нция
couple [къпл] *n* дво́йка, чифт; *v* свързвам
courage [къридж] *n* сме́лост, хра́брост
courageous [кърейджъс] *adj* смел, хра́бър
course [корс] *n* ход, курс, я́стие
court [корт] *n* двор, съд, те́нис игри́ще
cousin [къзън] *n* братовче́д
cover [къвър] *v* покри́вам, обхва́щам; *n* покри́вка, похлупа́к, прикри́тие
cow [кау] *n* кра́ва
crack [кра-к] *n* пукнати́на; *v* пу́квам, чу́пя
cracked [кра-кт] *adj* пу́кнат
craftsman [кра́фтсман] *n* занаятчи́я
crate [крейт] *n* ща́йга
crazy [крейзи] *adj* луд, побъркан, сма́хнат
cream [крийм] *n* смета́на, крем
create [криейт] *v* творя́, създа́вам
creature [кри́чър] *n* създа́ние
credit [кре́дит] *n* дове́рие, креди́т
creditor [кре́дитър] *n* креди́тор
crime [крайм] *n* престъпле́ние
criminal [кри́минъл] *adj* престъпе́н, кримина́лен; *n* престъпник
critic [кри́тик] *n* крити́к
critical [кри́тикъл] *adj* крити́чески, крити́чен
crop [кроп] *n* реко́лта, жътва
cross [крос] *n* кръст, кръсто́сване
crossing [кро́синг] *n* преси́чане, пресе́чка

crowd [крауд] *n* тълпа́, мно́жество; *v* тру́пам се, тълпя́ се

crown [кра́ун] *n* вене́ц, коро́на; *v* увенча́вам, короня́свам, завършвам

cruel [кру́ъл] *adj* жесто́к

cruelty [кру́ълти] *n* жесто́кост

crush [кръш] *v* сма́чквам, сма́звам, унищожа́вам

cry [край] *v* ви́кам, пла́ча; *n* вик, плач

crystal [кри́стъл] *adj* криста́лен

cube [кюб] *n* куб

cubic [кю́бик] *adj* куби́чески

cucumber [кю́къмбър] *n* кра́ставица

cuff [къф] *n* манше́т, ръкаве́л

cultivate [кѣлтивейт] *v* обрабо́твам, културви́рам

cultivation [кѣлтиве́йшън] *n* обрабо́тване, отгле́ждане

cultural [кѣлчъръл] *adj* култу́рен

culture [кѣлчър] *n* култу́ра

cup [къп] *n* порцела́нова ча́ша

cupboard [кѣбърд] *n* бюфе́т, шкаф

cure [кю́ър] *n* лек, леку́ване; *v* излеку́вам

curiosity [кюрио́сити] *n* любопи́тство, ря́дкост

curious [кю́риъс] *adj* любопи́тен, стра́нен

current [кѣрънт] *adj* теку́щ; *n* стру́я, тече́ние, ток

curse [кърс] *n* прокля́тие, ругатня́; *v* кълна́, руга́я

curtain [кӹртън] *n* заве́са, перде́
cushion [ку́шън] *n* възгла́вница за ся́дане
custom [кӹстъм] *n* на́вик, обича́й, ми́то
customer [кӹстъмър] *n* клие́нт
cut [кът] *v* ре́жа, крои́, сека́; *n* поря́зване, кро́йка
cycle [са́йкъл] *n* ци́къл, велосипе́д
cynical [си́никъл] *adj* скепти́чен, цини́чен
cynicism [си́нисизм] *n* неве́рие в добро́то, цини́зъм

D

dad [да-д] *n* та́тко
daily [де́йли] *adj* ежедне́вен
dairy [де́ъри] *n* мле́чни произведе́ния
damage [да́-мъдж] *n* вреда́, щета́, повре́да; *v* повре́ждам
dance [да-нс] *v* танцу́вам; *n* танц
dancer [да́-нсър] *n* танцьо́р, танцьо́рка
danger [де́йнджър] *n* опа́сност
dangerous [де́йнджъръс] *adj* опа́сен
dark [дарк] *adj* тъмен, че́рен; *n* тъмнина́, мрак
darkness [да́ркнис] *n* тъмнина́, мрак, неве́жество
data [де́йта] *noun pl* да́нни
date [дейт] *n* да́та, сре́ща; *v* дати́рам

daughter [дóтър] *n* дъщеря́

daughter-in-law [дóтър ин ло] *n* снаха́

day [дей] *n* ден, деноно́щие

dead [дед] *adj* мъ́ртъв, безчу́вствен

deaf [деф] *adj* глух

deal [дийл] *v* да́вам, търгу́вам, занима́вам се; *n* сде́лка, дял

dealer [ди́йлър] *n* търго́вец

dear [ди́ър] *adj* мил, драг, скъп

debt [дет] *n* дълг

decade [дéкейд] *n* десетилéтие

deceased [диси́йст] *adj* поко́ен, умря́л

deceit [диси́йт] *n* изма́ма

December [дисéмбър] *n* декéмври

decency [ди́сънси] *n* благоприли́чие

decent [ди́сънт] *adj* прили́чен, подходя́щ, задоволи́телен

decide [диса́йд] *v* реша́вам

decision [диси́жън] *n* решéние

decisive [диса́йсив] *adj* реши́телен, реша́ващ

declaration [дéклърéйшън] *n* изявлéние, деклара́ция

declare [диклéър] *v* заявя́вам, деклари́рам

decline [дикла́йн] *v* отка́звам, запа́дам, влоша́вам се

decorate [дéкърейт] *v* украся́вам, декори́рам

decoration [дéкърéйшън] *n* укра́са, украшéние, меда́л

decrease [дикри́йс] *v* намаля́вам
decrease [ди́кри́йс] *n* намаля́ване,
намале́ние
deep [дийп] *adj* дълбо́к
deer [ди́ър] *n* еле́н
defeat [дифи́йт] *v* побежда́вам, би́я,
прова́лям
defect [дифе́кт] *n* недоста́тък, дефе́кт
defective [дифе́ктив] *adj* дефе́ктен,
непъ́лен
defense [дифе́нс] *n* защи́та, отбра́на
defend [дифе́нд] *v* защища́вам, бра́ня
defendant [дифе́ндънт] *n* обвиня́ем,
отве́тник
define [дифа́йн] *v* определя́м, очерта́вам
definition [де́фини́шън] *n* определе́ние,
дефини́ция
degree [дигри́й] *n* сте́пен, гра́дус
delegate [де́лигит] *n* делега́т
delegation [де́лигейшън] *n* делега́ция
deliberate [дели́бърът] *adj* уми́шлен,
преднаме́рен
delicate [де́ликът] *adj* не́жен, изя́щен,
кре́хък
delicious [дели́шъс] *adj* прекра́сен, вку́сен,
сла́дък
delight [дила́йт] *v* ра́двам, очаро́вам,
възхища́вам *n* насла́да, възхище́ние
delightful [дила́йтфул] *adj* възхити́телен
delivery [дели́въри] *n* доста́вка, изна́сяне

demand [диманд] *v* искам; *n* искане, търсене

democracy [димокръси] *n* демокрация

democratic [демъкратик] *adj* демократичен

demonstrate [демънстрейт] *v* доказвам, демонстрирам

demonstration [демънстрейшън] *n* манифестация

denial [динайъл] *n* отказ, опровержение

dense [денс] *adj* гъст, плътен

density [денсити] *n* гъстота, плътност

dental [дентъл] *adj* зъбен

dentist [дентист] *n* зъболекар

deny [динай] *v* отричам, отказвам, опровергавам

depart [дипарт] *v* заминавам, тръгвам

department [дипартмънт] *n* отдел, факултет

departure [дипарчър] *n* заминаване, тръгване

depend [дипенд] *v* завися, разчитам

dependence [дипендънс] *n* зависимост, подчинение, доверие

deposit [дипозит] *v* влагам, утаявам, депозирам; *n* влог, нанос, утайка

depth [депт] *n* дълбочина

deputy [депюти] *n* заместник

derive [дирайв] *v* извличам, получавам, произлизам

describe [дискрайб] *v* описвам

description [дискри́пшън] *n* описа́ние, сорт, вид

desert [де́зърт] *n* пусти́ня; *adj* пуст, пусти́нен

design [диза́йн] *n* план, черте́ж *v* скици́рам, зами́слям

designer [диза́йнър] *n* проекта́нт

desire [диза́йър] *v* жела́я; *n* жела́ние

desk [деск] *n* бюро́, чин

despair [диспе́ър] *v* отча́йвам се; *n* отчая́ние

desperate [де́спърът] *adj* отча́ян, безразсъ́ден, безнаде́жден

despite [диспа́йт] *prep* въ́преки

dessert [дизъ́рт] *n* десе́рт

destination [де́стине́йшън] *n* местоназначе́ние, предназначе́ние

destiny [де́стини] *n* предопределе́ние, съдба́

destroy [дистро́й] *v* разруша́вам, унищожа́вам

destruction [дистръ́кшън] *n* разруше́ние, ги́бел

destructive [дистръ́ктив] *adj* разруши́телен, унищожи́телен

detail [ди́тейл] *n* подро́бност

detect [дите́кт] *v* откри́вам

deteriorate [дити́риърейт] *v* влоша́вам

determination [дитъ́рмине́йшън] *n* определе́ние, реши́телност

determine [дитъ́рмин] *v* опреде́лям, реша́вам

develop [дивéлъп] *v* развѝвам, проявя́вам, усъвършéнствувам

development [дивéлъпмънт] *n* развѝтие, развóй, събѝтие

device [дива́йс] *n* план, за́мисъл, срéдство, приспособлéние

devil [дéвъл] *n* дя́вол

devote [дивóут] *v* посвеща́вам, отда́вам

devotion [дивóушън] *n* прéданост, любов

dew [дю] *n* роса́

diagram [да́йъграм] *n* диагра́ма

dialect [да́йълект] *n* диалéкт, нарéчие

dialogue [да́йълъг] *n* диалóг

diameter [дая́митър] *n* диамéтър

diamond [да́йъмънд] *n* диама́нт, карó

diary [да́йъри] *n* днéвник

dice [дайс] *noun pl* за́рове

dictate [диктéйт] *v* дикту́вам

dictation [диктéйшън] *n* диктóвка

dictionary [дѝкшънъри] *n* рéчник

die [дай] *v* умѝрам

diet [да́йът] *n* храна́, диéта

differ [дѝфър] *v* различа́вам, изразя́вам несъгла́сие

difference [дѝфърънс] *n* ра́злика, спор, несъгла́сие

different [дѝфърънт] *adj* разлѝчен, друг, отдéлен

difficult [дѝфикълт] *adj* тру́ден, мъчен, тéжък

difficulty [дификълти] *n* трудност, мъчнотия

dig [диг] *v* копая, ровя

digestion [дайджесчън] *n* храносмилане

dignity [дигнити] *n* достойнство

dimension [дименшън] *n* измерение, размер

dine [дайн] *v* обядвам, вечерям

dinner [динър] *n* обед, вечеря

diplomacy [диплоумъси] *n* дипломация

direct [дайрект] *adj* пряк, непосредствен; *v* ръководя, отправям, насочвам

direction [дайрекшън] *n* посока

directly [дайректли] *adv* пряко, направо, веднага

director [дайректър] *n* директор, режисьор

dirt [дърт] *n* мръсотия, смет, пръст

dirty [дърти] *adj* мръсен

disappear [дисапиър] *v* изчезвам

disappearance [дисапиърънс] *n* изчезване

disappoint [дисъпойнт] *v* разочаровам

disappointment [дисъпойнтмънт] *n* разочарование

disarmament [дисармамънт] *n* разоръжаване

disaster [дизастър] *n* нещастие, бедствие

discipline [дисиплин] *n* дисциплина

discount [дискаунт] *n* намаление

discover [дискавър] *v* откривам, разкривам

discovery [дискавъри] *n* открытие, разкриване

discuss [дискъс] *v* разисквам, обсъждам

discussion [дискъ́шън] *n* разйскване, обсъждане

disease [дизййз] *n* бо́лест

disgust [дисгъ́ст] *n* отвраще́ние, погну́са; *v* отвраща́вам, възмуща́вам

dish [диш] *n* чинйя, съд, я́стие, блюдо

disk [диск] *n* диск, грамофо́нна пло́ча

display [дисплей] *v* изла́гам, пока́звам; *n* изло́жба, изла́гане

disregard [дйсрега́рд] *v* пренебре́гвам; *n* пренебреже́ние

distance [дйстънс] *n* разстоя́ние, далечина́

distant [дйстънт] *adj* дале́чен

distinguish [дистйнгуиш] *v* различа́вам, разграничавам

distinguished [дистйнгуишт] *adj* вйден, изтъкнат

distribute [дистрйбют] *v* разпределя́м, разда́вам

distribution [дйстрибю̀шън] *n* разпределе́ние, разпростране́ние

district [дйстрикт] *n* райо́н, о́бласт, око́лия

disturb [дистъ́рб] *v* безпокоя́, смуща́вам

dive [дайв] *v* гму́ркам се, спу́скам се; *n* гму́ркане, спу́скане

divide [дива́йд] *v* разделя́м

division [дивйжън] *n* деле́ние, дивйзия

divorce [диво́рс] *n* разво́д

do [ду] *v* пра́вя, върша

doctor [до́ктър] *n* до́ктор, ле́кар

document [до́кюмънт] *n* докуме́нт
dog [дог] *n* ку́че
doll [дол] *n* ку́кла
domestic [доме́стик] *adj* дома́шен
donkey [до́нки] *n* мага́ре
door [дор] *n* врата́
double [дабл] *adj* дво́ен; *v* удвоя́вам
doubt [да́ут] *v* съмня́вам се; *n* съмне́ние
down [да́ун] *adv* до́лу; *adj* нанадо́лен
dozen [да́зън] *n* дузи́на
draw [дро] *v* привли́чам, черта́я, рису́вам
drawer [дро́ър] *n* чекмедже́
drawing [дро́инг] *n* рису́нка
dream [дрийм] *v* съну́вам, мечта́я; *n* мечта́
dress [дрес] *v* обли́чам, украся́вам,
приго́твям *n* ро́кля, облекло́
drink [дринк] *v* пи́я; *n* питие́
drive [драйв] *v* ка́рам, шофи́рам, во́зя се;
n кампа́ния
driver [дра́йвър] *n* кола́р, шофьо́р
drought [дра́ут] *n* су́ша
drown [дра́ун] *v* уда́вям, заглуша́вам
drug [дръг] *n* лека́рство, опиа́т
dry [драй] *adj* сух, изсуше́н
duck [дък] *n* па́тица
duration [дюре́йшън] *n* времетра́ене
during [дю́ринг] *prep* през, по време
dust [дъст] *n* прах
dusty [дѣсти] *adj* пра́шен
duty [дю́ти] *n* дълг, ми́то

E

each [ийч] *adj* всѐки
eagle [ѝйгъл] *n* орѐл
ear [ѝър] *n* ухо́
early [ѐрли] *adv* ра́но; *adj* ра́нен
earn [ърн] *v* припечѐлвам, заслужа́вам
earring [ѝъринг] *n* обица́
earth [ърт] *n* земя́, пръст
earthquake [ѐрткуейк] *n* земетресѐние
ease [ийз] *n* леснина́, споко́йствие; *v* облекча́вам, отпу́скам се
easily [ѝйзили] *adv* лѐсно
east [ийст] *n* ѝзток
Easter [ѝйстър] *n* Велѝкден
eastern [ѝйстърн] *adj* ѝзточен
easy [ѝзи] *adj* лѐсен, свобо́ден, прия́тен
eat [ийт] *v* ям
economic [ѝкъно́мик] *adj* стопа́нски, икономѝчески
economy [ико́нъми] *n* стопа́нство, иконо́мика
edge [едж] *n* край, ръб, острие́
edition [едѝшън] *n* изда́ние
editor [ѐдитър] *n* реда́ктор
educate [ѐдюкейт] *v* образо́вам, възпита́вам
education [ѐдюкейшън] *n* образова́ние, възпита́ние

educational [е́дюке́йшънъл] *adj*
образова́телен, възпита́телен
effect [ифе́кт] *n* после́дствие, ве́щи
effective [ифе́ктив] *adj* действи́телен,
резулта́тен, ефе́ктен
efficiency [ифи́шиънси] *n* експедити́вност
efficient [ифи́шънт] *adj* резулта́тен,
ефика́сен
effort [е́фърт] *n* уси́лие
egg [ег] *n* яйце́
eight [ейт] *num* о́сем
eighteen [ейти́йн] *num* осемна́десет
eighty [е́йти] *num* осемдесе́т
either [а́йдър] *pron* еди́н от два́ма
elbow [е́лбоу] *n* ла́кът
elderly [е́лдърли] *adj* възста́р
election [иле́кшън] *n* и́збор
electric [иле́ктрик] *adj* електри́чески
electricity [електри́сити] *n* електри́чество
element [е́лъмънт] *n* еле́мент, част, стихи́я
elephant [е́лъфънт] *n* слон
elevator [елъве́йтър] *n* асансьо́р
eleven [иле́вън] *num* едина́десет
else [елс] *adv* и́наче, друг, о́ще
embassy [е́мбъси] *n* посо́лство
embrace [имбре́йс] *v* прегръщам,
обхва́щам; *n* прегръ́дка
emergency [имъ́рджънси] *n* непредви́дено
обстоя́телство, извънре́дно положе́ние
emigrate [е́мигрейт] *v* изсе́лвам се

emotion [имо́ушън] *n* чу́вство, емо́ция
emotional [имо́ушънл] *adj* емоциона́лен, темпераме́нтен
emphasis [е́мфъсис] *n* набля́гане, ударе́ние
emphasize [е́мфъсайз] *v* набля́гам
empire [е́мпайър] *n* импе́рия
employ [импло́й] *v* нае́мам на ра́бота, използу́вам
employee [е́мплойй] *n* слу́жещ
employer [импло́йър] *n* работода́тел
employment [емпло́ймънт] *n* ра́бота, слу́жба
empower [емпа́уър] *v* упълномоща́вам
empty [е́мпти] *adj* пра́зен; *v* изпра́звам
encore [ънко́р] *intej* бис
encyclopedia [енса́йклопи́дия] *n* енциклопе́дия
end [енд] *n* край, цел; *v* завъ́ршвам
endanger [инде́йнджър] *v* застраша́вам
endure [индю́ър] *v* пона́сям, издъ́ржам, тра́я
enemy [е́нъми] *n* неприя́тел, враг
energy [е́нърджи] *n* ене́ргия
engage [инге́йдж] *v* ангажи́рам, сгодя́вам
engagement [инге́йджмънт] *n* задълже́ние, годе́ж
engine [е́нджин] *n* маши́на, локомоти́в
engineer [е́нджини́ър] *n* инжене́р
enjoy [индж́ой] *v* наслажда́вам се, ра́двам се
enjoyment [индж́оймънт] *n* насла́да, удово́лствие

enough [инъф] *adj* достатъчен; *adv* достатъчно

enter [éнтър] *v* влизам, постъпвам

enterprise [éнтърпрайз] *n* предприятие, предприемчивост

entertain [éнтъртéйн] *v* забавлявам, каня гости

entertainment [éнтъртéйнмънт] *n* забавление

entire [ентáйър] *adj* цял

entrance [éнтрънс] *n* вход, влизане

entry [éнтри] *n* влизане, вписване

envelope [éнвълоуп] *n* плик

environment [енвáйърмънт] *n* среда, околна среда

envy [éнви] *n* завист; *v* завиждам

episode [éписоуд] *n* епизод

equality [екуóлити] *n* равенство

equation [екуéйшън] *n* уравнение

equip [екуйп] *v* снабдявам, екипирам

equipment [екуйпмънт] *n* снабдяване, съоръжения

erase [ирéйз] *v* изтривам, заличавам

err [ер] *v* греша

error [éрър] *n* грешка, заблуда

essence [éсънс] *n* същина

establish [естáблиш] *v* установявам, създавам

establishment [естáблишмънт] *n* създаване, заведение, институт

evaporate [евáпърейт] *v* изпарявам се

evaporation [евáпърейшън] *n* изпарéние

eve [ийв] *n* вéчер, навечéрие

even [úвън] *adj* рáвен, чéтен; *adv* дáже, дорú

evening [úвнинг] *n* вéчер

event [ивéнт] *n* събúтие, слýчай

ever [éвър] *adv* нáкога, вúнаги

every [éври] *adj* всéки

everybody [éврибъди] *pron* всéки, всúчки

everyday [éвридей] *adj* всекиднéвен, обикновéн

evidence [éвидънс] *n* доказáтелство, показáния

evil [úвъл] *adj* лош, зъл *n* зло

exact [игзáкт] *adj* тóчен; *v* изúсквам

exactly [игзáктли] *adv* тóчно

examination [игзáминéйшън] *n* úзпит, прéглед, проýчване

examine [игзáмин] *v* разглéждам, изпúтвам, проýчвам

example [игзáмпъл] *n* прúмер

excellent [éксълънт] *adj* отлúчен, превъзхóден

except [иксéпт] *prep* освéн, с изключéние на; *v* изключвам

exception [иксéпшън] *n* изключéние, възражéние

exchange [иксчéйндж] *n* размáна, бóрса; *v* размéням

excite [иксáйт] *v* възбýждам, вълнýвам

excitement [иксáйтмънт] *n* възбýда, вълнéние

excuse [икскю́з] *v* извинявам

excuse [икскю́с] *n* извинéние

exhibit [игзи́бит] *v* излáгам, проявявам; *n* експонáт

exhibition [éкзиби́шън] *n* изло́жба

exile [éксайл] *n* изгнáние, изгнáник; *v* прáщам в изгнáние

exist [игзи́ст] *v* съществýвам

existence [игзи́стънс] *n* съществýване

exit [éкзит] *n* излизане, и́зход

expand [икспáнд] *v* разширявам, развивам

expansion [икспáншън] *n* разширéние

expect [икспéкт] *v* очáквам, предполáгам

expedition [éкспиди́шън] *n* експеди́ция, бързинá, тóчност

expenditure [икспéндичър] *n* разнóски, рáзход

expense [икспéнс] *n* разнóски

expensive [икспéнсив] *adj* скъп

experience [икспи́риънс] *n* óпит, преживяване

experiment [икспéримънт] *n* прáвя óпит

experiment [икспéримънт] *n* óпит

expert [éкспърт] *adj* вещ; *n* экспéрт

explain [икспléйн] *v* обяснявам

explanation [éксплънéйшън] *n* обяснéние

explode [икспло́уд] *v* експлоди́рам, избýхвам, обо́рвам

exploration [е́ксплоре́йшън] *n* изсле́дване, проу́чване

explore [иксплóр] *v* изсле́двам, проу́чвам

explorer [иксплóрър] *n* изследова́тел

explosion [експлóужън] *n* експлóзия, избу́хване

export [експóрт] *v* изна́сям

export [е́кспорт] *n* и́знос

expression [икспре́шън] *n* и́зраз, изражéние

extend [икстéнд] *v* прости́рам, продължа́вам, разширя́вам

extension [икстéншън] *n* продължéние, разширя́ване

exterior [ексти́риър] *adj* вы́ншен

external [екстъ́рнъл] *adj* вы́ншен

extra [éкстра] *adj* допълни́телен

extreme [икстри́йм] *adj* кра́ен; *n* кра́йност

eye [ай] *n* окó; *v* глéдам, наблюда́вам

F

fabric [фá-брик] *n* тъ́кан, плат

face [фейс] *n* лицé; *v* обы́рнат съм с лицé към

fact [фа-кт] *n* факт, обстоя́телство

factor [фá-ктър] *n* фá́ктор, агéнт

factory [фá-ктъри] *n* фá́брика

faculty [фа́-кюлти] *n* факулте́т, спосо́бност, да́рба

fail [фейл] *v* пропа́дам, не сполу́чвам

failure [фе́йлиър] *n* неуспе́х, пропа́дание, фали́т

faint [фейнт] *n* припа́дък; *adj* слаб; *v* припа́дам, осла́бвам

faith [фейт] *n* вя́ра

faithful [фе́йтфул] *adj* ве́рен, то́чен

fall [фол] *v* па́дам, сти́хвам; *n* па́дане, вале́ж, е́сен, водопа́д

false [фолс] *adj* погре́шен, лъжли́в, фалши́в

fame [фейм] *n* сла́ва, изве́стност

family [фа́-мили] *n* семе́йство, род

famous [фе́ймъс] *adj* прочу́г, изве́стен

fan [фа-н] *n* ветри́ло, запаля́нко; *v* ве́я, разду́хвам

fantastic [фанта́-стик] *adj* фантасти́чен

fantasy [фа́-нтъси] *n* въображе́ние, фанта́зия

far [фар] *adv* дале́ч; *adj* дале́чен

farewell [фе́ъруе́л] *interj* сбо́гом; *adj* сбогу́ване

farm [фарм] *n* фе́рма, стопа́нство

farmer [фа́рмър] *n* земеде́лец, чифликчи́я

farming [фа́рминг] *n* земеде́лие

fashion [фа́-шън] *n* мо́да, стил, на́чин

fashionable [фа́-шънъбл] *adj* мо́ден

fast [фаст] *adj* бърз; *adv* бързо, здра́во

fat [фа-т] *adj* дебе́л, тлъст; *n* тлъстина́, мазнина́

fatal [фе́йтъл] *adj* съдбоно́сен, па́губен

fate [фейт] *n* съдба́, ги́бел

father [фа́дър] *n* баща́

fault [фолт] *n* гре́шка, дефе́кт, вина́

favor [фе́йвър] *n* благоскло́нност, услу́га, по́лза

fear [фи́ър] *n* страх; *v* страху́вам се

feather [фе́дър] *n* перо́, перуши́на

feature [фи́чър] *n* черта́, осо́беност

February [фе́брюри] *n* февруа́ри

feel [фийл] *v* чу́вствувам, смя́там

feeling [фи́йлинг] *n* чу́вство, усе́щане, отноше́ние

fellow [фе́лоу] *n* чове́к, друга́р

female [фи́мейл] *adj* же́нски

fertile [фъ́ртайл] *adj* плодоро́ден, плодови́т

fertility [фърти́лити] *n* плодоро́дност

fertilizer [фъртила́йзър] *n* изку́ствен тор

festival [фе́стивъл] *n* празненство́, фестива́л, пра́зник

fever [фи́вър] *n* тре́ска, температу́ра

few [фю] *adj* ма́лко

fiancé [фиа́нсе] *n* годени́к

fiancée [фиа́нсей] *n* годени́ца

fiction [фи́кшън] *n* белетри́стика, изми́слица

field [фийлд] *n* поле́, ни́ва, о́бласт

fifteen [фифти́йн] *num* петна́десет

fifty [фифти] *num* петдесе́т

fig [фиг] *n* смоки́ня

fight [файт] *v* би́я се, бо́ря се; *n* бой, борба́

fighter [фа́йтър] *n* боре́ц

figure [фи́гър] *n* фигу́ра, ци́фра; *v* изобразя́вам, представя́м си

fill [фил] *v* пълня, изпълвам, пломби́рам

film [филм] *n* филм, тънък слой

filter [фи́лтър] *n* фи́лтър; *v* филтри́рам

final [фа́йнъл] *adj* кра́ен, заключи́телен; *n* фина́лен мач, после́ден и́зпит

finally [фа́йнъли] *adv* на́й-по́сле, напълно

finance [файна́нс] *n* фина́нси, до́ходи; *v* финанси́рам

financial [файна́-ншъл] *adj* фина́нсов

find [файнд] *v* нами́рам

fine [файн] *adj* ху́бав, фин; *adv* чуде́сно

finger [фи́нгър] *n* пръст

fire [фа́йър] *n* о́гън, пожа́р, въодушеве́ност; *v* стре́лям, запа́лвам

fireplace [фа́йърплейс] *n* огни́ще, ками́на

fireworks [фа́йъруъркс] *noun pl* фойерве́рки

firm [фърм] *adj* твърд, постоя́нен, си́гурен; *adv* твърдо, непоколеби́мо; *n* фи́рма

first [фърст] *adj* пръв; *adv* на́й-напре́д, за първи път

fish [фиш] *n* ри́ба *v* ловя́ ри́ба

fist [фист] *n* юмрýк

five [файв] *num* пет

fix [фикс] *v* прикрéпвам, опредéлям, попрáвям

flag [фла-г] *n* знáме

flame [флейм] *n* плáмък

flat [фла-т] *adj* плóсък, рáвен; *n* плóскост, апартамéнт

flavor [флéйвър] *n* вкус; *v* подпрáвям

flesh [флеш] *n* месó, плът

flood [флад] *n* наводнéние, потóп; *v* наводнявам, залúвам

floor [флор] *n* под, етáж

flour [флáуър] *n* брашнó

flourish [флъ̀риш] *v* цъфтя́, процъфтя́вам, размáхвам

flow [флóу] *v* текá, лéя се, произтúчам; *n* течéние, прúлив

flower [флáуър] *n* цвéте, цъфтéне

fluid [флýид] *adj* тéчен, газообрáзен; *n* тéчност

fly [флай] *n* мухá; *v* летя́

focus [фóукъс] *n* фóкус; *v* съсредоточáвам се

fold [фóулд] *v* сгъвам; *n* гънка

folder [фóулдър] *n* пáпка

folk [фóук] *n* нарóд, хóра

follow [фóлоу] *v* слéдвам, вървя́ след, разбúрам

food [фýуд] *n* хранá

fool [фуул] *n* глупак, шут; *v* измамвам
foolish [фуулиш] *adj* глупав
foot [фуут] *n* крак, походка
for [фор] *prep* за, в полза на, по причина на
forbid [форбид] *v* забранявам
force [форс] *n* сила, войска
forecast [форкаст] *n* предсказване, прогноза
forehead [форид] *n* чело
foreign [форън] *adj* чуждестранен, външен
foreigner [форънър] *n* чужденец
forest [форист] *n* гора
forget [фъргет] *v* забравям
forgive [фъргив] *v* прощавам
fork [форк] *n* вилица, вила, разклонение
form [форм] *n* форма, вид, клас; *v* образувам, оформям
formal [формъл] *adj* формален, официален
formality [формалити] *n* формалност, официалност
formula [формюла] *n* формула
fortunate [форчънът] *adj* щастлив
fortune [форчън] *n* сполука, богатство, бъдеще
forty [форти] *num* четиридесет
forward [форуърд] *adj* преден; *adv* напред, нататък *v* подпомагам, изпращам
four [фор] *num* четири

fourteen [фóртийн] *num* четирина́десет
fox [фокс] *n* лиси́ца
frame [фрейм] *n* ра́мка; *v* офóрмям,
приспособя́вам
framework [фрéймуърк] *n* констру́кция,
ра́мки, структу́ра
frank [фра-нк] *adj* и́скрен, прям
frankly [фра́-нкли] *adv* и́скрено, откровéно
fraud [фрод] *n* изма́ма
free [фри] *adj* свобóден, безпла́тен; *v*
освобожда́вам
freedom [фри́йдъм] *n* свобода́
freight [фрейт] *n* прéвоз, товáр
frequent [фри́куънт] *adj* чест, многокра́тен
frequently [фри́куънтли] *adv* чéсто
fresh [фреш] *adj* прéсен, свеж, нов
freshness [фрéшнис] *n* свéжест
Friday [фра́йди] *n* пéтък
friend [френд] *n* прия́тел
friendly [фрéндли] *adv* прия́телски
friendship [фрéндшип] *n* прия́телство,
дру́жба
fright [фрайт] *n* страх, упла́ха, плаши́ло
frighten [фра́йтън] *v* изпла́швам
frog [фрог] *n* жа́ба
from [фром] *prep* от, из
front [франт] *n* прéдна част, фронт
fruit [фрут] *n* плод
fruitful [фру́тфул] *adj* плодорóден,
плодонóсен

fruitless [фру́тлис] *adj* безпло́ден, безполе́зен
fry [фрай] *v* пържа
fuel [фю́ъл] *n* гори́во; *v* снабдя́вам с гори́во
fulfil [фулфи́л] *v* изпълня́вам, извършвам, задоволя́вам
full [фул] *adj* пълен, цял
fully [фу́ли] *adv* напълно
fun [фън] *n* шега́, заба́ва
funeral [фю́нъръл] *n* погребе́ние
funny [фъни] *adj* сме́шен, стра́нен
furniture [фъ́рничър] *n* мебелиро́вка
further [фъ́рдър] *adv* по́-ната́тък; *v* съде́йствувам, придви́жвам
fuse [фюз] *adj* бушо́н
future [фю́чър] *n* бъдеще; *adj* бъдещ

G

gain [гейн] *v* пече́ля, избързвам; *n* печа́лба
gallery [га́-лъри] *n* гале́рия
game [ге́йм] *n* игра́, ди́веч
gang [га-нг] *n* гру́па, ба́нда
garage [гара́ж] *n* гара́ж; *v* гари́рам
garbage [га́рбидж] *n* смет
garden [га́рдън] *n* гради́на
garlic [га́рлик] *n* че́сън

gas [га–с] *n* бензи́н, газ
gasoline [га́–сълин] *n* бензи́н
gate [ге́йт] *n* по́рта, врата́
gay [гей] *adj* ве́сел
gender [дже́ндър] *n* род
general [дже́неръл] *adj* общ, обикнове́н, главе́н; *n* генера́л
generally [дже́неръли] *adv* о́бщо взе́то, обикнове́но
generation [дже́нерейшън] *n* поколе́ние
generosity [дже́нъро́сити] *n* ще́дрост
generous [дже́нъръс] *adj* ще́дър
gentle [дже́нтл] *adj* не́жен, благоро́ден, уме́рен
gently [дже́нтли] *adv* внима́телно, не́жно, ле́ко
genuine [дже́нюин] *adj* и́стински, неподпра́вен
geography [джио́гръфи] *n* геогра́фия
gesture [дже́счър] *n* жест
get [гет] *v* взе́мам, доби́вам, пече́ля, получа́вам
giant [джа́йънт] *n* велика́н, гига́нт
gift [гифт] *n* пода́рък, да́рба
gifted [ги́фтид] *adj* талантли́в, надаре́н
girl [гърл] *n* моми́че
give [гив] *v* да́вам, подаря́вам
glad [гла–д] *adj* ра́достен, дово́лен
gladly [гла́–дли] *adv* охо́тно, с удово́лствие
gland [гла–нд] *n* жлеза́

glass [глас] *n* стъклó
globe [глóуб] *n* кълбó, глóбус
glory [глóри] *n* слáва; *v* гордéя се, ликýвам
glove [глав] *n* ръкавúца
glue [глу] *n* лепúло; *v* лепя́
go [гóу] *v* отúвам, вървя́, двúжа се
goal [гóул] *n* цел, гол, вратá
goat [гóут] *n* козá
God [год] *n* бог, гóспод
gold [гóулд] *n* злáто; *adj* злáтен
good [гуд] *adj* добър, хýбав; *n* добрó, стóка
good-bye [гудбáй] *interj* сбóгом, довúждане; *n* сбогýване
good night [гýднáйт] *interj* лéка нощ
gospel [гóспъл] *n* евáнгелие, вéрую
gossip [гóсип] *n* клюка
government [гáвърмънт] *n* правúтелство, управлéние
governor [гáвърнър] *n* губернáтор
grace [грейс] *n* грáция, изя́щност, привлекáтелност, благоволéние
grade [грейд] *n* стéпен, клас
graduate [грá-джюейт] *v* завършвам учúлище úли университéт
graduation [грá-джюéйшън] *n* завършване на университéт
grammar [грáмър] *n* грамáтика
grandfather [грáндфадър] *n* дя́до
grandmother [грáндмáдър] *n* бáба

grandson [грáндсън] *n* внук
grass [грас] *n* тревá, пáсбище
gratitude [грáтитюд] *n* благодáрност, признáтелност
grave [грейв] *n* гроб; *adj* сериóзен
great [грейт] *adj* голям, велúк
greed [грийд] *n* áлчност, лакомúя
green [грийн] *adj* зелéн, незрял
greet [грийт] *v* поздравявам
greeting [грúтинг] *n* пóздрав
grey [грей] *adj* сив, побелял
grief [грийф] *n* скръб, печáл
grill [грил] *n* скáра за печéне на месó; *v* пекá на скáра
grocer [грóусър] *n* бакáлин
ground [грáунд] *n* земя, пóчва
grow [грóу] *v* растá, стáвам, отглéждам
guaranteee [гá-рантú] *n* гарáнция, поръчúтелство; *v* обезпечáвам
guard [гард] *v* пáзя, защищáвам; *n* охрáна
guest [гест] *n* гост, клиéнт
guide [гайд] *v* ръковóдя
guilt [гилт] *n* винá
guilty [гúлти] *adj* винóвен
guitar [гúтар] *n* китáра
gum [гъм] *n* венéц, клей, лепúло
gun [гън] *n* оръдие, пýшка, пистолéт
guy [гай] *n* човéк, момчé
gypsy [джúпси] *adj* цигáнски

H

habit [хá-бит] *n* нáвик
hail [хейл] *n* градýшка
hair [хéър] *n* косá
hairdresser [хéърдрéсър] *n* фризьóр
half [хаф] *n* половѝна
hall [хол] *n* зáла, хол
ham [ха-м] *n* шýнка, бут
hammer [хá-мър] *n* чук
hand [ха-нд] *n* рькá, почерк, часóвникова
стрелкá; *v* подáвам, връчвам
handkerchief [хá-ндкърчиф] *n* нóсна кърпа
handle [хá-ндъл] *n* дрьжка, рьчка; *v*
пѝпам, борáвя управлѝвам
handsome [хá-ндсъм] *adj* хýбав, щéдър
hang [ха-нг] *v* висѝ, закáчвам, обéсвам
hanger [хá-нгър] *n* закачáлка за дрéхи
happen [хá-пън] *v* слýчва се, стáва,
попáдам
happiness [хá-пинис] *n* щáстие
happy [хá-пи] *adj* щастлѝв, успéшен
hard [хард] *adj* твърд, корáв, тéжък,
трýден; *adv* сѝлно, усѝлено
hardware [хáрдуеър] *n* железарѝя
harm [харм] *n* вредá; *v* уврéждам, вредѝ
harmful [хáрмфул] *adj* врéден
harmless [хáрмлис] *adj* безврéден
harvest [хáрвъст] *n* жътва, рекóлта

hat [ха-т] *n* ша́пка
hate [хейт] *v* мра́зя; *n* омра́за
hatred [хе́йтрид] *n* омра́за
have [ха-в] *v* и́мам, нала́га ми се, тря́бва
he [хи] *pron* той
head [хед] *n* глава́, връх; *v* оглавя́вам, стоя́ наче́ло на
headache [хе́дейк] *n* главобо́лие
health [хелт] *n* здра́ве, здравеопа́зване
healthy [хе́лти] *adj* здрав, здравосло́вен
hear [хи́ър] *v* чу́вам, изслу́швам
hearing [хи́ъринг] *n* слух, изслу́шване
heart [харт] *n* сърце́, душа́, ку́па
heat [хийт] *n* горещи́на, гняв, разга́р
heater [хи́йтър] *n* нагрева́тел, отопли́тел
heaven [хевн] *n* небе́
heavy [хе́ви] *adj* те́жък, си́лен
heel [хийл] *n* пета́, ток
height [хайт] *n* височина́, възвише́ние
heir [е́ър] *n* насле́дник
hell [хел] *n* ад
hello [хъло́у] *interj* здраве́й, а́ло
help [хелп] *v* пома́гам; *n* по́мощ
hemisphere [хе́мисфиър] *n* полукълбо́
her [хъ] *pron* не́я, не́ин
here [хи́ър] *adv* тук, е́то
hereditary [хире́дитъри] *adj* насле́дствен
heredity [хире́дити] *n* насле́дственост
heritage [хе́ритидж] *n* насле́дство
hero [хи́роу] *n* геро́й

heroic [хиро́ик] *adj* геро́ичен
hesitate [хе́зитейт] *v* колеба́я се
hesitation [хе́зитейшън] *n* колеба́ние
hide [хайд] *n* ко́жа
high [хай] *adj* висо́к, възви́шен, отли́чен, си́лен
hill [хил] *n* хълм, ку́пчина пръст
him [хим] *pron* не́го, го
hint [хинт] *n* на́мек; *v* зага́твам
hip [хип] *n* бедро́, ши́пка
hire [ха́йър] *v* нае́мам
his [хиз] *pron* не́гов
historic [исто́рик] *adj* истори́чески
history [хи́стъри] *n* исто́рия
hit [хит] *v* у́дрям, улу́чвам; *n* у́дар, успе́х
hold [хо́улд] *v* държа́
hole [хо́ул] *n* ду́пка
holiday [хо́лидей] *n* пра́зник, вака́нция, о́тпуска, почи́вка
hollow [хо́лоу] *adj* кух, пра́зен, хлътнал; *n* хралу́па, вдлъбнатина́
holy [хо́ули] *adj* свят, свеще́н
home [хо́ум] *n* дом; *adj* дома́шен, въ́трешен
homeless [хо́умлис] *adj* бездо́мен
honest [о́нист] *adj* че́стен, открове́н, прям
honesty [о́нисти] *n* че́стност, открове́ност
honey [ха́ни] *n* пче́лен мед
honor [о́нър] *n* чест, по́чит, отли́чия; *v* почи́там, удостоя́вам

hook [хук] *n* ку́ка, сърп; *v* зака́чвам, хва́щам

hope [хо́уп] *n* наде́жда; *v* надя́вам се

hopeless [хо́уплис] *adj* безнаде́жден

horizon [хъра́йзън] *n* хоризо́нт

horizontal [хо́ризо́нтъл] *adj* хоризонта́лен

horrible [хо́рибл] *adj* ужа́сен

horrify [хо́рифай] *v* ужася́вам

horror [хо́рър] *n* у́жас

horse [хорс] *n* кон, кавале́рия

hose [хо́уз] *n* марку́ч, чора́пи

hospital [хо́спитъл] *n* бо́лница

hospitality [хо́спита́лити] *n* гостоприе́мство

host [хо́уст] *n* домаки́н, стопа́нин

hostile [хо́стайл] *adj* неприя́телски, вражде́бен, вра́жески

hostility [хости́лити] *n* вражде́бност

hot [хот] *adj* горе́щ, лют

hotel [хоуте́л] *n* хоте́л

hour [а́уър] *n* час

hourly [а́урли] *adj* ежеча́сен; *adv* ежеча́сно, все́ки час

house [ха́ус] *n* къ́ща, ка́мара

housewife [ха́усуайф] *n* домаки́ня, стопа́нка

housing [ха́узинг] *n* кварти́ра, жи́лище

how [ха́у] *adv* как

however [хауе́вър] *adv* ка́кто и да е, ко́лкото и; *conj* оба́че, при все това́

human [хю́мън] *adj* чове́шки

humane [хюме́йн] *adj* чове́чен, хума́нен
humanity [хюма́-нити] *n* чове́чество, хума́нност
humid [хю́мид] *adj* вла́жен
humidity [хюми́дити] *n* вла́га, вла́жност
humor [хю́мър] *n* ху́мор, настрое́ние
hunger [ха́нгър] *n* глад, си́лно жела́ние
hungry [ха́нгри] *adj* гла́ден
hunt [хънт] *v* тъ́рся, пресле́двам, хо́дя на лов; *n* тъ́рсене, лов
hunter [ха́нтър] *n* лове́ц
hunting [ха́нтинг] *n* лов
hurricane [ха́рикейн] *n* урага́н
hurry [ха́ри] *v* бъ́рзам; *n* бъ́рзане, бързина́
hurt [хърт] *v* наранявам, наскърбявам, боля́; *n* бо́лка, ра́на
husband [ха́збънд] *n* съпру́г
hut [хът] *n* коли́ба, хи́жа, бара́ка
hydrogen [ха́йдръджън] *n* водоро́д
hygiene [ха́йджин] *n* хигие́на
hymn [хим] *n* химн
hyphen [ха́йфън] *n* тире́
hypocrisy [хипо́кръси] *n* лицеме́рие

I

I [ай] *pron* аз
ice [айс] *n* лед, сладоле́д
ice-cream [а́йскри́йм] *n* сладоле́д

icon [áйкън] *n* икóна, изображéние
idea [áйдиа] *n* идéя, предстáва
ideal [айди́ъл] *adj* идеáлен; *n* идеáл
identity [айдéнтити] *n* самоли́чност,
еднáквост
idiom [и́диъм] *n* идиóм, гóвор, нарéчие
idol [áйдъл] *n* и́дол, божествó
if [иф] *conj* акó, дали́
ignite [игнáйт] *v* възпламеня́вам
ignorance [и́гнърънс] *n* невéжество,
незнáние
ignorant [и́гнърънт] *adj* невéж, несвéдущ
ignore [игнóр] *v* не зачи́там, пренебрéгвам
ill [ил] *adj* бóлен, лош
illegal [или́гъл] *adj* незакóнен,
противозакóнен
illiterate [или́търит] *adj* неграмóтен
illness [и́лнис] *n* бóлест
illustrate [и́лъстрейт] *v* илюстри́рам
illustration [и́лъстрéйшън] *n* илюстрáция,
рисýнка, при́мер
image [и́мидж] *n* óбраз, изображéние
imagination [имá-джинéйшън] *n* въображéние
imagine [имá-джин] *v* предстáвям си,
въобразя́вам си, предполáгам
immediate [ими́диът] *adj* незабáвен,
непосрéдствен
immediately [ими́диътли] *adv* веднáга,
незабáвно

immigrant [и́мигрънт] *n* пресе́лник, имигра́нт
immigration [и́мигре́йшън] *n* пресе́лничество, имигра́ция
immunity [имю́нити] *n* неприкоснове́ност, имуните́т
impatience [импе́йшънс] *n* нетърпе́ние
impatient [импе́йшънт] *adj* нетърпели́в
impetus [и́мпетъс] *n* у́стрем, тла́сък, импу́лс
implication [и́мпликейшън] *n* уча́стие, на́мек
imply [импла́й] *v* зага́твам, наме́квам
import [импо́рт] *v* вна́сям
import [и́мпорт] *n* внос
importance [импо́ртънс] *n* ва́жност, значе́ние
important [импо́ртънт] *adj* ва́жен, значи́телен
impose [импо́уз] *v* нала́гам
impossible [импо́сибл] *adj* невъзмо́жен
impression [импре́шън] *n* отпеча́тък, впечатле́ние
impressive [импре́сив] *adj* внуши́телен
improve [импру́в] *v* подобря́вам
improvement [импру́вмънт] *n* подобре́ние
impulse [и́мпълс] *n* тла́сък, подбу́да
in [ин] *prep* в, у, през
inability [и́нъби́лити] *n* неспосо́бност
incident [и́нсидънт] *n* слу́чка, произше́ствие, епизо́д, инциде́нт; *adj* присъщ

include [инклу́д] *v* включвам

income [и́нкъм] *n* при́ход, до́ход

incompetent [инко́мпътънт] *adj*
некомпете́нтен, неспосо́бен

inconvenience [и́нкънви́ниънс] *n* неудо́бство

inconvenient [и́нкънви́ниънт] *adj* неудо́бен,
ненавре́менен

increase [инкри́с] *v* увеличавам

increase [и́нкрис] *n* увеличе́ние,
нара́стване, расте́ж

independence [и́ндипе́ндънс] *n* незави́симост

independent [и́ндипе́ндънт] *adj* незави́сим

index [и́ндекс] *n* указа́тел, и́ндекс

indictment [инда́йтмънт] *n* обвини́телен акт

indifference [инди́фърънс] *n* безразли́чие,
равноду́шие

indignant [инди́гнънт] *adj* възмуте́н

indignation [и́ндигне́йшън] *n* възмуще́ние,
негодува́ние

individual [и́ндиви́джуъл] *adj* едини́чен,
отде́лен; *n* лице́, индиви́д

individuality [и́ндивиджуа́-лити] *n*
индивидуа́лност

industry [и́ндъстри] *n* проми́шленост,
прилежа́ние

inevitable [ине́витъбл] *adj* неизбе́жен,
немину́ем

infant [и́нфънт] *n* бе́бе, дете́

infect [инфе́кт] *v* заразя́вам

infection [инфе́кшън] *n* зара́за, инфе́кция

inflation [инфле́йшън] *n* наду́ване,
инфла́ция
influence [и́нфлуънс] *n* влия́ние,
възде́йствие; *v* влия́я, възде́йствувам
influential [инфлуе́ншъл] *adj* влия́телен
inform [инфо́рм] *v* уведомя́вам,
информи́рам
information [инфърме́йшън] *n* све́дения,
съобще́ние, информа́ция
innocence [и́нъсънс] *n* неви́нност
innocent [и́нъсънт] *adj* неви́нен
innovation [ино́уве́йшън] *n* нововъведе́ние,
нова́торство
insane [инсе́йн] *adj* безу́мен, неразу́мен
insanity [инса́-нити] *n* безу́мие, лу́дост
insect [и́нсект] *n* насеко́мо
inside [инса́йд] *n* вътрешност; *adj*
вътрешен; *adv* вътре
insist [инси́ст] *v* настоя́вам, набля́гам
inspect [инспе́кт] *v* разгле́ждам,
инспекти́рам
inspection [инспе́кшън] *n* разгле́ждане,
инспекти́ране
inspire [инспа́йър] *v* вдъхвам, внуша́вам,
подти́квам
install [инсто́л] *v* настаня́вам, инстали́рам
installation [инстъле́йшън] *n* инстала́ция
installment [инсто́лмънт] *n* вно́ска, част
instead [инсте́д] *adv* вме́сто
instinct [и́нстинкт] *n* инсти́нкт

institute [и́нститют] *n* институ́т; *v* учреда́вам

institution [и́нститю́шън] *n* учрежде́ние, учреда́ване

instruction [инстръ́кшън] *n* обуче́ние, наставле́ния, директи́ви

instructor [инстрѣ́ктър] *n* инстру́ктор, учи́тел

instrument [и́нструмънт] *n* инструме́нт, оръ́дие

insufficient [и́нсъфи́шънт] *adj* недоста́тъчен

insulate [и́нсюлейт] *v* изоли́рам

insult [и́нсълт] *n* оби́да, оскърбле́ние

insult [инсѣ́лт] *v* оби́ждам, оскърба́вам

insurance [иншу́ърънс] *n* застрахо́вка

insure [иншу́ър] *v* осигуря́вам, застрахо́вам

intellect [и́нтилект] *n* интеле́кт, ум

intellectual [и́нтиле́кчуъл] *adj* у́мствен, интелектуа́лен

intelligence [инте́лиджънс] *n* интелиге́нтност, ум, разузна́ване

intelligent [инте́лиджънт] *adj* интелиге́нтен, у́мен, сми́слен

intensity [инте́нсити] *n* си́ла, напреже́ние

intensive [инте́нсив] *adj* напре́гнат, интензи́вен

intention [инте́ншън] *n* намере́ние, цел

interest [и́нтрест] *n* интере́с, заинтересо́ваност, ли́хва; *v* заинтересу́вам

interesting [и́нтрестинг] *adj* интере́сен

interior [интириър] *n* вътрешност, интериор
internal [интърнъл] *adj* вътрешен
international [интърна́-шънъл] *adj*
международен
interpret [интърприт] *v* превеждам устно,
тълкувам
interpreter [интърпритър] *n* преводач
interrupt [интърът] *v* прекъсвам
interruption [интъръпшън] *n* прекъсване
interval [интървъл] *n* промеждутък,
интервал, пауза
interview [интървю] *n* интервю; *v*
интервюирам
intestine [интестин] *n* черва
intimacy [интимъси] *n* интимност
intimate [интимът] *adj* близък, интимен
into [инту] *prep* в
introduce [интрадюс] *v* въвеждам,
представям, запознавам
introduction [интрадъкшън] *n* въведение,
увод, запознаване
invasion [инвейжън] *n* нашествие
invent [инвент] *v* изобретявам, измислям
invention [инвеншън] *n* изобретение
inventor [инвентър] *n* изобретател
invest [инвест] *v* инвестирам
investment [инвестмънт] *n* вложение,
инвестиция
investor [инвестър] *n* вложител, инвеститор
invisible [инвизибл] *adj* невидим

invitation [инвитéйшън] *n* покáна
invite [инвáйт] *v* кáня, покáнвам
invoice [úнвойс] *n* фактýра
involve [инвóлв] *v* въвличам, замéсвам
iron [áйън] *n* желязо, ютия
irrigate [úригейт] *v* напоявам
irrigation [úригéйшън] *n* напояване
island [áйлънд] *n* óстров
isolation [áйсълéйшън] *n* изолáция,
уединéние
issue [úшю] *n* резултáт, край, изтúчане,
спóрен въпрóс, издáние; *v* издáвам,
разбúрам, произлúзам
itch [ич] *n* сърбéж; *v* сърбú ме
ivory [áйвъри] *n* слóнова кост

J

jacket [джá-кит] *n* жакéт, сакó, корá
jail [джейл] *n* затвóр; *v* затвáрям
jam [джа-м] *n* мармалáд, конфитюр; *v*
задрúствам
January [джá-нюъри] *n* януáри
jaw [джо] *n* чéлюст
jazz [джа-з] *n* джаз
jealous [джéлъс] *adj* ревнúв, завистлúв
jealousy [джéлъси] *n* рéвност, зáвист
jeans [джийнз] *noun pl* панталóни,
джúнси, дънки

jet [джет] *n* струя; *adj* реактивен
Jew [джу] *n* еврéин
jewel [джу́ъл] *n* скъпоцéнност, бижу́
job [джоб] *n* рáбота, слу́жба
join [джойн] *v* свързвам, присъединя́вам
joint [джойнт] *n* стáва; *adj* съвмéстен
joke [джóук] *n* шегá; *v* шегу́вам се
journal [джъ́рнъл] *n* списáние, днéвник
journalism [джъ́рнълизм] *n* журнали́зъм
journalist [джъ́рнълист] *n* журнали́ст
journey [джъ́рни] *n* пъту́ване, пътешéствие
joy [джой] *n* рáдост
judge [джъдж] *n* съдия́, познавáч; *v* съдя́,
преценя́вам
judicial [джуди́шъл] *adj* съдéбен
juice [джус] *n* сок
July [джулáй] *n* юли
jump [джъмп] *v* скáчам; *n* скок
June [джун] *n* юни
jungle [джъ́нгъл] *n* джу́нгла
jury [джу́ри] *n* съдéбни заседáтели, жу́ри
just [джъст] *adj* справедли́в, вéрен, тóчен,
заслу́жен; *adv* тóчно, сáмо
justice [джъ́стис] *n* справедли́вост,
правосъ́дие, съдия́

K

keep [кийп] *v* пáзя, държá, спáзвам,
продължáвам

key [ки] *n* ключ, клавиш
kid [кид] *n* дете; *v* шегувам се
kidney [кидни] *n* бъбрек
kill [кил] *v* убивам
kind [кайнд] *n* вид, сорт, същност; *adj* любезен, мил
kindness [кайнднис] *n* любезност, нежност
king [кинг] *n* крал, цар
kingdom [кингдъм] *n* кралство, царство
kiss [кис] *v* целувам; *n* целувка
kitchen [кичън] *n* кухня
knee [ний] *n* коляно
knife [найф] *n* нож
knob [ноб] *n* топка, дръжка
knock [нок] *v* чукам, тропам; *n* почукване, удар
know [ноу] *v* зная, познавам
knowledge [нолидж] *n* знание, наука

L

label [лейбъл] *n* етикет
laboratory [лъборътъри] *n* лаборатория
labor [лейбър] *n* труд, работа; *v* трудя се
lace [лейс] *n* дантела
lack [ла-к] *n* липса, недостиг, нужда; *v* липсва ми
ladder [ла-дър] *n* стълба
lady [лейди] *n* дама

lag [ла-г] *v* изоста́вам
lake [лейк] *n* е́зеро
lamb [ла-м] *n* а́гне, а́гнешко месо́
lamp [ла-мп] *n* ла́мпа
land [ла-нд] *n* земя́, су́ша, страна́; *v* приземя́вам се
landscape [ла́-ндскейп] *n* пейза́ж
lane [лейн] *n* але́я, у́личка
language [ла́-нгуидж] *n* ези́к, го́вор
large [лардж] *adj* голя́м, е́дър, ще́дър
last [ласт] *adj* после́ден, ми́нал; *v* тра́я, продължа́вам
lasting [ла́стинг] *adj* тра́ен, продължи́телен
late [лейт] *adj* късен, закъсня́л, поко́ен, бивш; *adv* късно
latitude [ла́-титюд] *n* геогра́фска ширина́
laugh [лаф] *v* сме́я се; *n* смях
laughter [ла́фтър] *n* смях
laundry [ло́ндри] *n* пера́лня, пране́
lavatory [ла́вътъри] *n* тоале́тна
law [ло] *n* зако́н, пра́во
lawyer [ло́йър] *n* юри́ст, адвока́т
layer [ле́йър] *n* пласт, слой
lazy [ле́йзи] *adj* лени́в, мързели́в
lead [лед] *n* оло́во
lead [лийд] *v* ръково́дя, предво́ждам, во́дя
leader [ли́йдър] *n* вода́ч, вожд, ръководи́тел
leadership [ли́йдършип] *n* вода́чество, ръково́дство

leaf [лийф] *n* лист

lean [лийн] *adj* слаб, мършав; *v* навеждам се, облягам се

learn [лърн] *v* уча, научавам

lease [лийс] *n* наем; *v* наемам

leather [лéдър] *n* обработена кожа

leave [лийв] *v* оставям, напускам, заминавам; *n* отпуска

lecture [лéкчър] *n* лекция; *v* поучавам, мъмря

left [лефт] *adj* ляв

leg [лег] *n* крак, бут, крачол

legal [лигъл] *adj* законен, юридически

legislation [лéджислéйшън] *n* законодателство

legislature [лéджислейчър] *n* законодателна власт

lemon [лéмън] *n* лимон

lemonade [лéмънейд] *n* лимонада

lend [ленд] *v* давам назаем, придавам

length [ленгт] *n* дължина

lens [ленс] *n* леща

lentil [лéнтил] *n* леща

less [лес] *adj* по-малък; *adv* по-малко *prep* без

lesson [лéсън] *n* урок, поука

let [лет] *v* позволявам, оставям, давам под наем

letter [лéтър] *n* буква, писмо

level [лéвъл] *n* равнѝще, нивó; *adj* хоризонтáлен, рáвен
liberate [лѝбърейт] *v* освобождáвам
liberation [лѝбърéйшън] *n* освобождéние
liberty [лѝбърти] *n* свободá, вóлност
library [лáйбръри] *n* библиотéка
licence [лáйсънс] *n* позволéние, разрешѝтелно
lick [лик] *v* лѝжа, бѝя
lid [лид] *n* похлупáк, капáк, клепáч
lie [лай] *n* лъжá; *v* лъ̀жа
lie [лай] *v* лежá, простѝрам се
life [лайф] *n* живóт
lift [лифт] *v* вдѝгам
light [лайт] *n* светлинá; *adj* свéтъл, блед
light [лайт] *v* осветя̀вам, запáлвам; *adj* лек
lightning [лáйтнинг] *n* светкáвица
like [лайк] *adj* подóбен; *prep* катó; *v* харéсвам, обѝчам, ѝскам, желáя
limb [лим] *n* крáйник, клон
line [лайн] *n* лѝния, чертá, връв, жѝца, редѝца, направлéние
link [линк] *n* връзка, звенó; *v* свързвам, съединя̀вам
lion [лáйън] *n* лъв
lip [лип] *n* ýстна; *adj* нейскрен
lipstick [лѝпстик] *n* червѝло за ýстни
liquid [лѝкуид] *n* тéчност; *adj* тéчен
liquor [лѝкър] *n* алкохóлно питиé
list [лист] *n* спѝсък; *v* прáвя спѝсък

listen [лисън] *v* слушам
listner [лисънър] *n* слушател
literary [литърӯри] *adj* литературен
literature [литрӯчър] *n* литература
little [литъл] *adj* малък; *adv* малко
live [лив] *v* живея
liver [ливър] *n* черен дроб
load [лоуд] *n* товар; *v* товаря
loan [лоун] *n* заем
lobby [лоби] *n* фоайе
local [лоукъл] *adj* местен
locate [лоукейт] *v* разполагам, намирам мястото
location [лоукейшън] *n* разположение, място
lock [лок] *n* ключалка; *v* заключвам, скопчвам
lodging [лоджинг] *n* квартира, жилище
logic [лоджик] *n* логика
logical [лоджикъл] *adj* логически
lonely [лоунли] *adj* самотен
long [лонг] *adj* дълъг
longitude [лонгитюд] *n* географска дължина
look [лук] *v* гледам, изглеждам; *n* поглед, изражение
loose [луус] *adj* свободен, хлабав, нехаен, разхлабен
loosen [лусън] *v* разхлабвам, освобождавам
lose [луз] *v* губя, изгубвам, изпускам
loss [лос] *n* загуба

lot [лот] *n* жребий, съдба, много
loud [лауд] *adj* силен, гръмогласен
love [лъв] *n* любов; *v* обичам, любя
lovely [лъвли] *adj* хубав, прекрасен
lover [лъвър] *n* любовник, любител
low [лоу] *adj* нисък, тих, низш, вулгарен
loyal [лойъл] *adj* лоялен, верен
luck [лък] *n* късмет, щастие
lucky [лъки] *adj* щастлив, с късмет
luggage [лъгидж] *n* багаж
lunch [лънч] *n* обед
lung [лънг] *n* бял дроб
luxury [лъкжъри] *n* разкош, лукс

M

machine [мъшийн] *n* машина
machinery [мъшийнъри] *n* машини,
машинария, механизъм
mad [ма-д] *adj* луд, обезумял, вбесен
madam [ма-дъм] *n* госпожа
madness [ма-днис] *n* лудост
magazine [ма-гъзийн] *n* списание
magic [ма-джик] *n* магия
magnet [ма-гнит] *n* магнит
magnetic [магнетик] *adj* магнитен,
привлекателен
mail [мейл] *n* поща; *v* изпращам по
пощата

main [мейн] *adj* гла́вен

mainly [ме́йнли] *adv* гла́вно, преди́мно

maintenance [ме́йнтънънс] *n* поддръ́жка, издръ́жка

major [ме́йджър] *n* майо́р, пълноле́тен чове́к

majority [мъджо́рити] *n* болшинство́, мнозинство́, пълноле́тие

make [мейк] *v* пра́вя, произве́ждам

male [мейл] *n* мъж

mammal [ма́-мъл] *n* боза́йник, млекопита́ещо живо́тно

man [ма-н] *n* мъж, чове́к

manage [ма́-нидж] *v* управля́вам, успя́вам, спра́вям се

management [ма́-ниджмънт] *n* ръково́дство, упра́ва

manager [ма́-ниджър] *n* упра́вител, дире́ктор

mankind [ма-нка́йнд] *n* чове́чество, мъже́

manner [ма́-нър] *n* на́чин, държа́не, обно́ски, нра́ви

manual [ма́-нюъл] *adj* ръчен, физи́чески; *n* наръ́чник

manufacture [ма́-нюфа́кчър] *v* произве́ждам, фабрику́вам; *n* произво́дство

manufacturer [ма́-нюфа́кчърър] *n* фабрика́нт, производи́тел

many [мéни] *adv* мнóго; *n* мнóжество, голя́м брой

map [ма-п] *n* геогрáфска кáрта

March [марч] *n* март

marine [мърúйн] *adj* мóрски; *n* флóта

mark [марк] *n* бéлег, следá, белéжка; *v* белéжа, оценя́вам

market [мáркит] *n* пазáр; *v* търгу́вам

marriage [мá-ридж] *n* женúтба, свáтба

marry [мá-ри] *v* ожéнвам се, омъ́жвам се

mask [маск] *n* мáска; *v* маскúрам, прикрúвам

mat [ма-т] *n* рогóзка, покрúвка

match [ма-ч] *n* кибрúт

match [ма-ч] *n* женúтба, мач; *v* подхóждам

material [мътúриъл] *n* материáл, плат

maternity [мътъ́рнити] *n* мáйчинство

mathematics [мá-темá-тикс] *n* математика

matter [мá-тър] *n* веществó, съ́щност, въпрóс

maximum [мá-ксимъм] *adj* максимáлен

May [мей] *n* май

may [мей] *v* мóга, разрешéно, мóже, нéка

maybe [мéйби] *adv* мóже би

mayor [мéйър] *n* кмет

meal [мийл] *n* я́дене

mean [мийн] *v* знáча, възнамеря́вам, úскам да кáжа

meaning [мúйнинг] *n* значéние; *adj* изразúтелен, многозначúтелен

measure [мéжър] *n* мя́рка; *v* мéря, измéрвам

measurement [мéжърмънт] *n* мя́рка, размéри, измéрване

meat [мийт] *n* месó

mechanic [микá-ник] *n* техни́к, механик

mechanism [мéкънизм] *n* механи́зъм, апарáт

medal [мéдъл] *n* медáл

medical [мéдикъл] *adj* медици́нски

medicine [мéдисин] *n* лекáрство, медици́на

medieval [мéдии́въл] *adj* средновекóвен

meet [мийт] *v* срéщам, запознáвам се

meeting [ми́йтинг] *n* събрáние, срéща

melody [мéлъди] *n* мелóдия

melon [мéлън] *n* пъпеш

melt [мелт] *v* топя́, стопя́вам

member [мéмбър] *n* член

membership [мéмбършип] *n* члéнство, члéнове

memory [мéмъри] *n* пáмет, спóмен

mental [мéнтъл] *adj* у́мствен, психи́чески

mention [мéншън] *v* споменáвам; *n* споменáване

menu [мéню] *n* меню́, лист за я́стия

merchandise [мέрчъндайс] *n* стóка

merchant [мέрчънт] *n* търгóвец на éдро, съдържáтел на магази́н

mercy [мέрси] *n* ми́лост, състрадáние

merge [мърдж] *v* смéсвам, сли́вам

message [месидж] *n* съобщéние, послáние, мúсия, поръчéние

metal [мéтъл] *n* метáл

method [мéтъд] *n* нáчин, спóсоб, мéтод, систéма

microphone [мáйкръфоун] *n* микрофóн

middle [мúдъл] *n* средá; *adj* срéден

midnight [мúднайт] *n* полунóщ

mild [майлд] *adj* мек, благ, лек

milk [милк] *n* млякó; *v* доя́

million [мúлиън] *num* милиóн

millionaire [мúлиънéър] *n* милионéр

mind [майнд] *n* ум, мнéние; *v* внимáвам, грúжа се

mine [майн] *n* мúна; *v* копáя, минúрам

miner [мáйнър] *n* миньóр

mineral [мúнъръл] *n* минерáл, рýда; *adj* минерáлен

minimum [мúнимъм] *n* мúнимум

minister [мúнистър] *n* минúстър, послáник, свещéник

ministry [мúнистри] *n* министéрство, духóвенство

minute [мúнит] *n* минýта, протокóл на заседáние

miracle [мúръкъл] *n* чýдо

mirror [мúрър] *n* огледáло

mischief [мúсчиф] *n* пáкост, немúрство, пáлавост

miserable [мúзъръбъл] *adj* жáлък, нещáстен

misery [мѝзъри] *n* нищета́, мизе́рия, нещастие

miss [мис] *v* пропу́скам, не улу́чвам, лѝпсва ми

Miss [мис] *n* госпо́жица

missing [мѝсинг] *adj* лѝпсващ, отсъ́ствуващ, загу́бен

mission [мѝшън] *n* зада́ча, мѝсия

mistake [мисте́йк] *n* гре́шка; *v* греша́, бъркам

Mister [мѝстър] *n* господѝн

misunderstand [мѝсъндърста́-нд] *v* разбѝрам погре́шно

misunderstanding [мѝсъндърста́-ндинг] *n* недоразуме́ние, неразбира́телство

mix [микс] *v* сме́свам

mixture [мѝксчър] *n* смес

model [мо́дъл] *n* образе́ц, моде́л

modern [мо́дърн] *adj* нов, съвре́менен, моде́рен

modest [мо́дест] *adj* скро́мен

modesty [мо́дисти] *n* скро́мност, уме́реност

moist [мойст] *adj* вла́жен

moisten [мо́йсън] *v* навлажня́вам

moisture [мо́йсчър] *n* вла́га, вла́жност

moment [мо́умънт] *n* моме́нт, миг

monastery [мо́нъстри] *n* манастѝр

Monday [мѐнди] *n* понеде́лник

money [мѐни] *n* парѝ

monkey [мѐнки] *n* майму́на

monopoly [мънóпъли] *n* монопóл

month [мънт] *n* мéсец

monthly [мѐнтли] *adj* мéсечен

monument [мóнюмънт] *n* пáметник

mood [мýуд] *n* настроéние, наклонéние

moon [мýун] *n* лунá, мéсец

moral [мóръл] *adj* нрáвствен, морáлен; *n* поýка

morality [морáлити] *n* морáл, нрáвственост

more [мор] *adj* пóвече

most [мóуст] *adj* нáй-мнóго, пóвечето; *adv* нáй-мнóго

mostly [мóустли] *adv* предúмно, глáвно

mother [мáдър] *n* мáйка

mother-in-law [мáдър ин ло] *n* свекѝрва, тѝща

motion [мóушън] *n* движéние, предложéние

motor [мóутър] *n* мотóр, двигáтел

motorist [мóутърист] *n* автомобилúст

mountain [мáунтин] *n* планинá

mourn [морн] *v* жалéя, оплáквам

mourning [мóрнинг] *n* скрѝб, трáур

mouse [мáус] *n* мúшка

mouth [мáут] *n* устá, ýстие, óтвор

move [мýув] *v* двúжа, мéстя, вълнýвам, трóгвам; *n* ход, постѝпка

movement [мýувмънт] *n* движéние

movie [мýви] *n* кúно

much [мач] *adj* голямо колúчество, мнóго

mud [мъд] *n* кал

multiply [мъ̀лтиплай] *v* умножа́вам, размножа́вам

murder [мъ̀рдър] *n* уби́йство; *v* уби́вам

murderer [мъ̀рдърър] *n* уби́ец

muscle [мъ̀съл] *n* му́скул

muscular [мъ̀скюлър] *adj* му́скулен, му́скулест

museum [мюзи́ъм] *n* музе́й

mushroom [мъ̀шрум] *n* гъ̀ба

music [мю̀зик] *n* му́зика

musical [мю̀зикъл] *adj* музика́лен; *n* опере́та

musician [мюзи́шън] *n* музика́нт

must [мъст] *v* тря́бва, длъ̀жен съм да

mutton [мъ̀тън] *n* о́внешно месо́

mutual [мю̀чуъл] *adj* взаи́мен, общ

my [май] *pron* мой

myself [майсе́лф] *pron* аз сами́ят, се́бе си

N

nail [не́йл] *n* но́кът, гво́здей, пиро́н; *v* закова́вам

naive [найв] *adj* наи́вен

naked [не́йкид] *adj* гол

name [нейм] *n* и́ме, репута́ция; *v* нари́чам, назова́вам

narrow [на-роу] *adj* тéсен, ограничéн; *v* стесня́вам

nation [нéйшън] *n* нарóд, нáция

national [нá-шънъл] *adj* нарóден, национáлен, държáвен

natural [нá-чуръл] *adj* естéствен, прирóден, вродéн

nature [нéйчър] *n* прирóда, естествó, харáктер

naval [нéйвъл] *adj* флóтски, мóрски

navy [нéйви] *n* флóта, марúна

near [нúър] *prep* близó до, при, почтú; *adj* блúзък; *v* приближáвам

near-by [нúърбай] *adj* наблúзо

nearly [нúърли] *adv* почтú

necessary [нéсесъри] *adj* необходúм, нýжен

neck [нек] *n* врат, шúя

necklace [нéклис] *n* огърлица, гердáн

need [нийд] *n* нýжда; *v* нуждáя се

needle [нийдл] *n* иглá

negative [нéгътив] *adj* отрицáтелен; *n* отрицáние, негатúв

neglect [ниглéкт] *v* пренебрéгвам; *n* пренебрежéние, небрéжност

negligence [нéглиджънс] *n* небрéжност, немарлúвост

negligent [нéглиджънт] *adj* небрéжен, нехáен, немарлúв

negro [нúгроу] *n* нéгър

neighbor [нéйбър] *n* съсéд, блúжен

neighborhood [нéйбърхуд] *n* окóлност, махалá

neither [нáйдър] *adv* нúто; *pron* нúто едúният, нúто дрýгият

nephew [нéфю] *n* плéменник

nervous [нъ̀рвъс] *adj* нéрвен, раздразнúтелен

nervousness [нъ̀рвъснис] *n* нéрвност

nest [нест] *n* гнездó

net [нет] *n* мрéжа; *v* улáвям в мрéжа

network [нéтуърк] *n* мрéжа

neutral [ню̀тръл] *adj* неутрáлен

never [нéвър] *adv* нúкога

new [ню] *adj* нов

news [нюз] *n* новинá

newspaper [ню̀зпейпър] *n* вéстник

next [некст] *adj* слéдващ, съсéден; *adv* след товá; *prep* до

nice [найс] *adj* хýбав, приятен

niece [нийс] *n* плéменница

night [найт] *n* нощ

nightgown [нáйтгаун] *n* нóщница

nine [найн] *num* дéвет

nineteen [нáйнтúйн] *num* деветнáдесет

ninety [нáйнти] *num* деветдесéт

no [нóу] *adj* нúкакъв

noise [нойз] *n* шум; *v* разгласявам

noisy [нóйзи] *adj* шýмен

none [нън] *adj* нúкакъв

nonsense [нóнсънс] *n* глýпости

normal [но́рмъл] *adj* обикнове́н, норма́лен
north [норт] *n* се́вер; *adj* се́верен
northern [но́рдърн] *adj* се́верен
nose [но́уз] *n* нос; *v* поду́швам
note [но́ут] *n* знак, беле́жка, но́та; *v* беле́жа, забеля́звам
notebook [но́утбук] *n* тетра́дка
notion [но́ушън] *n* иде́я, предста́ва
noun [на́ун] *n* съществи́телно и́ме
novel [но́въл] *n* рома́н
novelist [но́вълист] *n* романи́ст
November [нове́мбър] *n* ноември
now [на́у] *adv* сега́
number [нъ́мбър] *n* число́, брой, но́мер
numerous [ю́юмъръс] *adj* многобро́ен
nun [нън] *n* монахи́ня
nurse [нърс] *n* медици́нска сестра́
nut [нът] *n* о́рех, га́йка
nutrition [нютри́шън] *n* хра́нене, храна́

O

oak [о́ук] *n* дъб
oath [о́ут] *n* кле́тва
obey [обе́й] *v* покоря́вам се, подчиня́вам се
object [о́бджикт] *n* предме́т, обе́кт, цел, намере́ние, допълне́ние

object [ъбджéкт] *v* възразявам,
противопостáвям се

objection [ъбджéкшън] *n* възражéние

obligation [óблигéйшън] *n* задължéние

obligatory [облúгътъри] *adj* задължúтелен

obscure [ъбскюúр] *adj* неясен, смътен,
скрит, неизвéстен

obscurity [ъбскюúрити] *n* смътност,
неизвéстност

observe [ъбзъ́рв] *v* наблюдáвам,
забелязвам, спáзвам

observer [ъбзъ́рвър] *n* наблюдáтел

obtain [ъбтéйн] *v* получáвам, придобúвам

obvious [óбвиъс] *adj* очевúден, явен

occasion [ъкéйжън] *n* слýчай, пóвод,
причúна

occasionally [ъкéйжънъли] *adv* понякога,
от врéме на врéме

occupation [óкюпéйшън] *n* занимáние,
занятие

occupy [óкюпай] *v* заéмам, окупúрам

occur [ъкъ́р] *v* слýчвам се, úдва ми наýм

occurrence [ъкъ́рънс] *n* слýчка,
произшéствие

ocean [óушън] *n* океáн

October [ъктóубър] *n* октóмври

odd [од] *adj* нечéтен, тек, осóбен,
стрáнен, случáен

odor [óудър] *n* миризмá, аромáт,
репутáция

of [ов] *prep* на, за, с, от
off [оф] *prep* от, на разстояние от, извън
offense [ъфéнс] *n* нарушéние, простъпка, провинéние, оскърблéние
offend [ъфéнд] *v* оскърбявам, дразня
offer [óфър] *v* предлáгам; *n* предложéние
office [óфис] *n* слýжба, длъжност, кантóра
official [ъфúшъл] *adj* служéбен, официáлен; *n* служúтел
often [óфън] *adv* чéсто
oil [ойл] *n* мáсло, петрóл
O.K. [оукéй] *adv* добрé; *adj* правилен, в изпрáвност
old [óулд] *adj* стар, дрéвен
olive [óлив] *n* маслúна
omission [омúшън] *n* изпýскане, прóпуск
omit [омúт] *v* пропýскам, изпýщам
on [он] *prep* на, върхý, по, в, за, от
once [уáнс] *adv* веднъж, едúн път, някога
one [уáн] *adj* едúн, едúнствен; *n* човéк
onion [ѣниън] *n* лук
only [óунли] *adj* едúнствен; *adv* сáмо, едúнствено
open [óупън] *adj* отвóрен, открúт; *v* отвáрям, открúвам
opener [óупънър] *n* отварáчка
openly [óупънли] *adv* открúто, откровéно
opera [óупъра] *n* óпера
operation [óпърéйшън] *n* дéйствие, операция

operator [о́пърейтър] *n* меха́ник, опера́тор
opinion [ъпи́ниън] *n* мне́ние
opponent [ъпо́унънт] *n* проти́вник
opportunity [о́пъртю́нити] *n* възмо́жност,
удо́бен слу́чай
oppose [ъпо́уз] *v* противопоста́вям,
противоде́йствувам
opposite [о́пъзит] *adj* противополо́жен,
насре́щен, обра́тен
opposition [о́пъзи́шън] *n* противоде́йствие,
съпротивле́ние
oppression [ъпре́шън] *n* поти́скане, гнет
oppressive [ъпре́сив] *adj* поти́скащ, гнетя́щ
oppressor [ъпре́сър] *n* поти́сник, тира́нин
optimism [о́птимизм] *n* оптими́зъм
or [ор] *conj* или́
oral [о́ръл] *adj* у́стен
orange [о́риндж] *n* портока́л; *adj* ора́нжев
orchestra [о́ркистра] *n* орке́стър
order [о́рдър] *n* ред, наре́ждане, за́повед,
поръ́чка; *v* запо́вя́двам, поръ́чвам
ordinary [о́динъри] *adj* обикнове́н,
всекидне́вен
ore [ор] *n* ру́да
organ [о́ргън] *n* о́рган
organic [орга́-ник] *adj* органи́чен,
органи́чески
organism [о́ргънизм] *n* органи́зъм
organization [о́ргънайзе́йшън] *n* организа́ция
organize [о́ргънайз] *v* организи́рам

origin [о́риджин] *n* прои́зход, и́зточник, нача́ло

original [ори́джинъл] *adj* първонача́лен, оригина́лен, самоби́тен

ornament [о́рнъмънт] *n* украше́ние, орнаме́нт

orphan [о́рфън] *n* сира́к

orthodox [о́ртъдокс] *adj* правове́рен, общоприе́т, правосла́вен

other [а́дър] *adj* друг

our [а́уър] *pron* наш

ourselves [ауърсе́лвз] *pron* ни́е сами́те

out [а́ут] *prep* вън, навъ́н

outer [а́утър] *adj* въ́ншен

outline [а́утлайн] *n* очерта́ние, конту́ри; *v* скици́рам

output [а́утпут] *n* произво́дство, проду́кция

outside [а́утса́йд] *n* въ́ншна страна́, въ́ншност; *adj* въ́ншен; *adv* отвъ́н, навъ́н

oval [о́увъл] *adj* елипсови́ден, о́бъл

oven [ѣ́вън] *n* пещ, фу́рна

over [о́увър] *adv* наго́ре, по́вече; *prep* над, през, из, по, за, свръх

overlook [о́увърлу́к] *v* надзира́вам, недогле́ждам

owe [о́у] *v* дължа́

owner [о́унър] *n* со́бственик

ownership [о́унършип] *n* со́бственост, притежа́ние

oxide [о́ксайд] *n* о́кис
oxygen [о́ксиджън] *n* кислоро́д

P

pace [пейс] *n* кра́чка, върве́ж, ско́рост, темп; *v* вървя́, кра́ча
pack [па-к] *n* паке́т, вързо́п, глу́тница; *v* опако́вам
page [пейдж] *n* стра́ница
pain [пейн] *n* бо́лка, мъ́ка
painful [пе́йнфул] *adj* боле́знен, мъчи́телен
paint [пейнт] *n* боя́; *v* бояди́свам, рису́вам
painter [пе́йнтър] *n* худо́жник, бояджи́я
painting [пе́йнтинг] *n* живопи́с, рису́нка, карти́на
pair [пе́ър] *n* чифт, дво́йка; *v* чифто́свам
pal [па-л] *n* прия́тел
palace [па́-лъс] *n* двор́ец, пала́т
pale [пейл] *adj* бле́ден
palm [палм] *n* длан, па́лма
pan [па-н] *n* тига́н, тава́, те́нджера
panic [па́-ник] *n* па́ника; *v* панико́свам
pants [па-нтс] *noun pl* пантало́ни
paper [пе́йпър] *n* харти́я, докуме́нт, ве́стник, докла́д, сту́дия
paradise [па́-ръдайс] *n* рай
paragraph [па́-ръграф] *n* парагра́ф, нов ред, алине́я

parallel [па-ръ̀лел] *adj* у̀спореден; *n*
паралѐл *v* сравня̀вам
paralysis [пъра̀лисис] *n* пара̀лиза,
парализѝране
parcel [па̀рсъл] *n* пакѐт, колѐт; *v*
пакетѝрам, раздѐлям
pardon [па̀рдън] *n* про̀шка, извинѐние; *v*
проща̀вам
parent [пѐрънт] *n* родѝтел
park [парк] *n* парк; *v* гарѝрам
parliament [па̀рлъмънт] *n* парламѐнт
parrot [па̀-рът] *n* папага̀л
part [парт] *n* част, дял, ро̀ля, страна̀; *v*
деля̀, раздѐлям
participant [партѝсипънт] *n* уча̀стник
participate [партѝсипейт] *v* уча̀ствувам
participation [партѝсипѐйшън] *n* уча̀стие
particular [пъртѝкюлър] *adj* ча̀стен,
специа̀лен, осо̀бен; *n* подро̀бност
particularly [пъртѝкюлъли] *adv* осо̀бено,
специа̀лно, подро̀бно
partner [па̀ртнър] *n* партньо̀р, съдру̀жник
party [па̀рти] *n* гру̀па, па̀ртия, страна̀,
заба̀ва
pass [пас] *v* мина̀вам, пода̀вам,
прока̀рвам; *n* про̀ход
passenger [па̀-сънджър] *n* пъ̀тник, пасажѐр
passion [па̀-шън] *n* страст
passport [па̀спърт] *n* паспо̀рт

past [паст] *n* ми́нало; *adj* ми́нал; *adv* край, покра́й, след

patch [па-тч] *n* кръпка, петно́; *v* кърпя

patent [пе́йтънт] *n* пате́нт

path [пат] *n* пъте́ка, път

patience [пе́йшънс] *n* търпе́ние

patient [пе́йшънт] *n* пацие́нт; *adj* търпели́в

patriot [пе́йтриът] *n* патрио́т

pause [поз] *n* па́уза; *v* спи́рам

pavement [пе́йвмънт] *n* пава́ж, тротоа́р

pay [пей] *v* пла́щам; *n* запла́та, запла́щане

pea [пий] *n* грах

peace [пийс] *n* мир, поко́й, споко́йствие

peaceful [пи́йсфул] *adj* ми́рен, тих, споко́ен, миролюби́в

peach [пийч] *n* пра́скова

peak [пийк] *n* връх

peanut [пи́йнът] *n* фъстък

pear [пе́ър] *n* кру́ша

pearl [пърл] *n* пе́рла, би́сер

peasant [пе́зънт] *n* селянин

pedestrian [педе́стриън] *n* пешехо́дец

peel [пийл] *v* бе́ля, обе́лвам; *n* кора́

pen [пен] *n* перо́, пи́салка

penalty [пе́нълти] *n* наказа́ние, са́нкция

pencil [пе́нсъл] *n* мо́лив

peninsula [пини́нсюла] *n* полуо́стров

people [пи́пъл] *n* хо́ра, наро́д; *v* населя́вам

pepper [пе́пър] *n* пипе́р, чу́шка

percent [пърсе́нт] *n* проце́нт, на сто

perception [пърсéпшън] *n* възприе́мане, възприя́тие

perfect [пъ́рфект] *adj* съвърше́н, цял, завършен

perfect [пърфéкт] *v* усъвърше́нствувам

perform [пърфóрм] *v* изпълня́вам, извършвам

performance [пърфóрмънс] *n* изпълне́ние, представле́ние

performer [пъфóрмър] *n* изпълни́тел

perfume [пъ́рфюм] *n* парфюм

perhaps [пъха́-пс] *adv* мо́же би

period [пи́риъд] *n* перио́д, тóчка

permanent [пъ́рмънънт] *adj* постоя́нен

permission [пърми́шън] *n* разреше́ние

permit [пърми́т] *v* разреша́вам, позволя́вам

permit [пъ́рмит] *n* позволи́телно

persecute [пъ́рсикют] *v* пресле́двам

persecution [пъ́рсикю́шън] *n* пресле́дване

person [пъ́рсън] *n* лице́, чове́к

personal [пъ́рсънъл] *adj* ли́чен

personality [пърсъна́лити] *n* ли́чност

personnel [пърсъне́л] *n* персона́л, ли́чен съста́в

persuade [пърсуе́йд] *v* убежда́вам, приду́мвам, скла́ням

pet [пет] *n* люби́мо живо́тно, га́леник

phase [фейз] *n* фа́за

phenomenon [фенóмънън] *n* явле́ние

philosopher [филóсъфър] *n* философ

philosophy [фило́съфи] *n* филосо́фия
photograph [фо́утъграф] *n* сни́мка
photographer [фъто́гръфър] *n* фотогра́ф
photography [фъто́гръфи] *n* фотогра́фия
phrase [фрейз] *n* фра́за; *v* изразя́вам с
ду́ми
physician [физи́шън] *n* ле́кар
physics [фи́зикс] *n* фи́зика
pianist [пи́ънист] *n* пиани́ст
piano [пиа́ноу] *n* пиа́но
pick [пик] *v* бера́, изби́рам, крада́
picnic [пи́кник] *n* и́злет; *v* пра́вя и́злет
picture [пи́кчър] *n* карти́на, сни́мка, ки́но;
v преста́вям, изобразя́вам
pie [пай] *n* пло́дов сладки́ш, пай
piece [пийс] *n* парче́, къс, част
pig [пиг] *n* прасе́, свиня́
pile [пайл] *n* куп, кла́да; *v* тру́пам,
натру́пвам
pill [пил] *n* ха́пче
pillow [пи́лоу] *n* възгла́вница
pilot [па́йлът] *n* пило́т; *v* пилоти́рам
pin [пин] *n* топли́йка, карфи́ца; *v*
забо́ждам
pine [пайн] *n* бор
pipe [пайп] *n* тръба́, сви́рка, лула́
pistol [пи́стъл] *n* пистоле́т
pity [пи́ти] *n* ми́лост, жа́лост, състрада́ние
place [плейс] *n* мя́сто, ме́стност, къща;
v поста́вям, настаня́вам

plain [плейн] *adj* ясен, прост, обикновен;
n равнина

plan [пла-н] *n* план; *v* планирам

plane [плейн] *n* плоскост, самолет; *adj* плосък, равен

plant [плант] *n* растение, завод; *v* садя, поставям

plastic [пластик] *adj* пластичен, от пластмаса; *n* пластмаса

plateau [платоу] *n* плато

play [плей] *v* играя, свиря; *n* игра, пиеса

player [плейър] *n* играч, актьор, свирач

playground [плейграунд] *n* игрище

pleasant [плезънт] *adj* приятен

please [плийз] *v* задоволявам, радвам, искам, моля

pleasure [плежър] *n* удоволствие, радост

plenty [пленти] *n* изобилие, много, множество

plot [плот] *n* къс земя, заговор; *v* заговорнича

plug [плъг] *n* запушалка, щепсел; *v* запушвам

plum [плъм] *n* слива

plumber [плъмър] *n* водопроводчик

plural [плурър] *adj* множествен; *n* мн. число

plus [плъс] *prep* плюс

pneumonia [нюмоуниъ] *n* пневмония

pocket [пόкит] *n* джоб; *v* слάгам в джόба си

poem [пόуем] *n* стихотворέние, поέма

poet [пόует] *n* поέт

poetry [пόуетри] *n* поέзия

point [пойнт] *n* тόчка, връх, цел, същинά; *v* посόчвам, сόча

poison [пόйзън] *n* отрόва; *v* отрάвям, трόвя

poisonous [пόйзънъс] *adj* отрόвен

police [пълύйс] *n* полύция

policeman [пълύйсмън] *n* полицάй

policy [пόлиси] *n* полύтика, полύца

polish [пόлиш] *v* изглάждам, полύрам; *n* боя, лак

polite [пълάйт] *adj* учтύв, изύскан

political [пълύтикъл] *adj* политύчески

politician [пόлитύшън] *n* политύк

politics [пόлитикс] *n* политύка

poll [пόул] *n* брой на гласовέте; *v* гласύвам

pollute [пълю̀т] *v* замърся̀вам, поквάрям

pollution [пълю̀шън] *n* замърся̀ване

pool [пу́ул] *n* басέйн, вир, лόква

poor [пу́ър] *adj* бέден, недостάтъчен

pope [пόуп] *n* пάпа

popular [пόпюлър] *adj* нарόден, популя̀рен

popularity [пόпюлά-рити] *n* популя̀рност

population [пόпюлέйшън] *n* населέние

pork [порк] *n* свύнско месό

port [порт] *n* пристάнище

portable [пóртъбл] *adj* портати́вен
portrait [пóртрит] *n* портре́т
pose [пóуз] *v* пози́рам, поста́вям; *n* пóза, престру́вка
position [пъзи́шън] *n* положе́ние, пози́ция, длъжност
positive [пóзитив] *adj* положи́телен, си́гурен
possess [пъзéс] *v* притежа́вам, владе́я
possession [пъзéшън] *n* притежа́ние, владе́ние
possibility [пóсиби́лити] *n* възмóжност
possible [пóсибл] *adj* възмóжен
post [пóуст] *n* пост, длъжност; *v* поста́вям
post [пóуст] *n* пóща; *v* изпра́щам по пóщата
poster [пóустър] *n* афи́ш, плака́т
pot [пот] *n* тéнджера, съд, сакси́я
potato [пътéйтоу] *n* карто́ф
pottery [пóтъри] *n* грънча́рство, грънци, кера́мика
poultry [пóултри] *n* дома́шни пти́ци
pound [па́унд] *v* би́я, у́дрям
pour [пор] *v* нали́вам, лéя се
poverty [пóвърти] *n* бéдност
powder [па́удър] *n* прах, пу́дра, бару́т
power [па́уър] *n* си́ла, власт, енéргия
powerful [па́уърфул] *adj* могъщ, си́лен, мóщен

practical [прá-ктикъл] *adj* практи́чен, практи́чески

practice [прá-ктис] *n* прáктика, обичáй

practise [прá-ктис] *v* практику́вам, упражня́вам се

pray [прей] *v* мóля

prayer [прéйър] *n* моли́тва

preach [прийч] *v* проповя́двам, препоръчвам

precaution [прикóушън] *n* предпáзна мя́рка

precinct [при́синкт] *n* полицéйски учáстък

precise [присáйс] *adj* тóчен, преци́зен

precision [приси́жън] *n* тóчност, преци́зност

predecessor [при́дисéсър] *n* предшéственик

predict [приди́кт] *v* предскáзвам

prediction [приди́кшън] *n* предсказáние

prefer [прифъ́р] *v* предпочи́там

preference [прéфърънс] *n* предпочитáние

pregnant [прéгнънт] *adj* брéменна

prejudice [прéджудис] *n* предубеждéние, предразсъдък

preliminary [прили́минъри] *adj* предвари́телен, подготви́телен

preparation [прéпърéйшън] *n* подготóвка, препарáт

preparatory [припá-рътъри] *adj* подготви́телен, предвари́телен

prepare [припéър] *v* приготвям, подготвям

preposition [прéпъзи́шън] *n* предлóг

prescribe [прискрáйб] *v* предпи́свам

prescription [прискрѝпшън] *n* предписа́ние, реце́пта

presence [пре́зънс] *n* присъ́ствие, вид, въ́ншност

present [пре́зънт] *adj* присъ́ствуващ, настоя́щ; *n* пода́рък

present [призе́нт] *v* представя́м, подаря́вам

preservation [пре́зървѐйшън] *n* запа́зване

preserve [призъ́рв] *v* запа́звам, консерви́рам; *n* конфитю́р

presidency [пре́зидънси] *n* председа́телство

president [пре́зидънт] *n* председа́тел, президе́нт

press [прес] *n* пре́са; *v* пресо́вам, прити́скам, гла́дя

pressure [пре́шър] *n* на́тиск, наля́гане

pretend [прите́нд] *v* претенди́рам, престру́вам се

pretext [прѝтекст] *n* прете́кст, предло́г

pretty [прѝти] *adj* ху́бав, прия́тен; *adv* до́ста

prevent [приве́нт] *v* предотвратя́вам, осуетя́вам, пре́ча

prevention [приве́ншън] *n* предотвратя́ване

previous [прѝвиъс] *adj* преди́шен, предвари́телен

prey [прей] *n* пля́чка, же́ртва; *v* крада́, огра́бвам

price [прайс] *n* цена́

pride [прайд] *n* го́рдост, себелюбие

priest [прийст] *n* свещеник
primary [праймъри] *adj* първоначален, главен
primitive [примитив] *adj* първобитен, примитивен
prince [принс] *n* принц
princess [принсес] *n* принцеса
principal [принсипъл] *adj* главен; *n* директор
principle [принсипъл] *n* принцип
print [принт] *n* печат, отпечатък, шрифт, басма; *v* печатам, щампосвам
printer [принтър] *n* печатар
priority [прайорити] *n* предимство
prison [призън] *n* затвор
prisoner [призънър] *n* затворник
private [прайвит] *adj* частен, личен; *n* войник, редник
privately [прайвътли] *adv* тайно, поверително, насаме
privilege [привилидж] *n* привилегия
prize [прайз] *n* награда, премия; *v* ценя
probability [пробъбилити] *n* вероятност
probable [пробъбл] *adj* вероятен
problem [проблъм] *n* въпрос, проблем, задача
procedure [проусиджър] *n* процедура
proceed [проусийд] *v* продължавам, напредвам
process [проусес] *n* процес; *v* обработвам

produce [пръдю́с] *v* произве́ждам, предста́вям, причиня́вам

producer [пръдю́сър] *n* производи́тел, режисьо́р

product [про́дъкт] *n* произведе́ние, проду́кт

production [пръдъ́кшън] *n* произво́дство, постано́вка

profession [профе́шън] *n* профе́сия

professional [профе́шънъл] *adj* професиона́лен

professor [пръфе́сър] *n* профе́сор

profile [про́уфайл] *n* про́фил

profit [про́фит] *n* печа́лба, изго́да; *v* извли́чам печа́лба

profitable [про́фитъбл] *adj* изго́ден, до́ходен

program [про́уграм] *n* програ́ма

progress [про́угрес] *n* напре́дване, напре́дък, прогре́с

progress [проугре́с] *v* напре́двам

prohibit [проухи́бит] *v* забраня́вам, пре́ча

project [проуджект] *v* проекти́рам, хвърлям, изпъквам

project [про́уджект] *n* издатина́, проже́кция

prominent [про́минънт] *adj* изда́ден, забележи́телен, ви́ден

promise [про́мис] *n* обеща́ние; *v* обеща́вам

promising [про́мисинг] *adj* обеща́ващ, наде́жден

promote [прємо́ут] v повиша́вам, подпома́гам

promotion [пръмо́ушън] n повише́ние, промо́ция

pronoun [про́унаун] n местоиме́ние

pronounce [пръна́унс] v произна́сям, обявя́вам

pronunciation [пръне̌нсие́йшън] n произноше́ние

proof [пру́уф] n доказа́телство, изпита́ние, коректу́ра; adj импрегни́ран

propeller [пръпе́лър] n пе́рка, витло́

proper [про́пър] adj со́бствен, подходя́щ, прили́чен

properly [про́пърли] adv прили́чно, подходя́що

property [про́пърти] n со́бственост, сво́йство

proportion [пръпо́ршън] n пропо́рция

proposal [пръпо́узъл] n предложе́ние

propose [пръпо́уз] v предла́гам, възнамеря́вам

prose [про́уз] n про́за

prosecute [про́сикют] v продължа́вам, пресле́двам

prosecution [про́сикю̈шън] n съде́бно пресле́дване

prosper [про́спър] v преуспя́вам

prosperity [проспе́рити] n благополу́чие, преуспя́ване

protect [прътéкт] *v* пазя, закрилям
protection [прътéкшън] *n* покровителство, закрила
protest [проутéст] *v* заявявам, протестирам
protest [прóутест] *n* протéст
proud [прáуд] *adj* горд, надмéнен
prove [прýув] *v* докáзвам, окáзвам се
proverb [прóвърб] *n* послóвица, поговóрка
provide [пръвáйд] *v* снабдявам, предвиждам
province [прóвинс] *n* óбласт, провинция
provincial [пръвиншъл] *adj* провинциáлен
provoke [пръвóук] *v* предизвиквам
public [пъблик] *n* общéственост, хóра, пýблика; *adj* общéствен
publication [пъбликéйшън] *n* публикýване, публикáция, издáние
publicity [пъблисити] *n* глáсност, реклáма
publish [пъблиш] *v* публикýвам, издáвам
publisher [пъблишър] *n* издáтел
pull [пул] *v* дърпам, тéгля
pulse [пълс] *n* пулс; *v* пулсирам, бия
pump [пъмп] *n* пóмпа⁀ *v* пóмпя
punctual [пънкчуъл] *adj* тóчен
punctuality [пънкчуáлити] *n* тóчност
puncture [пънкчър] *n* спýскване на гýма; *v* пýквам
punish [пъниш] *v* накáзвам
punishment [пънишмънт] *n* наказáние
pupil [пюпъл] *n* учениќ

puppet [пѣпит] *n* кýкла
purchase [пѣрчъс] *v* купýвам; *n* покýпка
pure [пю̀ър] *adj* чист
purity [пю̀ърити] *n* чистотá
purple [пѣрпъл] *adj* лилáв, мóрав
purpose [пѣрпъс] *n* намерéние, цел
purse [пърс] *n* портмонé
push [пуш] *v* бýтам, тлáскам; *n* тлáскане
put [пут] *v* слáгам, постáвям

Q

qualification [куѣлификéйшън] *n*
квалификáция, ограничéние
qualify [куóлифай] *v* квалифицѝрам,
определям
quality [куóлити] *n* кáчество
quantity [куóнтити] *n* колѝчество
quarrel [куóръл] *n* кавгá, свáда; *v* кáрам се
queen [куѝйн] *n* царѝца, кралѝца
question [куéсчън] *n* въпрóс, проблéм; *v*
разпѝтвам, оспóрвам
quick [куѝк] *adj* бърз, жив, пъргав
quiet [куáйът] *adj* безшýмен, тих,
спокóен; *n* спокóйствие
quit [куѝт] *v* напýскам, спѝрам
quite [куáйт] *adv* съвсéм, напълно
quotation [куоутéйшън] *n* цитáт
quote [куóут] *v* цитѝрам, котѝрам

R

rabbit [ра́-бит] *n* за́ек
race [рейс] *n* надбя́гване; *v* надбя́гвам се
race [рейс] *n* ра́са
radiation [ре́йдие́йшън] *n* излъчване, радиа́ция
radiator [ре́йдиейтър] *n* радиа́тор
radio [ре́йдиоу] *n* ра́дио
rail [рейл] *n* парапе́т, закача́лка, ре́лса
railroad [ре́йлроуд] *n* желе́зница, жп. ли́ния
railway [ре́йлуей] *n* желе́зница, жп. ли́ния
rain [рейн] *n* дъжд; *v* вали́ дъжд
raise [рейз] *v* вди́га́м, повиша́вам, отгле́ждам
raisin [ре́йзин] *n* стафи́да
rally [ра́-ли] *n* събра́ние, ми́тинг
random [ра́-ндъм] *n* случа́йност; *adj* случа́ен, произво́лен
rape [рейп] *v* изнаси́лвам; *n* изнаси́лване
rapid [ра́-пид] *adj* бърз, стръмен
rare [ре́ър] *adj* ря́дък, необикнове́н
rarity [ре́ърити] *n* ря́дкост, разреде́ност
rash [ра-ш] *n* и́зрив, о́брив
raspberry [ра́збъри] *n* мали́на
rat [ра-т] *n* плъх
rate [рейт] *n* разме́р, сто́йност, ско́рост, сте́пен, съотноше́ние, та́кса

rather [ра́дър] *adv* по–ско́ро, доста́, твъ́рде

ratio [ре́йшиоу] *n* съотноше́ние, пропо́рция

raw [ро] *adj* суро́в, необрабо́тен

razor [ре́йзър] *n* бръсна́ч, самобрисна́чка

reach [рийч] *v* пося́гам, прости́рам, дости́гам; *n* о́бсег

react [риа́–кт] *v* реаги́рам, въздѐйствувам

reaction [риа́–кшън] *n* реа́кция

read [рийд] *v* чета́, у́ча

readiness [ре́динис] *n* гото́вност, охо́та, бързина́

reading [ри́йдинг] *n* че́тене, четиво́, тълкува́ние

ready [ре́ди] *adj* гото́в, скло́нен, бърз, навре́менен

real [ри́ъл] *adj* действи́телен, и́стински

reality [риа́–лити] *n* действи́телност, реа́лност

realize [ри́ълайз] *v* осъществя́вам, разби́рам

really [ри́ъли] *adv* действи́телно, наи́стина

reason [ри́йзън] *n* причи́на, основа́ние, ра́зум

receipt [рисий́т] *n* получа́ване, квита́нция, постъпле́ния

receive [риси́йв] *v* получа́вам, прие́мам

recent [ри́сънт] *adj* неотда́внашен, нов, съвре́менен

recipe [ре́сипи] *n* реце́пта, предписа́ние

recipient [риси́пиънт] *n* получа́тел; *adj* възприемчи́в

recognition [рѐкъгнѝшън] *n* разпознаване, признание

recognize [рѐкъгнайз] *v* разпознавам, различавам, признавам

recommend [рѐкъмѐнд] *v* препоръчвам, поверявам

recommendation [рѐкъмендѐйшън] *n* препоръка

record [рикорд] *v* записвам, отбелязвам

record [рѐкърд] *n* документ, рекорд, грамофонна плоча

recover [рикѐвър] *v* съвзѐмам се, възвръщам си

recovery [рикѐвъри] *n* съвзѐмане, възстановяване

red [ред] *adj* червен

reduce [ридюс] *v* намалявам, понижавам

reduction [ридъкшън] *n* намаляване, съкращение

refer [рифър] *v* отправям, насочвам, споменавам

referee [рѐфъри] *n* рефер, съдия

reference [рѐфърънс] *n* споменаване, справка

reflection [рифлѐкшън] *n* отражение, размишление

reform [риформ] *v* преустройвам; *n* преобразование, реформа

refresh [рифрѐш] *v* опреснявам, освежавам

refreshment [рифре́шмънт] *n* освежа́ване, заку́ска

refugee [ре́фюджи] *n* бежане́ц, емигра́нт

refund [рифъ́нд] *v* възстановя́вам

refuse [рифю́з] *v* отка́звам

regard [рига́рд] *v* счи́там, уважа́вам

regarding [рига́рдинг] *prep* отно́сно

region [ри́джън] *n* о́бласт, райо́н, сфе́ра

regret [ригре́т] *v* съжаля́вам; *n* съжале́ние, разкая́ние

regular [ре́гюлър] *adj* редо́вен, постоя́нен, пра́вилен

regularly [ре́гюлъли] *adv* редо́вно, постоя́нно, съвърше́но

rehearsal [рихъ́рсъл] *n* репети́ция

rehearse [рихъ́рс] *v* репети́рам, преповта́рям

reject [ридже́кт] *v* отказвам, отхвъ́рлям

rejection [ридже́кшън] *n* о́тказ, отхвъ́рляне

relation [риле́йшън] *n* отноше́ние, връ́зка, родни́на

relatively [ре́лътивли] *adv* относи́телно

relax [рила́-кс] *v* отпу́щвам, почи́вам се

relaxation [ри́ла-ксе́йшън] *n* отпу́щане, почи́вка

release [рили́йс] *v* освобожда́вам, пу́скам

reliable [рила́йъбл] *adj* си́гурен, наде́жден

reliance [рила́йънс] *n* дове́рие, упова́ние

relief [рили́йф] *n* облекче́ние, успокое́ние, по́мощ

relieve [рилийв] *v* облекчавам, подпомагам, сменям

religion [рилиджън] *n* религия, вяра

religious [религджъс] *adj* религиозен, верующ

reluctance [рилъктънс] *n* нежелание, неохота

reluctant [рилъктънт] *adj* неохотен, неподатлив

rely [рилай] *v* разчитам, осланям се

remain [римейн] *v* оставам, стоя; *n* останки, развалини

remark [римарк] *v* забелязвам; *n* забележка

removal [римувъл] *n* преместване, отстраняване, уволняване

remove [римув] *v* премествам, отстранявам, уволнявам

renew [риню] *v* подновявам, възобновявам

renewal [ринюъл] *n* подновяване, възобновяване

rent [рент] *n* наем, рента; *v* наемам, давам под наем

repair [рипеър] *v* поправям

repeat [рипийт] *v* повтарям, рецитирам

repetition [репитишън] *n* повторение

replace [риплейс] *v* възстановявам, заменям

reply [риплай] *v* отговарям, отвръщам; *n* отговор

report [рипорт] *v* съобщавам, докладвам; *n* доклад, гръм

reporter [рипо́ртър] *n* до́писник, репортьо́р

represent [ре́призе́нт] *v* предста́вям, представля́вам, опи́свам

representative [ре́призе́нтътив] *n* предста́вител

reproduce [ри́пръдю́с] *v* възпроизве́ждам

reproduction [ри́пръдъ̀кшън] *n* възпроизве́ждане, репроду́кция

reptile [ре́птайл] *n* влечу́го

republic [рипъ̀блик] *n* репу́блика

republican [рипъ̀бликън] *n* република́нец

reputation [ре́пютейшън] *n* и́ме, репута́ция

request [рикуе́ст] *n* и́скане, молба́, тъ̀рсене; *v* изи́сквам

require [рикуа́йър] *v* и́скам, изи́сквам, нужда́я се

requirement [рикуа́йърмънт] *n* изи́скване, ну́жда

research [рисъ̀рч] *n* изсле́дване, проу́чване; *v* проу́чвам

reserve [ризъ̀рв] *v* запа́звам; *n* запа́с, сдъ̀ржаност

reside [риза́йд] *v* живе́я, пребива́вам

residence [ре́зидънс] *n* местожи́телство, резиде́нция

resident [ре́зидънт] *n* жи́тел

residential [ре́зиде́ншъл] *adj* жи́лищен

resign [риза́йн] *v* изли́зам в оста́вка, оттéглям се

resignation [рéзигнейшън] *n* остáвка,
примирéние
resist [ризúст] *v* съпротивля́вам се,
устоя́вам
resistance [ризúстънс] *n* съпротúва, отпóр
respect [риспéкт] *n* уважéние, отношéние;
v почúтам
respectability [риспéктъбúлити] *n* почтéност
respectable [риспéктъбл] *adj* почтéн,
прилúчен
respective [риспéктив] *adj* съотвéтен
respiration [рéспирéйшън] *n* дúшане
respond [риспóнд] *v* отговáрям, реагúрам
response [риспóнс] *n* óтговор, óтзив
responsibility [риспóнсибúлити] *n*
отговóрност
responsible [риспóнсибл] *adj* отговóрен
rest [рест] *n* почúвка, покóй; *v* почúвам
rest [рест] *n* остáтък
restaurant [рéстъран] *n* ресторáнт
restrict [ристрúкт] *v* ограничáвам
restriction [ристрúкшън] *n* ограничéние
result [ризъ́лт] *v* послéдвам, произтúчам;
n послéдица, резултáт
retail [рúтейл] *n* продáжба на дрéбно
retire [ритáйър] *v* оттéглям, излúзам в
остáвка
retired [ритáйърд] *adj* пенсионúран
retirement [ритáйърмънт] *n* остáвка,
оттéгляне

return [ритъ́рн] *v* връ́щам; *n* връ́щане
revenge [риве́ндж] *v* отмъща́вам; *n* отмъще́ние
revenue [ре́виню] *n* приход, постъпле́ния
review [ривю́] *v* разгле́ждам, рецензи́рам; *n* пре́глед, реце́нзия
revise [рива́йз] *v* прегле́ждам, попра́вям
revolution [ре́вълюшън] *n* въртѐне, револю́ция
reward [риуо́рд] *n* награ́да; *v* възнагражда́вам
rhyme [райм] *n* ри́ма, стихотворе́ние
rib [риб] *n* ребро́
ribbon [ри́бън] *n* па́нделка, ле́нта
rice [райс] *n* ори́з
rich [рич] *adj* бога́т, разко́шен
richness [ри́чнис] *n* бога́тство
rid [рид] *v* освобожда́вам, изба́вям
ride [райд] *v* я́здя, во́зя се
rifle [ра́йфъл] *n* пу́шка
right [райт] *adj* прав, ве́рен, де́сен; *n* дя́сно; *adv* вя́рно, пра́во
ring [ринг] *n* пръ́стен, ринг, кръг; *v* звъня́
rise [райз] *v* ста́вам, изди́гам се, изгря́вам
risk [риск] *n* опа́сност, риск; *v* риску́вам
risky [ри́ски] *adj* опа́сен, риско́ван
rival [ра́йвъл] *n* съпе́рник, конкуре́нт; *v* съпе́рнича, конкури́рам
rivalry [ра́йвълри] *n* скъпе́рничество
river [ри́вър] *n* река́

road [ро́уд] *n* шосе́, път
roast [ро́уст] *v* пека́; *n* пе́чено месо́
rob [роб] *v* гра́бя, огра́бвам
robber [ро́бър] *n* кра́дец
robbery [ро́бъри] *n* грабе́ж
rock [рок] *n* скала́, канара́
rocket [ро́кит] *n* раке́та
rodent [ро́удънт] *n* гриза́ч
role [ро́ул] *n* ро́ля
Roman [ро́умън] *adj* ри́мски
romance [роума́-нс] *n* рома́нтика, рома́нс
romantic [роума́-нтик] *adj* романти́чен
roof [ру́уф] *n* по́крив, подсло́н
room [ру́ум] *n* ста́я, мя́сто
rooster [ру́стър] *n* пете́л
root [ру́ут] *n* ко́рен
rope [ро́уп] *n* въже́
rose [ро́уз] *n* ро́за; *adj* ро́зов
rot [рот] *n* гни́ене; *v* гни́я
rotate [роуте́йт] *v* въртя́
rotation [роуте́йшън] *n* върте́не, кръгова́т
rough [ръф] *adj* груб, бу́рен, необрабо́тен
round [ра́унд] *adj* кръ́гъл; *n* кръг,
обико́лка, тур *v* закръгля́м; *prep* зад,
о́коло
route [рут] *n* път, маршру́т
row [ро́у] *n* реди́ца, ред
royal [ро́йъл] *adj* кра́лски, великоле́пен
royalty [ро́йълти] *n* кра́лска осо́ба,
а́вторски хонора́р

rub [ръб] *v* трия, търкам
rubber [ръбър] *n* гума, каучук
rubbish [ръбиш] *n* боклук, смет, глупости
rude [руд] *adj* груб, неучтив
rug [ръг] *n* килим
ruin [руин] *v* разрушавам, разорявам; *n* гибел, развалина
rule [рул] *v* управлявам, решавам; *n* правило, власт
ruler [рулър] *n* владетел, линия
rum [ръм] *n* ром
rumor [румър] *n* слух, мълва; *v* пръскам слух
run [рън] *v* тичам, движа се
runner [ръннър] *n* бегач, пратеник
rural [руръл] *adj* селски
rush [ръш] *v* втурвам се, спускам се, прибързвам, нахлувам
rust [ръст] *v* ръждясвам; *n* ръжда
rusty [ръсти] *adj* ръждясел, ръждив, извехтял

S

sack [са-к] *n* чувал *v* уволнявам
sacred [сейкрид] *adj* свещен
sad [са-д] *adj* тъжен, мрачен
safe [сейф] *adj* невредим, сигурен; *n* сейф

safety [сéйфти] *n* сигурност, безопасност
sail [сейл] *n* кóрабно платнó, мóрско пътýване; *v* пътýвам по морé
sailor [сéйлър] *n* моряк
saint [сейнт] *n* светéц
salad [сá-лъд] *n* салáта
salary [сá-лъри] *n* заплáта
sale [сейл] *n* продáжба
salesman [сéйлзмън] *n* продавáч
salt [солт] *n* сол; *v* посолявам
salty [сóлти] *adj* солéн
same [сейм] *adj* същ
sample [сá-мпл] *n* мóстра; *v* изпрóбвам
sanction [сá-нкшън] *n* одобрéние, сáнкция; *v* одобрявам
sand [са-нд] *n* пясък
sandal [сá-ндъл] *n* сáндал
sandwich [сá-ндуич] *n* сáндвич; *v* притискам
sanitation [сá-нитéйшън] *n* здравеопáзване
Santa Claus [сáнта клóз] *n* Дядо Мраз
sarcasm [сáрка-эм] *n* саркáзъм
satire [сá-тайър] *n* сáтира
satisfaction [сá-тисфá-кшън] *n* задовóлство, удовлетворéние
satisfactory [сá-тисфá-ктъри] *adj* задоволителен
satisfy [сá-тисфай] *v* задоволявам, убеждáвам
Saturday [сá-търди] *n* събота

saucer [со́усър] *n* чини́йка за ча́ша
sausage [со́сидж] *n* сала́м, на́деница
save [сейв] *v* спася́вам, спестя́вам; *prep* осве́н
saving [се́йвинг] *adj* пестели́в; *n* спестя́вания
say [сей] *v* ка́звам
scale [скейл] *n* маща́б, ска́ла, везни́
scandal [ска́-ндъл] *n* сканда́л, клю́ка
scandalize [ска́-ндълайз] *v* шоки́рам
scare [ске́ър] *v* пла́ша; *n* па́ника
scene [сийн] *n* сце́на, гле́дка
scenery [си́йнъри] *n* деко́ри, приро́да
sceptic [ске́птик] *n* скепти́к
school [скул] *n* учи́лище, шко́ла; *v* обуча́вам
schoolboy [ску́лбой] *n* учени́к
schoolgirl [ску́лгърл] *n* учени́чка
science [са́йънс] *n* нау́ка
scientific [са́йънтифик] *adj* нау́чен
scientist [са́йънтист] *n* у́чен
scissors [си́зърс] *noun pl* но́жици
score [скор] *n* сме́тка, резулта́т, музика́лна партиту́ра
scratch [скра́-ч] *v* дра́скам; *n* драскоти́на
scream [скрийм] *v* пи́скам; *n* пи́сък
screen [скрийн] *n* парава́н, екра́н
screw [скру] *n* винт, витло́; *v* зави́нтам
sculptor [скъ́лптър] *n* ску́лптор
sculpture [скъ́лпчър] *v* ва́я; *n* скулпту́ра

sea [сий] *n* морé
seal [сийл] *n* печáт, тюлéн; *v* запечáтвам
search [сърч] *v* тъ́рся; *n* тъ́рсене,
претъ́рсване
season [сúйзън] *n* сезóн, годúшно врéме; *v*
подпрáвям
seat [сийт] *n* мя́сто, седалище
second [сéкънд] *a* втóри; *n* секýнда
secret [сúкрит] *adj* тáен; *n* тáйна
secretary [сéкрътъри] *n* секретáр
seduce [сидю́с] *v* прелъстя́вам, привлúчам
see [сий] *v* вúждам, разбúрам
seed [сийд] *n* сéме
seek [сийк] *v* тъ́рся, дúря
seem [сийм] *v* изглéждам
select [силéкт] *v* подбúрам
selection [силéкшън] *n* подбóр, селéкция
self [селф] *pron* сам, сéбе си
selfish [сéлфиш] *adj* егоистúчен
selfishness [сéлфишнис] *n* егоúзъм
sell [сел] *v* продáвам, измáмвам
senate [сéнит] *n* сенáт
senator [сéнътър] *n* сенáтор
send [сенд] *v* изпрáщам
senior [сúниър] *adj* стар, стáрши
sensation [сенсéйшън] *n* усéщане, сензáция
sensational [сенсéйшънъл] *adj* сензациóнен
sense [сенс] *n* чýвство, сетивó, рáзум,
значéние
sensible [сéнсъбл] *adj* разýмен

sentence [сéнтънс] *n* изречéние, присъ́да; *v* осъждам

separate [сéпърит] *adj* отдéлен

separate [сéпърейт] *v* раздéлям

separation [сéпърéйшън] *n* отдéляне, раздя́ла

September [септéмбър] *n* септéмври

series [сúрийз] *n* сéрия, редúца

serious [сúриъс] *adj* сериóзен

sermon [съ́рмън] *n* прóповед

servant [съ́рвънт] *n* слугá, прислýжник

serve [съ́рв] *v* слýжа на, сервúрам

service [съ́рвис] *n* слýжба, услýга, сервúране

session [сéшън] *n* заседáние, сéсия

set [сет] *v* заля́звам, постáвям, втвърдя́вам; *n* сервúз, апарáт

seven [сéвън] *num* сéдем

seventeen [сéвънтúйн] *num* седемнáдесет

seventy [сéвънти] *num* седемдесéт

several [сéвърл] *adj* ня́колко, разлúчен

sew [сóу] *v* шúя, зашúвам

sex [секс] *n* пол, секс

shadow [шáдоу] *n* ся́нка; *v* засéнчвам, следя́

shake [шейк] *v* клáтя се, разколебáвам

shaky [шéйки] *adj* несúгурен, колеблúв

shall [шал] *v* ще

shame [шейм] *n* срам, позóр; *v* засрáмвам

shape [шейп] *n* фо́рма, о́браз, калъ́п; *v* оформям

share [ше́ър] *n* дял, пай, уча́стие, а́кция; *v* поде́лям

sharehold [ше́ърхо́улдър] *n* акционе́р

shark [шарк] *n* аку́ла

sharp [шарп] *adj* о́стър, си́лен, у́мен

sharpen [ша́рпън] *v* о́стря

shave [шейв] *v* бръ́сна се

she [ши] *pron* тя

sheep [шийп] *n* овца́

sheet [шийт] *n* лист, чарша́ф

shelf [шелф] *n* поли́ца, рафт

shell [шел] *n* черу́пка, ги́лза; *v* обстре́лвам

shield [шийлд] *n* щит; *v* закри́лям

shine [шайн] *v* гре́я, блистя́

ship [шип] *n* ко́раб; *v* експеди́рам

shipment [ши́пмънт] *n* пра́тка, експеди́ране

shirt [шърт] *n* ри́за

shiver [ши́вър] *v* трепе́ря; *n* тръ́пка

shoe [шу] *n* обу́вка, подко́ва

shoot [шу́ут] *v* стре́лям, изра́ствам

shop [шоп] *n* магази́н, работи́лница, цех; *v* пазару́вам

shopping [шо́пинг] *n* пазару́ване

shore [шор] *n* бряг

short [шорт] *adj* къс, кра́тък, ни́сък

shoulder [шо́улдър] *n* ра́мо

shout [ша́ут] *v* ви́кам; *n* вик

shovel [шъ́вьл] *n* лопа́та

show [шóу] *v* покáзвам; *n* излóжба, представлéние

shower [шáуър] *n* преваляване, душ

shut [шът] *v* затвáрям

shy [шай] *adj* срамежлѝв, стеснѝтелен

shyness [шáйнис] *n* свенлѝвост

sick [сик] *adj* бóлен, повръщащ

side [сайд] *n* странá

sight [сайт] *n* зрéние, глéдка, забележѝтелности

sign [сайн] *n* знак, прѝзнак, нáдпис; *v* дáвам знак, подпѝсвам

signal [сѝгнъл] *n* сигнáл, знак; *v* сигнализѝрам

signature [сѝгнъчър] *n* пóдпис

significance [сигнѝфикънс] *n* значéние

significant [сигнѝфикънт] *adj* значѝтелен, вáжен

silence [сáйлънс] *n* мълчáние, тишинá

silent [сáйлънт] *adj* мълчалѝв, тих

silk [силк] *adj* копрѝнен

silver [сѝлвър] *n* сребрó

similar [сѝмилър] *adj* подóбен, схóден

similarity [сѝмилá-рити] *n* прѝлика, схóдство

simple [сѝмпъл] *adj* прост, обикновéн, откровéн, глýпав

sin [син] *n* грях; *v* прегрешáвам

since [синс] *prep* от; *conj* откáкто, тъй катó

sincere [синси́ър] *adj* и́скрен
sincerity [синсе́рити] *n* и́скреност
sing [синг] *v* пе́я, възпя́вам
singer [си́нгър] *n* певе́ц
sink [синк] *v* потъ́вам, спа́дам; *n* ми́вка
sir [сър] *n* господи́не
siren [са́йрън] *n* сире́на
sister [си́стър] *n* сестра́
sit [сит] *v* седя́
situation [си́чюе́йшън] *n* местоположе́ние, длъ́жност
six [сикс] *num* шест
sixteen [си́кстийн] *num* шестна́десет
sixty [си́ксти] *num* шестдесе́т
size [сайз] *n* разме́р, но́мер
skate [скейт] *n* кънка́; *v* пързя́лям се с кънки́
skeleton [ске́литън] *n* скеле́т, ски́ца
ski [ский] *v* ка́рам ски
skill [скил] *n* сръ́чност, уме́ние
skin [скин] *n* ко́жа
skirt [скърт] *n* пола́
skull [скъл] *n* че́реп
sky [скай] *n* небе́
slang [сла́-нг] *n* сланг, жарго́н
slap [сла-п] *v* пля́скам; *n* плесни́ца
slave [слейв] *n* роб
sleep [слийп] *v* спя; *n* сън
sleeve [слийв] *n* ръка́в, му́фа
slice [слайс] *n* ре́зен, фили́я; *v* ре́жа

slight [слайт] *adj* незначителен, слаб
slim [слим] *adj* строен, слаб
slip [слип] *v* хлъзгам
slipper [слипър] *n* чехъл
slow [слоу] *adj* бавен
small [смол] *adj* малък, дребен
smart [смарт] *adj* елегантен, умен
smell [смел] *v* мириша; *n* миризма
smile [смайл] *v* усмихвам; *n* усмивка
smoke [смоук] *n* пушек; *v* пуша
smoker [смоукър] *n* пушач
smooth [смуут] *adj* гладък, равен
snack [сна-к] *n* лека закуска
snake [снейк] *n* змия
sneeze [снийз] *v* кихам
snore [снор] *v* хъркам; *n* хъркане
snow [сноу] *n* сняг; *v* вали сняг
so [соу] *adv* така, толкова; *conj* така че
soap [соуп] *n* сапун; *v* сапунисвам
sober [соубър] *adj* трезвен, сериозен
soccer [сокър] *n* футбол
socialism [соушълизм] *n* социализъм
socialist [соушълист] *adj* социалистически
society [съсайъти] *n* общество,
дружество,компания
sock [сок] *n* къс чорап, стелка
soda [соуда] *n* сода, газирана вода
sofa [соуф] *n* канапе
soft [софт] *adj* мек, тих, нежен, лек
softness [софтнис] *n* мекост, нежност

soil [сойл] *n* по́чва; *v* изца́пвам
soldier [со́улджър] *n* войни́к
sole [со́ул] *n* подме́тка; *adj* еди́нствен
solid [со́лид] *adj* твърд, здрав
solve [солв] *v* разреша́вам
some [съм] *pron* ня́кой, ня́какъв, ня́колко
somebody [съмбъди] *pron* ня́кой
something [съмтинг] *pron* не́що
son [сън] *n* син
song [сонг] *n* пе́сен
son—in—law [сън ин ло] *n* зет
soon [су́ун] *adv* ско́ро, ведна́га
sorrow [со́роу] *n* тъга́; *v* тъгу́вам
sorry [со́ри] *adj* жа́лък, изпи́тващ
съжале́ние
soul [со́ул] *n* душа́
sound [са́унд] *n* звук, шум; *v* звуча́; *adj*
здрав, си́лен
soup [су́уп] *n* су́па
sour [са́уър] *adj* кисел, раздразни́телен
south [са́ут] *n* юг
southern [са́дърн] *adj* ю́жен
sow [со́у] *v* се́я
space [спейс] *n* простра́нство, ко́смос
spare [спе́ър] *v* щадя́, икономи́свам; *adj*
оскъ́ден, резе́рвен
spark [спарк] *n* и́скра
sparrow [спа́-роу] *n* врабче́
speak [спийк] *v* гово́ря

speaker [спийкър] *n* оратор, говорител, спикер

speaking [спийкинг] *adj* говорещ

special [спешъл] *adj* особен, специален

specialist [спешълист] *n* специалист

species [спийшийз] *n* вид, порода

specific [песифик] *adj* специфичен, определен

spectator [спектейтър] *n* зрител

speech [спийч] *n* говор, реч

speed [спийд] *n* бързина, скорост

spell [спел] *v* прочитам буква по буква

spelling [спелинг] *n* правопис

spend [спенд] *v* харча, израсходвам

sphere [сфиър] *n* сфера, кълбо, област

spice [спайс] *n* подправка за ястие

spider [спайдър] *n* паяк

spill [спил] *v* разливам

spinach [спинидж] *n* спанак

spine [спайн] *n* гръбнак, бодил

spirit [спирит] *n* дух, призрак, смелост, спирт

spit [спит] *v* плюя

spite [спайт] *n* злоба

split [сплит] *v* цепя; *n* разцепление

spoil [спойл] *v* развалям, разглезвам; *n* плячка

spokesman [споуксмън] *n* говорител

sponge [спъндж] *n* гъба

spoon [спуун] *n* лъжица

sport [спорт] *n* спорт
spot [спот] *n* петно́, мя́сто
spouse [спа́уз] *n* съпру́г
spray [спрей] *v* пръ́скам
spread [спред] *v* разсти́лам, прости́рам; *n* разпростране́ние
spring [спринг] *v* ска́чам; *n* пружи́на, и́звор, про́лет
spy [спай] *v* шпиони́рам; *n* шпио́нин
square [скуе́ър] *n* квадра́т, площа́д
squeeze [скуи́йз] *v* сти́скам, изце́ждам
stability [стъби́лити] *n* устойчи́вост
stable [стейбл] *adj* устойчи́в
stadium [сте́йдиъм] *n* стадио́н
staff [стаф] *n* щаб, персона́л
stage [стейдж] *n* сце́на, фа́за, ета́п; *v* поста́вям
stair [сте́ър] *n* стъпа́ло, стълба́
staircase [сте́ъркейс] *n* стъ́лбище
stamp [ста-мп] *n* по́щенска ма́рка
stand [ста-нд] *v* стоя́, нами́рам, търпя́; *n* пози́ция, щанд
standard [ста́-ндърд] *n* станда́рт, но́рма; *adj* станда́ртен
star [стар] *n* звезда́
start [старт] *v* тръ́гвам, запо́чвам
starve [старв] *v* гладу́вам
state [стейт] *n* състоя́ние, държа́ва, щат; *v* заявя́вам; *adj* държа́вен
statement [сте́йтмънт] *n* изявле́ние

statesman [стéйтсмън] *n* държáвник
station [стéйшън] *n* гáра, стáнция
statistics [стътúстикс] *n* статúстика
statue [стá-тю] *n* стáтуя
status [стéйтъс] *n* положéние
stay [стей] *v* остáвам, престоя́вам; *n*
престóй
steak [стейк] *n* пържóла
steam [стийм] *n* пáра
steel [стийл] *n* стомáна
step [степ] *n* стъ́пка; *v* стъ́пвам
stick [стик] *n* пръ́чка, пáлка
stick [стик] *v* пъ́хам, лепя́
still [стил] *adj* тих, неподвúжен
stillness [стúлнис] *n* тишинá
stitch [стич] *n* бод; *v* шúя
stockholder [стóкхóулдър] *n* акционéр
stomach [стъ́мък] *n* стомáх
stone [стóун] *n* кáмък, костúлка
stop [стоп] *v* спúрам, престáвам; *n*
спúране, спúрка
storage [стóридж] *n* съхранéние, склад
store [стор] *n* запáс; *v* складúрам
storm [сторм] *n* бýря
story [стóри] *n* прúказка
straight [стрейт] *adj* прав, пряк, чéстен,
úскрен; *adv* тóчно
strange [стрейндж] *adj* стрáнен, чужд
stranger [стрéйнджър] *n* непознáт
strategy [стрá-тиджи] *n* стратéгия

strawberry [стро́бъри] *n* я́года
stream [стрийм] *n* пото́к; *v* тека́, струя́
street [стрийт] *n* у́лица
strength [стрент] *n* си́ла
strengthen [стре́нтън] *v* заси́лвам, укре́пвам
stretch [стреч] *v* опъ́вам
strict [стрикт] *adj* строг
strictly [стри́ктли] *adv* стро́го, то́чно
strike [страйк] *v* у́дрям, стачку́вам; *n* ста́чка
string [стринг] *n* връв, стру́на
strip [стрип] *n* и́вица, ле́нта
stroll [строл] *v* разхо́ждам се; *n* разхо́дка
strong [стронг] *adj* си́лен, твърд, як
struggle [стръ́гъл] *v* бо́ря се, мъ́ча се; *n* борба́
student [стю́дънт] *n* студе́нт
studio [стю́диоу] *n* сту́дио, ателие́
study [стъ́ди] *v* у́ча, сле́двам; *n* кабине́т, сту́дия
stuff [стъф] *n* вещество́, мате́рия
stupid [стю́пид] *adj* глу́пав, тъп
style [стайл] *n* стил, на́чин, мо́да
subject [съ́бджикт] *n* по́даник, по́длог, те́ма, предме́т
submit [събми́т] *v* подчиня́вам се, предста́вям
subscribe [събскра́йб] *v* абони́рам се
subscription [събскри́пшън] *n* абонаме́нт

substance [сѝбстънс] *n* субстáнция, вещество́

substitute [сѝбститют] *v* замéням; *n* замéстник, замести́тел

substitution [сѝбститю̀шън] *n* замéстване

subway [сѝбуей] *n* метро́

succeed [съкси́йд] *v* успя́вам, наследя́вам

success [съксéс] *n* успéх

successful [съксéсфул] *adj* успéшен, сполучли́в

such [съч] *pron* такѝв, такѝва

suck [сък] *v* сѝча, смѝча

sudden [сѝдън] *adj* внезáпен

sue [сю] *v* дáвам под съд

suffer [сѝфър] *v* страдам

sufficient [съфѝшънт] *adj* достáтъчен

sugar [шу́гър] *n* зáхар

suggest [съджéст] *v* подскáзвам, внушáвам, предлáгам

suicide [сю̀сайд] *n* самоубѝйство

suit [сют] *n* костю́м, комплéкт, процéс; *v* подхо́ждам, задоволя́вам

suitcase [сю̀ткейс] *n* кѝфар

suite [суи́йт] *n* апартамéнт

sum [съм] *n* су́ма, сбор

summer [сѝмър] *n* ля́то

summit [сѝмит] *n* връх, врѝхна то́чка

sun [сън] *n* слѝнце

Sunday [сѝнди] *n* недéля

sunrise [сѝнрайз] *n* ѝзгрев

sunset [сънсет] *n* за́лез

superficial [су́пърфи́шъл] *adj* повъ́рхностен

superior [супи́ърър] *adj* по́-висш

superiority [супи́ърио́рити] *n* превъзхо́дство

superstition [су́пърсти́шън] *n* суеве́рие

supervise [су́първайз] *v* надзира́вам

supervision [су́първи́жън] *n* надзо́р

supper [съ́пър] *n* вече́ря

supply [съпла́й] *v* снабдя́вам, доста́вям; *n* снабдя́ване, предла́гане

support [съпо́рт] *v* поддъ́ржам, издъ́ржам; *n* поддръ́жка, опо́ра

supporter [съпо́ртър] *n* поддръ́жник

suppose [съпо́уз] *v* предпола́гам, ми́сля

sure [шу́ър] *adj* си́гурен, уве́рен; *adv* разби́ра се

surface [съ́рфис] *n* повъ́рхност

surgeon [съ́рджън] *n* хиру́рг

surgery [съ́рджъри] *n* хиру́ргия

surname [съ́рнейм] *n* пре́зиме

surprise [съпра́йз] *n* изнена́да, учу́дване; *v* изнена́двам

survival [сърва́йвъл] *n* оцеля́ване

survive [сърва́йв] *v* оцеля́вам

suspect [съ́спект] *n* заподозря́но лице́

suspect [съспе́кт] *v* подози́рам

suspicion [съспи́шън] *n* подозре́ние

suspicious [съспи́шъс] *adj* подозри́телен

swallow [суо́лоу] *v* гъ́лтам

swear [суе́ър] *v* кълна́ се, псу́вам

sweat [суéт] *n* пот; *v* потя́ се
sweater [суéтър] *n* пуло́вер
sweep [суи́йп] *v* мета́
sweeper [су́йпър] *n* мета́ч
sweet [су́йт] *adj* сла́дък, мил; *n* бонбо́н, сладки́ш
sweetness [су́йтнис] *n* сла́дост
swell [суéл] *v* поду́вам се
swift [су́йфт] *adj* бърз
swiftness [су́йфтнис] *n* бързина́
swim [су́йм] *v* плу́вам; *n* плу́ване
swimmer [су́ймър] *n* плуве́ц
sword [суо́рд] *n* меч, са́бя
syllable [си́лъбл] *n* сри́чка
symbol [си́мбъл] *n* знак, си́мвол
symmetry [си́митри] *n* симе́трия
sympathize [си́мпътайз] *v* съчу́вствувам
sympathy [си́мпъти] *n* съчу́вствие
symphony [си́мфъни] *n* симфо́ния
synonym [си́нъним] *n* синони́м
syrup [са́йръп] *n* сиро́п
system [си́стъм] *n* систе́ма

T

table [те́йбъл] *n* ма́са, та́блица
tact [та-кт] *n* такт
tactics [та́-ктикс] *noun pl* та́ктика

tag [та-г] *n* етике́т
tail [тейл] *n* опа́шка, край, тура́
tailor [те́йлър] *n* шива́ч
take [тейк] *v* взе́мам, зана́сям, заве́ждам
talent [та́-лънт] *n* тала́нт
talk [ток] *n* ра́зговор, бесе́да; *v* разгова́рям, гово́ря
tall [тол] *adj* висо́к
tank [та-нк] *n* танк, резервоа́р
tap [та-п] *n* кран, чешма́, поту́ване; *v* то́ча питие́, поту́пвам
tape [тейп] *n* ле́нта; *v* завъ́рзвам
target [та́ргит] *n* цел, мише́на
tariff [та́-риф] *n* тари́фа
task [та-ск] *n* зада́ча
taste [тейст] *n* вкус; *v* опи́твам
tax [та-кс] *n* да́нък; *v* обла́гам с да́нък
taxation [та-ксе́йшън] *n* обла́гане, да́нъчна систе́ма
taxi [та́-кси] *n* такси́
taxpayer [та́-кспейър] *n* данъкопла́тец
tea [тий] *n* чай
teach [тийч] *v* обуча́вам, препода́вам
teacher [ти́йчър] *n* учи́тел, преподава́тел
team [тийм] *n* отбо́р, тим, кома́нда
tear [ти́ър] *n* сълза́
tear [те́ър] *v* къ́сам, дера́
teaspoon [ти́йспун] *n* ча́ена лъжи́чка
technical [те́кникъл] *adj* техни́чески

technology [текно́лъджи] *n* те́хника, техноло́гия

telephone [те́лифоун] *n* телефо́н; *v* телефони́рам

television [те́ливижън] *n* телеви́зия

tell [тел] *v* ка́звам, разка́звам, различа́вам

temperature [те́мпричър] *n* температу́ра

temporary [те́мпъръри] *adj* вре́менен

tempt [темпт] *v* изкуша́вам, съблазня́вам

temptation [темпте́йшън] *n* изкуше́ние, събла́зън

ten [тен] *num* де́сет

tenant [те́нънт] *n* наема́тел, квартира́нт

tender [те́ндър] *adj* не́жен, кре́хък

tenderness [те́ндърнис] *n* не́жност

tennis [те́нис] *n* те́нис

tension [те́ншън] *n* напреже́ние

tent [тент] *n* пала́тка

term [търм] *n* срок, те́рмин, усло́вия

terrible [те́ръбл] *adj* ужа́сен

terrify [те́рифай] *v* ужася́вам

territory [те́ритъри] *n* терито́рия

terror [те́рър] *n* у́жас, теро́р

test [тест] *n* прове́рка, изпита́ние; *v* изпи́твам, проверя́вам

testify [те́стифай] *v* свиде́телствувам, удостоверя́вам

text [текст] *n* текст

textbook [те́кстбук] *n* уче́бник

textile [те́кстайл] *n* тексти́л

than [да-н] *conj* отколкото
thank [та-нк] *v* благодаря́
that [да-т] *pron* то́зи, о́нзи, ко́йто; *conj* че, за да
theater [ти́ътър] *n* теа́тър
theatrical [тиа́-трикъл] *adj* театра́лен
theft [тефт] *n* кра́жба
their [де́ър] *pron* те́хен
them [дем] *pron* тях, ги
theme [тийм] *n* те́ма
themselves [демсе́лвз] *pron* се́бе си, се
then [ден] *adv* тога́ва, след това́
theory [ти́ъри] *n* тео́рия
there [де́ър] *adv* там
thermometer [търмо́митър] *n* термоме́тър
these [дийз] *pron* те́зи
they [дей] *pron* те, ня́кой
thick [тик] *adj* дебе́л, гъст
thickness [ти́книс] *n* гъстота́
thief [тийф] *n* краде́ц
thigh [тай] *n* бедро́
thin [тин] *adj* тъ́нък, слаб, ря́дък
thing [тинг] *n* не́що, ра́бота, предме́т
think [тинк] *v* ми́сля, смя́там
thirst [търст] *n* жа́жда
thirsty [тъ́рсти] *adj* жа́ден
thirteen [тъ́ртийн] *num* трина́десет
thirty [тъ́рти] *num* триде́сет
this [дис] *pron* то́зи, та́зи, то́ва
thorn [торн] *n* трън

thorough [тъ́ръ] *adj* пъ́лен, съвърше́н

those [до́уз] *pron* оне́зи

thought [тот] *n* ми́съл

thousand [та́узънд] *num* хиля́да

thread [тред] *n* коне́ц

threat [трет] *n* запла́ха

three [три] *num* три

throat [тро́ут] *n* гъ́рло

throw [тро́у] *v* хвъ́рлям; *n* хвъ́рляне

thumb [тъм] *n* па́лец

thunder [тъ́ндър] *n* гръм; *v* гърмя́

thunderstorm [тъ́ндърсторм] *n* бу́ря с гръмоте́вици

ticket [ти́кит] *n* биле́т, етике́т

tide [тайд] *n* при́лив и о́тлив

tidy [та́йди] *adj* спре́тнат

tie [тай] *v* връ́звам; *n* вратовръ́зка

tiger [та́йгър] *n* ти́гър

tight [тайт] *adj* як, сте́гнат, опъ́нат

tile [тайл] *n* кереми́да

time [тайм] *n* вре́ме, епо́ха

timetable [та́ймтейбл] *n* разписа́ние

tin [тин] *n* кала́й, тенеки́я, консе́рвна кути́я; *v* консерви́рам

tiny [та́йни] *adj* мъ́ничък

tip [тип] *n* край, връ́хче, бакши́ш

tire [та́йър] *n* въ́ншна гу́ма на колело́; *v* уморя́вам, омръ́зва ми

tissue [ти́шю] *n* тъ́кан

title [та́йтъл] *n* загла́вие, ти́тла

to [ту] *prep* към, за, в, според, до, по;
conj за да

tobacco [тъба́-коу] *n* тютю́н

today [тъде́й] *adv* днес

toe [то́у] *n* пръст

together [тъге́дър] *adv* за́едно

tolerance [то́лърънс] *n* търпи́мост,
толера́нтност

tolerate [то́лърейт] *v* търпя́, поня́сям

toll [тол] *n* та́кса

tomato [тъма́тоу] *n* дома́т

tomb [тум] *n* гроб

tomorrow [тъмо́роу] *adv* у́тре

ton [тан] *n* тон

tone [то́ун] *n* тон, нюа́нс

tongue [танг] *n* ези́к

tonight [тъна́йт] *adv* та́зи ве́чер, дове́чера

too [ту] *adv* съ́що, твъ́рде

tool [ту́ул] *n* инструме́нт

tooth [ту́ут] *n* зъб

toothache [ту́утейк] *n* зъбобо́л

top [топ] *n* връх; *adj* го́рен, на́й-голя́м

topic [то́пик] *n* предме́т, те́ма

torture [то́рчър] *n* мъче́ние; *v* измъ́чвам

total [то́утъл] *adj* пъ́лен, цял

touch [тъч] *v* пи́пам, доко́свам

tough [тъф] *adj* тру́ден, упори́т

tour [ту́ър] *n* обико́лка, пътеше́ствие; *v*
пъту́вам

tourist [ту́ърист] *n* тури́ст

towards [тъуо́рдз] *prep* към, по отноше́ние на, о́коло, приблизи́телно

towel [та́уъл] *n* къ́рпа за лице́

tower [та́уър] *v* изди́гам се; *n* ку́ла

town [та́ун] *n* град

toy [той] *n* игра́чка

trade [трейд] *n* търгови́я, занаят; *v* търгу́вам

trade union [тре́йд ю́ниън] *n* професиона́лен съ́юз

tradition [тръди́шън] *n* тради́ция, преда́ние

traditional [тръди́шънъл] *adj* традицио́нен

traffic [тра́-фик] *n* движе́ние

tragedy [тра́-джиди] *n* траге́дия

tragic [тра́-джик] *adj* траги́чен

train [трейн] *n* влак; *v* обуча́вам, трени́рам

trainer [тре́йнър] *n* треньо́р

transform [трансфо́рм] *v* преобразя́вам, превръ́щам

transformation [тра́-нсформе́йшън] *n* преобразя́ване, преустро́йство

translate [тра-нсле́йт] *v* преве́ждам

translation [тра-нсле́йшън] *n* прево́д

translator [тра-нсле́йтър] *n* преводач

transmission [тра-нсми́шън] *n* трансми́сия, преда́ване

transmit [тра-нсми́т] *v* преда́вам

transport [тра-нспо́рт] *v* прена́сям, прево́звам

transport [тра́-нспорт] *n* пре́воз, транспо́рт

travel [трá-вгл] *v* пътýвам; *n* пътýване
traveler [трá-вглгр] *n* пгтник
tray [трей] *n* тáбла, пóднос
treasure [трéжгр] *n* съкрóвище
treat [трийт] *v* отнáсям се; *n* удовóлствие
treatment [трийтмгнт] *n* отношéние,
лечéние
treaty [трийти] *n* дóговор
tree [трий] *n* дървó
tremble [трéмбл] *v* трепéря
trend [тренд] *n* тендéнция, насóка
trial [трáйгл] *n* изпитáние, дéло
triangle [трáйа-нгъл] *n* триъгълник
tribe [трайб] *n* плéме, род
trick [трик] *n* хитрост, фóкус
trip [трип] *v* спъвам; *n* пътýване
triumph [трáйгмф] *n* сполýка, триýмф; *v*
тържествýвам
trouble [трабл] *n* неприятности; *v*
безпокоя
trousers [трáузгрз] *noun pl* панталóни
truck [трък] *n* камиóн
true [тру] *adj* вéрен, истински; *adv* тóчно
trunk [трънк] *n* стъблó, ствол
trust [тръст] *n* довéрие, отговóрност; *v*
доверявам, вярвам
truth [трут] *n* истина
try [трай] *v* опитвам, изпитвам
tube [тюб] *n* тýба
Tuesday [тюзди] *n* втóрник

tuition [тюйшън] *n* обуче́ние, уче́бна та́кса
tunnel [тѣнъл] *n* туне́л
turn [търн] *v* въртя́, преврѣ́щам; *n* обра́т
twelve [туе́лв] *num* двана́десет
twenty [туе́нти] *num* двадесе́т
twin [туи́н] *n* близна́к; *adj* една́къв
twist [туи́ст] *v* изви́вам, изкривя́вам; *n*
изкривя́ване, осо́беност
two [ту] *num* две
type [тайп] *n* вид, тип, шрифт; *v* пи́ша
на пи́шеща маши́на
typewriter [та́йпра́йтър] *n* пи́шеща маши́на
typical [ти́пикъл] *adj* типи́чен, характе́рен
typist [та́йпист] *n* машинопи́сец,
машинопи́ска

U

ugliness [ѣглинис] *n* грозота́
ugly [ѣгли] *adj* гро́зен
umbrella [ѫмбре́ла] *n* чадѣ́р
unable [ейбл] *adj* неспосо́бен
uncle [ѣнкъл] *n* чи́чо, ву́йчо
uncomfortable [ѫнкѣмфѫтъбл] *adj* неудо́бен
under [а́ндър] *prep* под, на, по́-ма́лко от,
при, в
underclothes [а́ндърклоудз] *noun pl* до́лни
дре́хи

understand [а́ндърста́-нд] *v* разби́рам
underwear [а́ндъруеър] *n* до́лни дре́хи
unemployed [ѣнимпло́йд] *adj* безрабо́тен
unemployment [ѣнимпло́ймънт] *n*
безрабо́тица
unfair [ѣнфе́ър] *adj* несправедли́в,
непочте́н
uniform [ю́ниформ] *adj* еднообра́зен; *n*
унифо́рма
union [ю́ниън] *n* съ́юз, обедине́ние
unit [ю́нит] *n* едини́ца
unity [ю́нити] *n* еди́нство
universal [ю́нивѣ́рсъл] *adj* собщ,
универса́лен
universe [ю́нивърс] *n* вселе́на
university [ю́нивѣ́рсити] *n* университе́т
unknown [ѣнно́ун] *adj* непозна́т,
неизве́стен
unlock [ѣнло́к] *v* отключвам
until [ънти́л] *prep* до; *conj* докато́
unusual [ъню́жуъл] *adj* необикнове́н
up [ап] *adv* го́ре, ста́нал прав, нади́гнал
се; *prep* наго́ре
upper [апър] *adj* го́рен, висш
urgent [ѣ́рджънт] *adj* неотло́жен
us [ъс] *pron* нас
use [юс] *n* по́лза, употре́ба
use [юз] *v* изпо́лзувам, употребя́вам
useful [ю́сфул] *adj* поле́зен
useless [ю́слис] *adj* безполе́зен

usual [южуъл] *adj* обикновѐн, обичѐен
usually [южуъли] *adv* обикновѐно

V

vacancy [вѐйкънси] *n* вакѐнтно мѝсто
vacation [въкѐйшън] *n* освобождѐване,
вакѐнция
vaccination [вѐ-ксинѐйшън] *n* ваксинѐция
valid [вѐ-лид] *adj* валѝден, в сѝла
valley [вѐ-ли] *n* долинѐ
valuable [вѐ-люъбл] *adj* цѐнен
value [вѐ-лю] *n* стѐйност, ценѐ
vapor [вѐйпър] *n* пѐра
variety [връѐйъти] *n* разнообрѐзие,
разновѝдност
various [вѐриъс] *adj* разлѝчен,
разнообрѐзен
vary [вѐ-ри] *v* менѝ се, варѝрам
vase [ваз] *n* вѐза
vast [васт] *adj* обшѝрен, огрѐмен
veal [вийл] *n* тѐлешко месѐ
vegetable [вѐджитъбл] *n* растѝтелен,
зеленчѐков; *n* зеленчѐк
vegetation [вѐджитѐйшън] *n* растѝтелност,
растѐне
vehicle [вѝйкъл] *n* превѐзно срѐдство, колѐ
verb [върб] *n* глагѐл

verdict [вѐрдикт] *n* присъ̀да
verse [върс] *n* стих, поѐзия
version [вѐржън] *n* вѐрсия
vertical [вѐртикъл] *adj* вертика̀лен
very [вѐри] *adv* мно̀го
vessel [вѐсъл] *n* съд
veteran [вѐтърън] *n* ветера̀н
via [ва̀йъ] *prep* през
vibration [вайбрѐйшън] *n* трепѐрене
vicinity [висѝнити] *n* око̀лност
victim [вѝктим] *n* жѐртва
victory [вѝктъри] *n* побѐда
view [вю] *n* ѝзглед, мнѐние
village [вѝлидж] *n* сѐло
vinegar [вѝнигър] *n* оцѐт
violate [ва̀йълейт] *v* наруша̀вам
violation [ва̀йълѐйшън] *n* наруша̀ване
violence [ва̀йълънс] *n* насѝлие
violent [ва̀йълънт] *adj* сѝлен, бу̀ен
violin [ва̀йълин] *n* цигу̀лка
visible [вѝзъбл] *adj* очевѝден
vision [вѝжън] *n* зрѐние
visit [вѝзит] *n* посещѐние, вѝзита; *v* посеща̀вам
visitor [вѝзитър] *n* посетѝтел, гост
vocabulary [въка̀-бюлъри] *n* рѐчник, запа̀с от ду̀ми
vocal [во̀укъл] *adj* гла̀сен
voice [войс] *n* глас, зало̀г
volcano [волкѐйноу] *n* вулка̀н

volume [во́люм] *n* том, кни́га, обе́м
voluntary [во́лънтъри] *adj* доброво́лен
volunteer [во́лънти́ър] *n* доброво́лец; *v* предла́гам доброво́лно
vote [во́ут] *n* глас, гласу́ване; *v* гласу́вам
voter [во́утър] *n* избирател, гласоподава́-тел
vowel [ва́уъл] *n* гла́сна
voyage [во́ядж] *n* пъту́ване

W

wage [уе́йдж] *n* на́дница
waist [уе́йст] *n* та́лия
wait [уе́йт] *v* ча́кам, прислу́жвам
waiter [уе́йтър] *n* сервитьо́р
wake [уе́йк] *v* събу́ждам се
walk [уо́к] *n* разхо́дка; *v* хо́дя
wall [уо́л] *n* стена́
wallet [уо́лит] *n* портфе́йл
want [уо́нт] *v* и́скам, нужда́я се
war [уо́р] *n* война́
wardrobe [уо́рдроуб] *n* гардеро́б
warehouse [уе́ърхаус] *n* склад
warm [уо́рм] *adj* то́пъл, сърде́чен
warning [уо́рнинг] *n* предупрежде́ние
wash [уо́ш] *v* ми́я, пера́; *n* пране́
washing [уо́шинг] *n* пране́

waste [уейст] *v* хабя́, прахо́свам; *n* отпа́дъци

watch [уо́ч] *v* наблюда́вам, внима́вам; *n* ръ́чен часо́вник

water [уо́тър] *n* вода́

waterfall [уо́търфол] *n* водопа́д

watermelon [уо́търмелън] *n* ди́ня

wave [уе́йв] *n* вълна́, ма́хане с ръка́; *v* разма́хвам, развя́вам

way [уе́й] *n* път, начи́н

weak [уи́йк] *adj* слаб

weakness [уи́книс] *n* сла́бост

wealth [уе́лт] *n* бога́тство, изоби́лие

wealthy [уе́лти] *adj* бога́т

weapon [уе́пън] *n* оръ́жие

wear [уе́ър] *v* но́ся

weather [уе́дър] *n* вре́ме

wed [уе́д] *v* венча́вам

wedding [уе́динг] венча́вка, сва́тба

Wednesday [уе́нзди] *n* сря́да

week [уи́йк] *n* се́дмица

weigh [уе́й] *v* те́гля, тежа́

weight [уе́йт] *n* тежина́, тегло́

welcome [уе́лкъм] *interj* добре́ дошъ́л; *v* приве́тствувам

well [уе́л] *n* кла́денец; *adv* добре́

west [уе́ст] *n* за́пад

western [уе́стърн] *adj* за́паден

wet [уе́т] *adj* мо́кър; *v* мо́кря

what [уóт] *pron* каквó, щó, какъ́в, товá, коéто

wheat [уи́йт] *n* пшени́ца, жи́то

wheel [уи́йл] *n* колелó

when [уéн] *conj* когáто

which [уи́ч] *pron* кой, кóйто

while [уáйл] *conj* докатó

whisky [уи́ски] *n* уи́ски

whistle [уи́съл] *n* сви́рка; *v* свиря́ с устá

white [уáйт] *adj* бял, блéден

who [ху] *pron* кой, кóйто

whole [хóул] *adj* цял

wholesale [хóулсейл] *n* продáжба на éдро

whose [хуз] *pron* чий, чи́йто

why [уáй] *adv* защó

wide [уáйд] *adj* ширóк, голя́м, обши́рен

widen [уáйдън] *v* разширя́вам

widow [уи́доу] *n* вдови́ца

width [уи́дт] *n* широчинá

wife [уáйф] *n* съпрýга

wild [уáйлд] *adj* див, необуздáн

will [уи́л] *v* ще, и́скам, желáя, завещáвам; *n* вóля, завещáние

win [уи́н] *v* печéля

wind [уи́нд] *n* вя́тър

window [уи́ндоу] *n* прозóрец

wine [уáйн] *n* ви́но

wing [уи́нг] *n* крилó, кули́си

winner [уи́нър] *n* победи́тел

winter [уи́нтър] *n* зи́ма; *v* зимýвам

wipe [уайп] *v* бърша, трия
wire [уайър] *n* жици, телеграма; *v* слагам жици, телеграфирам
wisdom [уиздъм] *n* мъдрост
wise [уайз] *adj* мъдър, умен
wish [уиш] *n* желание; *v* желая
with [уит] *prep* с, у, при, от
without [уидаут] *prep* без, извън
witness [уитнис] *n* свидетел, доказателство; *v* свидетелствувам
wolf [улф] *n* вълк
woman [уман] *n* жена
wonder [уандър] *v* чудя се, учудвам се
wonderful [уандърфул] *adj* чуден, чудесен
wood [уд] *n* дърво, гора
wool [ул] *n* вълна
woollen [улън] *adj* вълнен
word [уърд] *n* дума
work [уърк] *n* работа, произведение; *v* работя
worker [уъркър] *n* работник
world [уърлд] *n* свят
worry [уъри] *v* безпокоя
worse [уърс] *adj* по-лош
worst [уърст] *adj* най-лош
worth [уърт] *adj* на стойност, заслужаващ; *n* цена, стойност
wound [унд] *n* рана; *v* ранявам
wrestle [ресл] *v* боря се; *n* борба
wrestler [реслър] *n* борец

wrist [рист] *n* китка
write [райт] *v* пиша
writing [райтинг] *n* писание, съчинение
wrong [ронг] *adj* крив, погрешен; *adv* криво, погрешно; *n* неправда; *v* онеправдавам

X

X-ray [ексрей] *n* рентгенови лъчи

Y

yacht [йат] *n* яхта
yard [ярд] *n* двор, ярд
yawn [йон] *v* прозявам се; *n* прозявка
year [йър] *n* година
yellow [йелоу] *adj* жълт
yes [йес] *adv* да
yesterday [йестърдей] *adv* вчера
you [ю] *pron* ти, вие
young [йънг] *adj* млад, малък

Z

zebra [зибра] *n* зебра
zero [зироу] *n* пула

zone [зо́ун] *n* зо́на
zoo [зу́у] *n* зоологи́ческа гради́на
zoology [зоо́лъджи] *n* зооло́гия

Hippocrene Foreign Language Dictionaries

Modern • Up-to-date • Easy-to-use • Practical

ALBANIAN-ENGLISH/ENGLISH-ALBANIAN
PRACTICAL DICTIONARY
**416 pages • 16,000 entries • ISBN 0-7818-0419-1 •
$14.95pb • (483)**

ENGLISH-ALBANIAN COMPREHENSIVE
DICTIONARY
**938 pages • 60,000 entries • ISBN 0-7818-0792-1 •
$35.00pb • (305)**

BOSNIAN-ENGLISH/ENGLISH-BOSNIAN
CONCISE DICTIONARY
**331 pages • 8,500 entries • ISBN 0-7818-0276-8 •
$14.95pb • (329)**

BULGARIAN-ENGLISH/ENGLISH-
BULGARIAN COMPACT DICTIONARY
**322 pages • 8,000 entries • ISBN 0-7818-0535-X •
$8.95pb • (623)**

BYELORUSSIAN-ENGLISH/ENGLISH-
BYELORUSSIAN CONCISE DICTIONARY
**290 pages • 6,500 entries • ISBN 0-87052-114-4 •
$9.95pb • (395)**

CZECH-ENGLISH/ENGLISH-CZECH
STANDARD DICTIONARY
10th Revised Edition
**1,072 pages • 40,000 entries • ISBN 0-7818-0653-4 •
$39.50hc • (740)**

**AMERICAN ENGLISH-CZECH
COMPREHENSIVE DICTIONARY**
1,183 pages • 40,000 entries • ISBN 80-238-0456-1 •
$55.00hc • (654)

**CZECH-ENGLISH/ENGLISH-CZECH
CONCISE DICTIONARY**
594 pages • 7,500 entries • ISBN 0-87052-981-1 •
$11.95pb • (276)

CZECH HANDY EXTRA DICTIONARY
186 pages • 2,600 entries • ISBN 0-7818-0138-9 •
$8.95pb • (63)

**GREEK-ENGLISH/ENGLISH-GREEK
STANDARD DICTIONARY**
686 pages • 25,000 entries • ISBN 0-7818-0600-3 •
$16.95pb • (695)

**GYPSY-ENGLISH/ENGLISH-GYPSY
CONCISE DICTIONARY**
229 pages • 6,000 entries • ISBN 0-7818-0775-1 •
$12.95pb • (191)

**HUNGARIAN-ENGLISH/ENGLISH-
HUNGARIAN CONCISE DICTIONARY**
267 pages • 7,000 entries • ISBN 0-7818-0317-9 •
$14.95pb • (40)

**LADINO-ENGLISH/ENGLISH-LADINO
CONCISE ENCYCLOPEDIC DICTIONARY**
602 pages • 17,000 entries • ISBN 0-7818-0658-5 •
$19.95pb • (742)

MACEDONIAN-ENGLISH/ENGLISH-MACEDONIAN CONCISE DICTIONARY
180 pages • 10,000 entries • ISBN 0-7818-0516-3 • $14.95pb • (619)

POLISH-ENGLISH UNABRIDGED DICTIONARY
3,800 pages • 250,00 entries • ISBN 0-7818-0441-8 • $200.00hc • (526)
CD-ROM **(requires Windows 95) • ISBN 0-7818-0627-5 • $55.00 • (951)**

POLISH-ENGLISH/ENGLISH-POLISH PRACTICAL DICTIONARY
703 pages • 31,000 entries • ISBN 0-7818-0085-4 • $11.95pb • (450)

POLISH-ENGLISH/ENGLISH-POLISH CONCISE DICTIONARY
With complete phonetics
408 pages • 8,000 entries • ISBN 0-7818-0133-8 • $9.95pb • (268)

POLISH HANDY EXTRA DICTIONARY
125 pages • 2,800 entries • ISBN 0-7818-0504-X • $11.95pb • (607)

ROMANIAN-ENGLISH/ENGLISH-ROMANIAN STANDARD DICTIONARY
567 pages • 18,000 entries • ISBN 0-7818-0444-2 • $17.95pb • (99)

SERBIAN-ENGLISH/ENGLISH-SERBIAN
CONCISE DICTIONARY
**394 pages • 7,500 entries • ISBN 0-7818-0556-2 •
$14.95pb • (326)**

SERBO-CROATIAN-ENGLISH/
ENGLISH-SERBO-CROATIAN
PRACTICAL DICTIONARY
**527 pages • 24,000 entries • ISBN 0-7818-0445-0 •
$16.95pb • (130)**

SLOVAK-ENGLISH/ENGLISH-SLOVAK
CONCISE DICTIONARY
**359 pages • 9,000 entries • ISBN 0-87052-115-2 •
$11.95pb • (390)**

SLOVAK HANDY EXTRA DICTIONARY
**200 pages • 3,000 entries • ISBN 0-7818-0101-X •
$12.95pb • (359)**

UKRAINIAN-ENGLISH/ENGLISH-
UKRAINIAN PRACTICAL DICTIONARY
**406 pages • 16,000 entries • ISBN 0-7818-0306-3 •
$14.95pb • (343)**